D1274623

AMERICAN IMPERIALISM
Viewpoints of United States
Foreign Policy, 1898-1941

Reproduced with the cooperation of the
Hoover Institution of War, Revolution and Peace,
Stanford University, Stanford, California

BANANA GOLD

Carleton Beals

ARNO PRESS & THE NEW YORK TIMES
New York ★ 1970

Collection Created and Selected
by
CHARLES GREGG OF GREGG PRESS

Reprinted by permission of Doubleday & Co., Inc.
Reprinted from a copy in The Klausner Library

Library of Congress Catalog Card Number: 72-111708
ISBN 0-405-02002-3

ISBN for complete set: 0-405-02000-7

Reprint Edition 1970 by Arno Press Inc.
Manufactured in the United States of America

BANANA
GOLD

CARLETON BEALS *is one of those men whose lives are rich with the foreign names of the places they have been, the things they have done and the people they meet. He has slept in the hovels of the Indians and the palaces of the governments. He really knows Central Amercia.* MEXICAN MAZE, *published in* 1931, *a choice of the Book League of America, is the amazing jigsaw of war and revolution and peace in Mexico.* BANANA GOLD *is the story of the patriotism, politics, heat, and corruption of Central America.*

CARLOS MÉRIDA *is the descendant of two worlds —through his mother from a Spanish sacerdote and through his father from a prince of the Maya-Quiché dynasty. Born in Guatemala City in* 1892, *he went to Paris when he was twenty-two and studied under Van Dongen. Ten years later he returned to Mexico and became one of the famous Syndicate of Painters with Rivera, Orozco, Siqueiros and Charlot. The frontispiece of* BANANA GOLD *is reproduced from his Paris Portfolio.*

BANANA GOLD

CARLETON BEALS

Illustrations
by
CARLOS
MERIDA

J. B. Lippincott Company
PHILADELPHIA & LONDON
1932

CONTENTS

I Bugles 9

II Seventeen Children 16

III The Quetzal Kingdom 25

IV Kaiser Koffee 34

V Indian Runners 40

VI Missionaries and Mangos 44

VII A Tale of Two Cities 48

VIII Saints and Sinners 55

IX The Cacique's Revenge 63

X Head of a Traitor 68

XI Mattresses for Bananas 75

XII Mistaken Identity 79

XIII Salvador 83

XIV "Ssst . . . Honey" 89

XV Anathema 97

XVI The Raw Tropics 102

XVII Lost Soul 106

XVIII An Ancient Eruption 111

XIX Imperial Intrigue 120

XX Auto, Train and Sail Boat 129

XXI Baron Banana 139

XXII The Song of the Carvers of Gods 148

XXIII Balum Votan 155

XXIV The Lacandones 163

XXV Four Leaf Clover 169

XXVI Off for Sandino 178

XXVII My Diplomatic Letter 184

5

CONTENTS

XXVIII	*Arrest*	189
XXIX	*Honduras Trails*	195
XXX	*To Jacaleapa*	202
XXXI	*Danli*	206
XXXII	*The Sandino Underground*	210
XXXIII	*A New Guide*	215
XXXIV	*Night Rain*	219
XXXV	*Revenge*	224
XXXVI	*God Knows*	229
XXXVII	*The Thread Broken*	239
XXXVIII	*Dead Men's Cigarettes*	246
XXXIX	*Sandino's Camp*	253
XL	*Sandino*	264
XLI	*Valley of Youth*	272
XLII	*Marine Intelligence*	279
XLIII	*Undiplomatic Letters*	291
XLIV	*How the News Is Made*	302
XLV	*Across Lake Nicaragua*	308
XLVI	*The Canal Route*	317
XLVII	*Greytown*	324
XLVIII	*Ladies for Strangers*	329
XLIX	*Bluefields*	337
L	*Guatemala Ho!*	347
	Index	353

BANANA
GOLD

1

At six o'clock in the morning I stepped from the "Queen's Own" train between Mexico City and Vera Cruz into the long shadows of tropic Córdoba. Muddy streets twisted up from a mean, dirty station into a sprawling town, overhung with dense, dripping vegetation, from which oozed a powerful, orchid-like scent. A tousled Indian boy, barefoot, clad in white cotton "drawers," pounced upon my baggage. His sturdy body and deer-slender legs darted across the street to a ramshackle hotel-restaurant.

At an oil-cloth, wire-tripod table, I drank hot milk impregnated with coffee-essence, read the Vera Cruz *Dictamen* about a renters' strike, and had my shoes shined by brown arms agitating a pink shirt, tails out.

The pace here in Córdoba is slow. Though so early in the morning, the Indian waitress—a fat little girl, black braids dangling, her red celluloid comb glittering with glass diamonds—dragged her bare brown feet listlessly over the red flaggings. But though drooping, or rather melting, in movement, her inky doe-like eyes sparkled with high lights; her straight hawk-wing hair gave fierce severity to her otherwise broad, gentle countenance.

At my greeting, she paused, one dark toe fumbling a crack. "You've come down from Mexico City? I've been there," she said with pride. "That's where I learned

9

BANANA GOLD

my speed." Then she set a plate of fried eggs in front of me with a gesture as leisurely and studied as though she were caressing the rock of ages.

To my baggage boy I gave a twenty-dollar gold piece to be exchanged for Mexican silver pesos "at the very best rate" in the nearest *coyote's* (money-changer's) den, then strolled out to see the town.

Already at seven in the morning, I was glad to keep on the shady side of the street just to prove Mexicans are quite wrong when they say "only Americans and dogs" like to walk in the sun.

My first visit to this place occurred shortly after the 1920 revolution. The town had been badly shattered, recurrently swept with steel and fire for ten years. Now there were evidences of attempts at civic beautifying. Along a road rambling up from the station, a new park has been laid out. Uncomfortable red mosaic benches line its stiff paths. Further up the hill, the plaza, eight years before hard ground, was now adorned with flower beds and white shells patterned in cement, with rococo taste. Red earth paths curved between red cement benches.

The municipal campaign was on. My *Dictamen* had said Córdoba was imitating Chicago, two men had been bumped off for talking too much about their "honorable" candidate who was going to give everybody jobs except his political enemies; the latter would have to handle baggage instead of sitting on the red plaza benches. Big labor candidate posters were plastered on the frowsy walls—a fat black-skin moron peered out of a red and black circle.

Women, each a study in brown and blue—blue *rebozos* over dark brown cheeks; light brown terra cotta

10

ollas cuddled against blue blouses or carried on erect heads—pattered along the grassy cobbled streets, now and then pausing to chatter in soft Spanish or Huasteco dialect. A boy, two twenty-gallon milk cans slung across a burro, jogged by.

At the head of a lane which dipped down between enormous palms, sapotas and orchards, and low adobe houses, rainbow calcimined, a bugle broke the morning stillness. Mexicans are always blowing bugles furiously; it makes them think they are saving the fatherland three hundred and sixty-five days a year; and the further south you go, and the smaller the country, the louder, earlier, and more frequently people blow bugles.

This particular hot morning, squat Indian soldiers in slouchy leggings emerged listlessly from a faded church converted into barracks. The local palace guard, if you please. Attention. Roll call. I focused my kodak. The bepaunched officer twisted his long black mustaches and drew his sword, ready for an imaginary charge. Properly photographed, he marched his men around and around the block to the furious rat-a-tat-tatting of tight snare drums, tumultuously important. Back inside the nigger-blue church, they blew more bugles.

Beyond the town, now framed in a colonial arch, now set between adobe walls, rose the virginal white brow of Mount Orizaba—Citlaltepetl—Mountain of the Star, the highest peak in Mexico, its sides swift and sleek, cut sharp in the morning light against the pale turquoise sky. On that heaven-flung summit of snowy chastity, Quetzalcoatl, the ancient white god of the wind, the patron of arts and crafts, was consumed in divine fire. And the sons of the ancient legend makers blow bugles and wait Quetzalcoatl's resurrection.

2

We rattled south from Córdoba towards the Isthmus of Tehuantepec, through hilly country. Just after the Obregón revolution, I once took this same route; the roadbed then was almost lost under the growth of vegetation, and we had arrived at the Isthmus twelve hours late. Six miles an hour had been our average.

Now the roadbed was improved. The engineer took the curves on high; we jerked around alarmingly between sprouting fence posts and uninhabited country—long miles of gorse-grown land. Only occasionally some thatched village was set in a ring of tropic trees or in the crook of a silver stream.

Noon found us at the Tierra Blanca junction, eternally hot, a dry, piercing heat. The station drowsed. The dogs drowsed. White-clad Indians with mild lovable faces drowsed, shirt-tails out. The flies did not drowse. They had appointments with manure, exposed food, and human bodies.

We dragged through the heat over to a restaurant open to the street. At the common washstand we scrubbed off what dust of travel we could and wiped the remainder on the grimy towel.

The restaurant flaunted typical middle-class decorations; gilt-frame enlargements of the family ancestors, wearing their most wooden expressions; Millet's "The Reapers," cheap color-print landscapes, and a Swiss lake in a bamboo frame. This lake competes with the bugles in popularity: it is encountered all over Mexico, peddled perhaps by some homesick, hard-up Swiss.

In the deep garden grinned a caged monkey; turkey-cocks gobbled; and a straw-tinted dog, whose color had run slightly in the rain, bit his fleas.

In a corner of the restaurant, a voluptuous girl with an ash skin was whanging at a cracked piano, bulging breasts quivering, thin bloodless lips creased hard. Her silk stockings were clocked; her white high-heeled satin shoes were scuffed and soiled. She threw me a provocative, unsmiling glance, then tossed her mop of black hair and pounded harder.

A typical Mexican meal—greasy soup, fried rice, fried eggs with chili sauce, lettuce chopped fine and drowned in oil; a paper-thin steak with tinny flavor, mashed black beans and bitter black coffee. The dark waitress, frizzy-haired, clad in a frayed Mother Hubbard, clattered, bare legs over stone floor, on single-strap wooden soles. Her sandals, her long red earrings, her one-piece dress scarcely concealing her rounded body, were all her clothing. But nine years old, in body and manner she was already a woman.

Behind a counter, in front of shelves with rows of amber "XX" beer bottles, the proprietress, a huge woman with naked ham arms and shoulders, leaned on the counter with her elbows, fat chin in hand and smiled lazily at everybody, never changing this set pose, even when she scolded the waitress in a shrill parrot voice, with grim yet half-indifferent persistence.

3

South from Tierra Blanca to the Isthmus the train carried a new assortment of passengers. A German from

Tampico, headed for the new Minatitlán oil fields, exhibited mild Saxon amusement at everything, pointing out passing objects with thick thumb instead of forefinger. A bright-eyed Japanese dentist talked in the alert jerky manner of his race.

Two wealthy *hacendados* walked aboard with blatant ease—big-bodied fellows in *charro* costumes, broad hats, guns at the hip. Their loud, healthy voices, punctuated with gross laughter, describe a beautiful German woman who knew no Spanish but was very, very generous.

Most voluble was the Cuban, son of a French mother and a Catalan father. He was aggressive, ignorant, humorless, a dynamic jumping-jack with a tiny Charlie Chaplin mustache. His white duck suit, soiled to a dirty gray, in no way restrained his self-importance. His present interest in life was selling Paludismol. To the whole car, in a shrill effeminate voice, he poured out all the virtues of this curative, which would both prevent and control malaria, endemic in this region. As Paludismol had no quinine it was especially good for pregnant women. He gave me a sly wink and hauled out a large poster—with which he was plastering the country-side—bearing a gigantic blue bottle labeled "Paludismol." Paludismol was such a wonderful product, he was going to sell many thousands of cases in a few short months. And as he had the exclusive agency for the entire state of Vera Cruz, in a very few months he would make fifty thousand dollars. Then he would get married. When he had done all this, he was going down to Chiapas and buy two carloads of cattle which he would peddle in Vera Cruz.

From time to time, a mestiza girl in a pale blue silk dress, covered with steel beads, turned around to smile at me. I commented on a passing coffee plantation, whereupon she boldly moved back to my seat. Two years ago she had gone up to Mexico City to "do business." Like the Cuban she had her ambitions: now she was going back to her native Chiapas town to buy a little house and orchard and marry comfortably—somebody, whom she "could handle."

Queer mongrel types—the backwash of East and West, the combings of the centuries—tossed here against these lofty tangled jungles (now rushing past the car windows) and tossed back again in some lost eddy of timelessness.

1

IN MAY, THE CHIAPAS coast south from Tehuanté-pec, is nearly as desolate as Mojave desert. From San Gerónimo Junction, the Pan-American Railway drags on interminably through an expanse of cactus, mesquite, jagged gray horizon mountains, and thatched towns, hour after dreary hour.

Near the Isthmus, the stations are crowded with beautiful tall Tehuana women in long red *enaguas,* ending at the ankles in a wide flounce of exquisite lace; red or blue gold-embroidered *huipiles* expose their brown arms and ample brown bosoms. These women flock down to the trains, baskets on shoulders or heads; they walk with swaying motion, full skirts held out daintily on both sides or flowing into delightful patterns with their free stride, with the movement of legs and hips; the white lace rustles and foams about their bodies. They are voluptuous, flirtatious, bold, black-eyed, ready tongued, and so far as I know, not knock-kneed. Among themselves, they chatter in Zapotec, a keen, half-Chinese speech; they address travelers in racy Spanish.

They are selling plums, bananas, cocoanuts, pineapples, sugar-cane, candy, and cooked foods; hard-boiled eggs, roast chicken, tortillas, rolled meat, or cheese-filled *tacos,* hot with chili. To ride in a Mexican train is to sit at a continuous banquet, a new course spread at each station.

At each town the characteristic food changes, also, the type of passenger. The exuberant talkative Vera Cruzano has given way to a more serious sensuous type. The Tehuanas, though jolly, always maintain reserve, dignity. The Chiapas highlander is still another type, arrogant, leonine.

I hobnobbed with hard-faced politicians going up to the State capital. They spoke in booming voices or soft, purring voices; guns were strapped about their big paunches; they wore gray suits and sporty shirts. Their talks were of intrigue, of deals with militarists and labor politicians. They compared their ornate pistols, the silver-embroidered holsters, the carved leather cartridge belts; and they talked of killings. "In Tixtla, I killed . . . in Ciudad Gómez, I killed . . . in La Cruz, I killed . . ." It was done this way and that way; each obviously had a private graveyard. Eloquence was stimulated by frequent rounds of *tequila,* the native firewater.

The only other foreigner in the car was an American with big biceps and a shifty glance, accompanied by a repulsively neat little Mexican, effeminate and softvoiced. This American avoided talking to anybody, and sat on his spine, a troubled yet bored expression clouding his face.

The dust whirled over us in choking white alkaline clouds. In spite of the heat, the windows had to remain closed. Even the water in the Pullman, drawn from the passing stations, was full of yellow silt. Gray with dust, faces streaked, we clambered out for a station lunch.

17

When in the midst of our *mole* (turkey with sauce and many spices), the train started off without any warning. *Mole* is a smeary dish. Even with the greatest care the yellow brown sauce drips at the corners of one's mouth and gets on one's fingers. We were a pretty sight as we dashed madly after the train, the Pullman conductor and myself in the lead, behind us a woman with babe in arms, two of the politicians, and the American and his fifi companion. The conductor and I hit the last car at the same moment. No cord to call the engineer, so the train ran on for nearly a mile before word was finally passed up to his cab. Grumblingly the train backed into the station to collect its passengers.

On again. Blazing heat, dust, hours fretful with the squalling baby, everybody lolling listlessly in their seats, coats off.

By late afternoon, when we were mummies with haggard eyes peering out of caked dust, the landscape changed. In Santa Rosa, thatched houses clambered up a steep hill. To the right a large salt lagoon stretched in from the far gray sea. The late sun was a dazzling globe tangled in jungle-growth. Its yellow rays clutched at faded golden sails. The salt shore glistened purple and gold. Dug-out canoes drifted about, the paddles shaped like water-lily leaves. Fish nets hung like batwings from wall and stake. A marimba band greeted us with *Honey Boy*, then fortunately switched to *Borrachita*.

Native women, costumes drabber than those of the Tehuanas, ran along the train selling sizzling hot fish wrapped in green banana leaves. Terra cotta cups held refreshingly cold pineapple *tepacho*, and the tired day cooled to a quiet symphony of sea and jungle.

2

Five hours late, at one in the morning, we reached Tapa-chula, the largest town in this rich coffee region. Here the Pullman was taken off. Bones aching, stumbling sleepily, cursing, we dragged ourselves and baggage into the first-class coach for the two-hour run into the frontier town of Suchiate.

The hotel there was a ramshackle two-story building. The landlord, a confused little Spaniard, ran around like a chicken with its head off, as though he had never received any guests before in his life. He didn't even have the beds made up. Everybody made demands on him, hauling him here and there. Not to be behind any-body else, I insisted on "a large, airy room."

"You'll get that all right," he sneered and dashed off.

Presently he was back again in a rage. "A large airy room, eh; well, you'll get that, but I don't know whether you'll get a bed."

The clock ticked on. Beds finally were made up. With two amiable Spaniards, an Italian, and an Austrian, I was ushered into the "large airy" without any windows. But the floor was full of cracks and holes and the wash-basins were on the verandas, so we could not douse the inmates of the rooms below. Slops were thrown over the rail into the vegetable garden. Idyllic plumbing. I lay me down in a squeaky cot, utterly weary but un-able to sleep because of heat and mosquitoes. Right then and there I decided it was much simpler to stay back home, marry the sweetest girl on earth, like the ones you see in lingerie ads, sprout radios and autocars, and raise babies.

Hardly in bed, when the Italian came over to hold a whispered conversation with me and the Austrian.

"Is the Suchiate River the Guatemalan frontier?" he asked. "Which direction is it? How do you get to it? How deep is it? Is it guarded?

"I'm wading the river to-night," he said to the Austrian, whom he had never seen before. "Will you take my suitcase across through the customs? I'll meet you several stations down on the Guatemalan side."

The Austrian, embarrassed, finally agreed.

A nightmare of a night. Roll and toss! Roll and toss! The mosquitoes were voracious. At half past four, a cat, trapped between ceiling and roof, announced his predicament to the world in hair-raising yowls. The proprietor, cursing, entered our room with a lantern and a stepladder to release the crazed animal.

Wakened again by a candle lighted, I saw the Italian pasting some document inside the cover of a map. He was, I decided at once, a dangerous Bolshevik. Only Bolsheviks paste documents inside maps. Now and then he peered around at us nervously. Finally, he rummaged in his suitcase, snapped it shut, set it by the side of the Austrian's bed and tip-toed out of the room.

"Some sleep at last!" I thought.

The return train north was due to leave at six, and the racket began before five. Cars bumped, brakes screeched. The switch-engine whistle split the night. Bedlam all night long.

Eyes smarting, tempers addled, we went down to breakfast at oil-cloth tables. Already the heat made us jumpy.

But our proprietor was now all smiles. Talkative in a jerky, nervous way, his protruding teeth suggested a perpetual laugh, his side-burns an episcopalian deacon. He became ingratiating. He interested himself in the details of our passports. He inquired whether we had any gold, warning us to change it into American paper money if we didn't want it confiscated by the Mexican customs. Generously he offered to perform this trifling service at a ruinous rate.

I was carrying two hundred dollars in American gold, but kept my mouth shut, well knowing that if I told him without letting him exchange them, he would probably tip off the officials and get a rake-off.

Between sentences, he shouted insulting orders to his fat, lazy but clean wife, waiting on table. Or he drove off the swarm of dogs that tagged into the hotel.

"They belong to the street," he said mournfully, "but how the blazes is one going to keep them out?" He waved his hand despondently. His good humor was only brought forth for money-changing; he shouted angrily at his offspring, a flock of girls almost as numerous as the dogs.

He groaned dismally. "A hell of a hole this."

I agreed.

He looked around, suspiciously, lowering his voice. "They hate all foreigners. They've been trying to hamstring me ever since I came here. I've got forty acres of land, but they tried to divide it up for the peons. I blocked that, with money. Now they've ordered a street cut through my property, right through the center of the hotel. Pure spite. I'm a foreigner. What do they want a street through here for? There's only a jungle back there." He waved his hand toward the rear.

"This is a rummy hotel. But is there any better? And why should I fix it up when the next day they'll ruin me? It's just because I'm a foreigner and work, and so they hate me. They all want something for nothing. Some night they'll stick a knife in my ribs. Just you wait and see."

"Some late nights when you don't have your beds made up, one of your guests will do that," I told him. "But a man who works in this heat ought to be knifed anyway. So you are likely to get it coming and going."

"You're right," he agreed gloomily.

3

The Austrian and I walked to the station. A groggy traveler, who had preferred to sit up and hug his suitcase on the platform rather than pay for a few hours at the hotel, sat there sunk in ill-humor. An Indian girl was selling hot coffee and kicking at the dogs. At a Chinese store I bought cigarettes. "Americans belly lich!" said Hop Wing with a shake of his head.

A splinter of a boy staggered under my bags to the immigration office. Each moment it grew hotter. Perspiration poured off us. A surly immigration officer stamped our passports.

At the *aduana*, an open, palm-thatched roof on the river bluff, no one showed the least interest in inspecting our baggage. We crouched in the patch of shade, mopping our brows. Hot, goddam hot.

Again the officials looked at our passports with a curious air, as though they had never seen such documents before. This seemed to exhaust their energy.

They smoked black cigarettes and discussed their personal affairs. A ratty looking official, creased face, sparse stiff mustache, complained of his rheumatism—caused by La Viuda. He'd tried sea baths; they'd only made it worse. To judge by his grimy neck, the sea baths had happened long ago.

In due time, our baggage was carted down to the river's edge, to be loaded on to flat-bottomed *piraguas*.

4

The Mexican side of the river was harsh and barren. The scattered, palm-thatched houses wilted in the blazing tropic sun. Few trees. The bluffs were red scars, uninviting.

The Guatemalan side was a mass of tall river trees, shrubs and vines. Under a thatched roof, barefoot Indian soldiers in blue white-braid dungarees received us courteously speaking a mongrel Spanish. My Anglo-Saxon name amused them. My vaccination certificate was examined upside down.

We followed our baggage carriers across flat stifling river sands under cottonwood trees to the Comandancia.

The Austrian and I entered laughing. The plump, self-important official was annoyed by our levity. As punishment, he examined my passport with insulting scrupulousness. "It isn't Spanish, I can't read it," he snapped. "Not my fault," I assured him. After carefully looking over a *persona non grata* list and expressing disappointment at not finding my name upon it, he had me fill out a blank form, big as a pillow case.

Troubles are never over at Latin frontiers. At the

customs I was taxed twenty pesos for the inspecting of my baggage; an alarming amount, until the official reassured me that twenty Guatemalan pesos represented less than forty cents.

At the police station, more arrogance. Another enormous questionnaire. My sense of humor came to my aid. To "married?" I now replied, "Six times." "How many children?"—"Seventeen." The police chief looked over my questionnaire, gravely and lengthily. Probably I'll be shot at sunrise for my replies . . . But without comment, he signed it laboriously as one barely able to write. Again my passport was stamped. It would be delivered later to me at the hotel. To the Austrian I remarked, "The smaller and the hotter country, the greater the red tape and self-importance of its officials."

He grunted, mopping his neck.

The Hotel Seville proved another and larger two-story frame structure, little green rooms, screen-doors opening out upon narrow verandas. The walls, which did not reach to the ceiling, were completed by two feet of screening to permit the free circulation of air and the noise of neighborly occupations of divers moralities. The furniture consisted of a canvas cot, a tiny chair, a small table, and washbasin.

A bottle of cold black Munich beer, and life again seemed endurable.

III THE QUETZAL KINGDOM

1

SOMEWHERE DURING THE frontier ordeals, I had torn the seat of my trousers. I showed the rent to the Austrian. He grunted, passing a moist palm over a moister brow.

The hotel boy led me half across the town to "the best tailor." I requested the "best tailor" to mend my trousers and press my suit while I waited. But the thatched roof harbored only one large room; present were his wife and two buxom daughters. Calmly he indicated a reed-bottomed chair, near his work-bench. Apprehensively I glanced at the other occupants, then pulled off my trousers and sat me down in my shirt tails and B.V.D.'s. With nonchalance equal to theirs, I smoked a black Guatemalan cigarette and chatted to them about babies and pigs, a new litter of which gamboled about the feet of the "best tailor."

2

Latin American countries are much alike, yet any one passing from Mexican Suchiate to Guatemalan Ayutla would immediately know, even had he faced no ordeal of official red tape, that he was in new country. On the Guatemalan side, the thatched roofs are differently made; they have a different slant. The walls are white-washed. Things are more orderly, neater, cleaner. Officialdom is more in evidence. Law seems always at one's elbow. Little of the Mexican casualness and easily gained camaraderies.

I took pictures with the sweat dripping upon the finder: Thatched roofs, a deaf and dumb female beggar, buzzards, nude women washing clothes at the river; then with the Austrian and one of the Spaniards, went to take a swim. Everywhere women, wholly or partially nude, were washing clothes on the stones under little squares of thatch or canvas to protect them from the fierce sun. But a mile down the river, near a pretty little wooded island, we found a suitable and solitary place.

When we were gleefully splashing and feeling a bit cooler, a runty Guatemalan soldier appeared on the bank. Angrily he ordered us out, demanding what we meant by going in bathing. Gravely we assured him that in our respective countries it was quite customary to take a bath. He ignored the insult, dignifiedly informing us bathing was permitted only in one place.

"But there are women all along there!" we protested.

He could not comprehend why this was an obstacle and added, "In your country, don't you have regulations about bathing in frontier rivers?"

We assured him that in "our country" we could do exactly as we pleased.

Politely but firmly he intimated that we were liars. "Probably you came across without passports," he told us insultingly. "Come out and get dressed.

"Where are your passports?"

"With the chief of police."

26

"We'll see," and he marched us back to town like so many convicts.

3

The rest of the afternoon, we drank cold beer at the hotel *cantina* and wrote postcards.

All afternoon the cantina had been in charge of a gray-haired, doddering wretch, who mumbled to me he had the itch, which could be bettered only by a certain patent medicine procurable in no other place than Guatemala City. Forthwith, though he had never before seen me in his life, he gave me a dollar to send a bottle of it to him as soon as I got there.

About seven in the evening the burly Málaga proprietor took charge in person. He scolded the old man harshly; cursing, he rewrote all the accounts because the old fellow's handwriting was so shaky. Looking over at me forlornly in the midst of this task, he said, "In this world one has to have patience." Presently, he scolded the boy who waited in the restaurant, and receiving a saucy reply, batted the lad over the head with the long wooden stick attached to the doorkey of the back-lot toilets. Again turning dolefully to me, he repeated, "In this world one has to have patience."

The dumb beggar woman shuffled into the cantina, making gruesome gestures and guttural noises. The proprietor shoved her out angrily with loud curses. Then he turned to me and repeated gently, "In this world one must have patience."

About nine o'clock the American adventurer and the Mexican fifi came into the bar with the chief of police and a bunch of satellites armed to the teeth. The Amer-

ičan and his companion, not knowing about police regis-
tration, had been obliged at this late hour to search the
town high and low for the Chief; and now had to
spend the evening buying him drinks so they might
leave on the morning train.

4

Before dawn, we were herded into a bus to be jolted
down to the station and the orange-colored narrow-
gauge train. Cane-bottom seats allow two passengers
on one side of the aisle, but a single passenger on the
other. Though narrow gauge, this train was far more
efficient than the Pan-American over which we had
just traveled. It rolled along quite determinedly past
stations neat, well-kept, and freshly painted.

The police were ubiquitous. At every stop they passed
through the train, scrutinizing each and every passenger,
especially foreigners, with hostile eye. Passport inspec-
tion at the first two stations by bright ignoramuses who
moved their mouths when they read, contributed to
our consciousness of watchful officialdom. What a lot
of pother and useless energy spent on such folderol.
All immigration, customs officials, and police of all
countries look upon the traveler as a potential enemy.
Good citizens stay home and raise babies. The real
enemies of any existing state are always careful to have
all their documents and luggage in proper order. It is
the innocent and unwary traveler who is molested,
grafted upon, and treated with discourtesy. And Guatemala is about the worst country I know in this respect.

At the third station, our clandestine Italian friend

put in an appearance. He had almost drowned himself in the river, was shot at by guards and lost his shoes. Afterwards, to get to this third station, he walked barefoot all day and all night, then secured a new pair of shoes at a *finca* store, but as they were quite too large for him, his feet were terribly blistered.

He now explained his conduct. All his money was in gold, and having been told it would be confiscated, he preferred to ford the river clandestinely. I pulled out of my pocket the two hundred dollars which I had risked rather than submit to the Suchiate hotel keeper's extortionate exchange rates. The Italian looked sheepish.

5

Everything is cleaner and tidier in the Guatemala uplands than in Mexico. Here the second-class coaches are not strewn with filth. The Quiché Indians, in multicolored clothes, sit in orderly rows. The *ladinos,* or people of mixed blood, are more disciplined though a softer type than the Mexican mestizos. Protected with their omnipresent law, these *ladinos* move with jovial assurance. They are business men, small proprietors, traders.

Ladino was the name originally applied to Spanish Jews. To-day, among the mestizos, the profiles tell the story; the Jewish nose is often obvious; probably inherited from Jews exiled from Spain during the Inquisition. The process has been continued in more recent years by a new infusion of German Jews: Lowenthal, Schwartz, Zaccisshon, Knoth, Sclubacher, are names encountered in high financial and governmental circles.

The Jews are lovers of law, perhaps that is why law is so much more in evidence there than in Mexico.

In Mexico, a hundred cross-currents swirl and mill about. A dozen conflicting psychologies leap over restraints—everything is brutally in the making; many lives, many voices, many customs.

In comparison (at least on the surface), Guatemala is a finished product with a preciseness of category almost Western European. Things pigeon-hole. Events are well oiled. Here in Guatemala is a covert restraint, bespeaking the dignity of Spanish super-state tradition handed down unbroken since independence. Guatemala has been ruled by a long line of supermen—Carrera, Barrios, Cabrera, Orellana—a concentration of power reflected in the lowest gendarmes who seem to dispose of cocky but illimitable authority. The country is an effective little toy no larger than the state of Louisiana, yet enjoying international status.

After the desolate stretches of Chiapas, the Guatemala countryside is vivid; the bleak coast of Chiapas gives way to the rich coffee *fincas* of the Guatemala coast. The train roars over the rushing streams, steep *barrancas* clogged with the dense masses of tropical trees, gourds, big-leaved plants. Droves of plump cattle appear. In the towns, beggars are rare. Prosperity reaches out a benevolent hand. Everything is smiling, well regulated—precision and order are set against majestic natural scenery ever disorderly.

Authority accounts for much. Authority, here as everywhere, is rough-shod, aggressive. The raw seamy side of life is not allowed to protrude. It is brutally beaten back into the shadows.

At one station, a poverty-stricken Indian with blistered feet was lying beside the track. Two soldiers ordered him to get up. He protested he could not walk. The soldiers hammered him with the butts of their guns. Groaning and whining he writhed to his feet, staggered a few yards, then fell heavily on his face, bleeding. The soldiers, now convinced that he really could not walk, called two *cargadores* to carry him away.

"Dump him in some alley out of sight," they commanded.

"Who will pay us?" demanded one of the *cargadores*. For answer, a soldier struck him across the side of the head and he lifted the sick Indian up forthwith.

6

Guatemala's tradition of long-term dictatorship has been broken by short interludes of grave disorder, usually during a transition from Conservative to Liberal party or vice versa. The first long dictatorship was that of Carrera, who came into power as a mere youth and soon showed himself a Caligula.

On the occasion of his first fall in 1848, the Liberals seized the reins and retained control four months and a half. Congress immediately divided into two bitter Liberal groups which quarreled violently and were not averse to shooting at each other. In their brief interval of control, they elected four presidents. The Conservatives laughed and bided their time.

First, the Liberals put in Juan Antonio Martínez, then promptly pulled him down; next, José Bernado Escobar. Immediately he was faced by a revolt of fellow Liberals, the Cruz brothers, one in the east, the

other in the west. Twice Escobar resigned. The second
time, having no supplies or money with which to put
down the Cruz rebellion, he absolutely refused to re-
consider his resignation. It was accepted on December
31, 1848. Congress put in Lico Tejada.

On being chosen, Tejada leapt violently from his
seat. His face lengthened. His eyes bulged. Trembling
he begged for the floor.

"No, gentlemen! No!" he cried out. "In my hands
the Fatherland would sink. No, a thousand times, no!
I do not wish it, I will not accept this high post. The
situation is the most difficult imaginable; and I, the
most stupid person you could designate to settle such
complicated problems. I implore you, name another.
Do not give me this post, the Fatherland would sink—"

Breaking off, he placed two hands on the railing in
front of his seat, vaulted over, and rushed hatless to
his home "as though a wild bull were chasing him." He
barred himself in a room. Rather than the presidency,
he preferred death.

Lico Tejada's flight left the deputies in a plight. They
had accepted the resignation of Escobar, and Tejada,
during that night and part of the following day, was
undoubtedly president of Guatemala. Then Congress
convened and called upon Escobar to continue pro tem.

On New Year's Day, 1849, a new attempt was made
to elect a president. The chamber now divided into
half a dozen factions, supporting five candidates. Two
ballots gave no one a majority. They voted again and
again in vain. The session was suspended. Between snuff
and *tusa* cigarettes, the fathers of the country tried to
agree. The session was renewed.

Finally the Liberals united on Mariano Paredes. A

friend in the balconies hurried to Paredes' house to tell him of the high honor. Paredes rushed to his stable, saddled a good mule, and jumping on its back, spurred violently in the direction of La Parroquia, a suburb of the capital.

He called back to his friend, "Tell the deputies to name as president any of their distinguished grandmothers. I'm not going to be their jumping-jack." And he disappeared like smoke.

When the deputies arrived at Paredes' house to notify him officially of his election, and found the bird had flown, several of them jumped on horses to pursue the fugitive. At full gallop, they finally overtook him in Rodriguitos, and called on him to halt. Paredes refused to return. He preferred to ride clear to the north coast and wait for a boat to take him to Africa rather than see himself settled in the presidential chair.

Almost by main force, his friends dragged him back to the capital, directly to the Chamber of Deputies, where Escobar pressed the staff of command into his unwilling hands.

Two months later Colonel Paredes brusquely changed his policy, forgot his Liberal doctrines, abolished freedom of the press. At the end of three months, he abolished all liberties. At the end of six months, he recalled the Conservative dictator, Carrera. The Liberals fled from the country panic stricken. At the end of seven months not a Liberal could be found in all Guatemala.

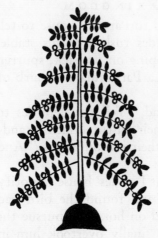

IV   KAISER KOFFEE

1

MANUEL ESTRADA CABRERA, also for many years dictator of Guatemala, was once asked why he reëlected himself.

"Because I wanted to finish the railway to the Atlantic. Ever since I was a poor child that was my golden dream. I always believed I could amount to something and be able to dispose of authority and power sufficient to unite the two oceans. I reëlected myself, and I fulfilled my ambition."

And, within three years after his reëlection, Don Manuel set January 1, 1908, for the solemn inauguration of the Inter-oceanic Railway. No expenditure was avoided to make the ceremony complete, impressive, and sumptuous. One critic of the time said: "The celebration of the inauguration of the railway was like throwing the house out of the window."

The official chroniclers overdid themselves. Declared the leading newspaper: "The Dawn which, like Ninon, is eternally young, has prepared to receive the visit of the Sun. She has fastened a rose in her bodice, a carnation in her hair, and she has sunk into the light of her royal lover, like Ayesha of Haggard, in the column of fire that made her immortal. It was in the place close to El Fiscal where the last spike was driven in the line."

34

2

Periods of dictatorship during the colonial period were tempered by recurrent crown inspections. The terror of the governors of the Indies was the royal *Visitador*, usually men of high integrity imbued with a spirit of justice; but on occasion instruments of unsavory plotters against honest local régimes.

After the death of Barrios Leal, the famous Conquistador of Petén, Gabriel Sánchez de Berrospe was named governor, captain general and president of the Audiencia, the colonial governing body. Elderly Sánchez de Berrospe was a very mild, kindly man, but somewhat lazy. People did with him pretty much as they liked, but his government was tempered. He remained calmly in office four years until Visitador Francisco Gómez de la Madriz arrived.

A worse devil than Gómez could not be imagined. Gambling, orgies, women, gold. Inordinately ambitious. Previously he had requested the Spanish court to make him an *Oidor* of the Audiencia. But lacking merits, he was turned down. Nevertheless, he managed to reach Guatemala. Soon he divided the country into two factions and through the recommendations of influential people succeeded in being named Visitador to judge the acts of Sánchez de Berrospe.

In 1697 several *cabos*, or sergeants, had been put in prison. The soldiers of their regiment, quartered in San Gerónimo, resented this imprisonment and under the leadership of Bartolomé Amezquita they overpowered the prison guards and released the captives. Amezquita was an enemy of the Audiencia and an enemy of Sánchez. He uncovered frauds in the Honduras mines. As a result, Gómez de la Madriz was named Visitador.

Promptly (February 19, 1700), he ordered the confinement of Governor Sánchez in Patulul, pending investigation.

Sánchez happened to be in the Pacific coast town of Esquintla, taking baths in Las Aguas Vivas, attempting to recover his health, somewhat broken on account of his heavy duties and his age. As Gómez well knew, Patulul was famed for its insalubrity.

Nevertheless, Sánchez announced his willingness to comply with the order. Leisurely he took the road for Chimaltenango and continued through Patzún, in no particular hurry to arrive at his place of confinement. He eyed the beautiful panorama, recited verses along the road and made merry with the Indian girls encountered on the way.

He journeyed and journeyed and finally arrived at Panajachel, where he begged temporary hospitality of a monastery. The good friars comforted his spirit and opened for him a special window so that he could look at the sky. They offered to keep him there with affection and safety and advised him not to go on to Patulul where he would contract malaria or some other dread disease. The fallen governor accepted their counsels and remained in the monastery until the investigations were over.

By then, the citizenry, outraged by the acts of the Visitador, demanded that the governor return.

Justice had been vindicated, probably served better by the slow jogging of Sánchez' mule than it would have been by railroads, airplanes and hotels with regiments of servants.

3

We halted in the Pacific coast coffee-region. Here is little of the industrialized haste, the feverish, raw-product extraction, the flourish of dollars and man-power, that features the Atlantic banana region. Banana is the plebeian of Guatemala; coffee is the aristocrat. The coffee-berry ripens leisurely under the shade of noble Guajiniquil trees; the fruit is picked cautiously; skillful fingers select and grade. From Ayutla in the west, all along the coastal foothills to Jutiapa near the Salvador frontier, an older feudal atmosphere prevails.

Here in the south, the peons toil under a paternal régime for a few cents a day and rations of beans and corn—corn, that seed from which, so the natives believe, sprang the first man. True, the peon is in debt to his master, as will be his children after him; he is subject to abuses and robberies; he must purchase everything in the company *tienda de raya*; he must toil long hours; often he is paid with company tag-metal instead of real cash. Sale ads of coffee ranches are reminiscent of Gogol's Russia—so many souls with the outfit:

FOR SALE: COFFEE RANCH, DEPARTMENT OF SUCHITEPEQUEZ; TEN THOUSAND FINE ACRES; ADMINISTRATION HOUSE; STABLES, WAREHOUSE, WORK CABINS, TWO HUNDRED AND TWENTY HANDS.

The peon's lot is that of his enslaved brother during the Díaz epoch in Mexico. He is not a component part of the modern state. He is a part of the paternal feudalism of the coffee coast, a feudalism so powerful that frequently plantation owners flout the orders of the Center.

Yet at times he need not work too strenuously, and he has some assurance that he will not starve. His masters are sometimes benevolent. And now that the *fincas* or ranches are chain-owned by large companies, mostly German, if malaria attacks him, his manager will send him up to recover on the cooler plantations in the highlands, where he will be set to work digging pits through the volcanic ash to replant the coffee bushes destroyed in the last eruption of the slim Santa María volcano. On the coffee coast the law is the rhythm of the slow-ripening berry and the long simmer of coffee, the companion of leisurely talk.

The condition of the coffee peon is less pitiful than that of the casual worker. When in need of harvest hands, the *finca* administrator appeals to the nearest Jefe Político, who at once orders the surrounding Indian villages to contribute the necessary number of "brazos" —"arms"—on a given date, *"sin excusa ni pretexto."* If the village defaults, trouble breaks. The system still surviving, in spite of the fall of dictator Cabrera, is described by Guillermo Rodríguez in his *Guatemala:*

And even more abusive and habitual is the arrival of the mounted and infantry escorts to capture the workers; by day and by night, in their homes or at their work, without asking permission of any one, the workers are hunted down, like deer, caught, bound, and carried off . . . The manner of securing workers consists in paying the Jefe Político a sum for each day's work for each laborer sent to the *finca* . . . The tariff is well known, for example: twenty pesos (thirty-three cents) for each day's work. A hundred laborers working fifteen days makes thirty thousand pesos, which sum is delivered to the Jefe. The interested party has nothing further to do. The Jefe receives the money and pays the worker what he wishes, for example: a peso and a half a day (two and a half cents). Of the thirty thousand pesos received, he thus pays the Indians twenty-five hundred and distributes a similar amount among those executing his orders. There remains twenty-five thousand pesos for the Jefe.

Naturally the native villages near the coffee *fincas* suffer worst; but in all the villages the Indians are hunted down by soldiers with guns and ropes to provide fodder for the army or for the building of railways, power-plants, roads for factory work, etc. Most concessions given to foreign capitalists contain clauses that the government shall provide the labor supply.

V INDIAN RUNNERS

1

From Mulua in Guate-mala to the capital, I rode in the company of the papal delegate Caruana, whom I had met before his expulsion from Mexico. I expressed my surprise at seeing him out of his jurisdiction—Mexico and the West Indies.

"On a vacation," he said.

Noting that Guatemala seemed to me a curious place for him to take a vacation in, he added, "I have been arranging things with the Guatemalan government. Ex-President Orellana, as you know, followed Mexico's lead in religious matters, deported priests and made other difficulties. President Chacón is easier to deal with. We have arranged now to create two archbishoprics in Guatemala instead of one—the capital and Quetzalte-nango. And, as in France, our appointments will be rati-fied by the government before becoming final. I am arranging too for facilities for transit of foreign priests and nuns through the country, a matter now scarcely tolerated.

"Once, I myself determined to come to Guatemala, boldly, openly, in clerical collar and vest. But when the boat anchored in Puerto Barrios the manager of the United Fruit Company happened aboard and exclaimed, 'My goodness, Father, they won't let you off in the garb. Haven't you an ordinary collar?' I was prepared

40

and hurriedly changed. The manager said, 'Come with me,' and took me off the boat with him personally, baggage and all, saying I was a company employee. The officials never even opened my effects. He then gave me free passage on the railway up to Guatemala City."

I noticed that now also Caruana was traveling with a pass, not a purchased ticket.

"The United States Fruit Company and the railroad," declared Caruana, "have always been very helpful to us. We, in turn, settle a few unpleasantnesses for them."

And he mentioned a claim against the company which they had forced a Catholic student to withdraw.

2

At each station our conversation was interrupted. Several newcomers immediately came over to kiss Monsignor's hand.

Resumed Caruana, "These Indians of Guatemala are curious folk, they haven't learned to spend money."

"They haven't much to spend," I remarked.

"No, but take the matter of traveling on the railways. Second-class is relatively cheap. Nevertheless, they go on foot for days from Quetzaltenango to the Mexican frontier, sleeping on the ground, suffering great hardship. By coming down to Muluá, they could go by train in a few hours for a small sum."

"You have been a good observer since you came to Guatemala," I remarked.

He looked at me sharply.

"And those Indians," I asked, "do they carry loads to the frontier?"

"Some of them, heavy loads."

"And correspondence?"

He shot me another glance.

"I shouldn't be surprised."

I tried a frontal attack. "And is that one of the things you have been arranging in Guatemala?"

He smiled again. "Why should I conceal the facts? We are not especially loved in Mexico. We have no way of keeping in touch with our people, except secretly."

He told me of his expulsion from Mexico. "You see, I had a perfect right to go there. Although the Mexican government had expelled a previous papal delegate, relations with the Papacy had not been formally broken off."

"But isn't it customary diplomatic practice for a government to declare *persona grata* whoever is named as representative, before he enters the country?"

"Ordinarily, but the circumstances were very special. To have questioned the Mexican government beforehand would definitely have caused a rupture difficult to bridge. By not precipitating such a rupture, I hoped to patch things up satisfactorily with the authorities. So I preferred to go quietly and establish my status on the ground."

"But you were expelled."

"Yes, my immigration card was tampered with."

"Then you did not enter as a professor and a Protestant as the press stated?"

"As a professor, yes. I stated that. I am a professor; I have taught in seminaries. But I never for an instant stated that I was a Protestant. This declaration was written in later on the card in another handwriting.

This was then used as an excuse to deport me. Never did I sign such a declaration.

"In the States after being deported I was seriously ill. The Mexican government, though, was prepared. They handled their publicity against me superbly. I was a babe in the woods at that sort of thing. When I got my version of the expulsion out, the news was stale. The government spread its side of the story over the front pages of the press; mine, a week later, was buried in the back pages for brief mention.

"When I went up to the Eucharistic Congress in Chicago, I was warned that the Mexican Consul would attempt to make trouble for me. Indeed, the police officials took charge of my visiting schedule, fearing personal aggression. A high police official told me, 'If the Mexican Consul so much as opens his mouth or gives out a word to the press while you are here, we'll beat him up and run him out of town. This Congress is going to be a hundred percent show.' "

1

ESCUINTLA IS A JUNCTION
town just before the steep
ascent to the capital. The
bright orange mangos are
three times the size of those
of Mexico. Instead of bottled
soda water and beer, one drinks cocoanut milk. The
cocoanuts are hacked down with machetes to the paper-
thin inner shell. A slight pressure of the thumb gives
access to the milk, which is sucked through a straw. In
Palín, on the sharp upward climb to the plateau, sweet-
meats are sold in gaudy little wooden boxes.

The real glory of the ascent is Lake Amatitlán,
reached towards the end of the afternoon—an enormous
body of water, sprawling around through the mountains, and dominated by the two slim volcanos of Fire
and Water—the latter having been called by the natives
Hunahpuh, "spray of flowers," from the spectacle of its
earlier fiery eruptions. Hot springs flow out by the side
of the track, steam oozes up around the car wheels.

An American, a fellow traveler, with a squdgy, ill-
shaped body, remarked in a cheery tone, "Very beautiful . . . You have never been in Guatemala, I take it."

Earlier I had sized up the man and had avoided him.
But he had intruded. "You will find it a remarkable
country." He beamed at me, a cat-like beam from steel-
rim, thick-lense glasses, set like headlights on his round,
pasty face. His left eye constantly exuded yellow mat-

ter that ran down his cheek bone. "I should like to help you here if I can. It is always difficult for one not knowing the language."

"I speak Spanish," I replied, watching the twilight on the lake.

"You will find several of the hotels good," he volunteered.

"I'm stopping at the Washington, thank you. It's cheap and native."

"Well, I dare say it is quite all right, of course. I'm accustomed to that sort of thing." He paused, wishing me to take the lead in inquiring about his personal business. "I'm a missionary," he finally announced. "It's a life of real hardship." He had to sleep in houses where there were bedbugs. Food was frightful. His stomach was always getting upset. Once, he had gotten into a house where there was only one bed and he had to sit up until three o'clock in the morning until the man of the house went off to work in the fields, and then had to use the same dirty blankets. He shuddered in memory.

He talked about his family. He had named his baby David because that could be either English or Spanish—handy to have a name like that, especially for a future missionary. His own name, "Harry," was not so easy for the natives to pronounce.

"Morals here are very bad," he shook his head mournfully. "Most of the people do not even get married, they live together—horrible! Still, when they do get married, it's well done; first, a eugenic license then both a civil and religious ceremony, priest and judge."

"How much would it cost to acquire a eugenic license?" I asked.

"Two dollars," I was told.

"And the marriage license?"

He was not quite sure about the fee.

"And the priest and the judge?"

It would cost between five and ten dollars to get married. The peon in Guatemala receives between fifteen and thirty cents a day; five dollars is a sum he has never known. I pointed this out to him. "I don't see how morality has much to do with it."

"Well," said the missionary lamely, "they could manage somehow to get properly married if they really wanted to. . . . Another trouble here, there is no divorce." He said this in a most daring whisper as though he was venturing on the bolshevistic. "Divorce here needs seven counts. Just to find a wife in bed with another man is not enough." He smacked his lips.

His mind jumped. His conversation jerked. He told me that Ford motors had been installed in the street cars which, a few years ago, had been hauled by horses. He wiped his cheek and once more returned to his favorite theme, the hardships of a missionary, traveling through the countryside.

Above all, he suffered from a lack of canned fruit. "I've just sent for three cases of California peaches. So nice to serve at afternoon tea."

We came to a stop. A Quiché woman lifted up a basket of beautiful mangos, plums and bananas resting on cool green banana leaves.

2

At the Guatemala station I was taken in tow by the runner of the Hotel Washington who hired a coach for me, piled my suitcases into it, shoved me in excitedly, and we dashed off over the cobblestones. The streets, village fashion, have the gutter down the center instead of at the curbs. Here and there were little pivot bridges for pedestrians to cross the street during summer deluges.

The Hotel Washington had a charming patio, a mass of vines, plants, and a splashing fountain.

My room gave me a good view of the city, including the Church of Calvario on a far hill and many of the flat roofs of this little place of one hundred thousand odd inhabitants. The town seemed like a drowsy third class Mexican city, backward, lost in a lazy dream.

I woke up the next morning, staring at the ceiling. The beams were very slight, almost sticks. Houses are advertised for rent or sale, not as fire proof but as earthquake proof. Fifteen years before, the city had been wiped out of existence by an earthquake. A row of buzzards topped the roof-trees across the street. Earthquakes and buzzards. Fires, too, are a special calamity.

There is no fire department. If any one permits a fire in his house, he is promptly arrested. Not long since, a shoemaker ran to the police to announce that his place was burning up. The policeman took him off to jail without giving a whoop about the fire, which burned down half a block. The water supply of Guatemala City is deficient, so when there is a fire, it goes to its god-appointed end. People come out to watch it, as they might a play; they wring their hands and exclaim, "What a pity there is no water!" Six months rolled by before the shoemaker got out of jail.

1

CORPUS CHRISTI DAY. I walked out through the Santa Carmen Parroquia, up to the church on the hill, with its enormous white cross. Below in the plaza were booths and a winding procession carrying the sacred heart of Jesus. The galloping beat of marimba bands pulsed through the languid air. In every restaurant, café, saloon, of Guatemala every few doorways, the slithering tune of the marimba hammers out in the clear night. On the country roads time and again one meets up with three or four marimba players carrying their bulky instrument from town to town. At the slightest suggestion they will set it up and pound out tunes, content to receive a few pennies.

The houses had decorations over the door, pictures of Jesus and great red hearts. I photographed a saloon; over the half-open door in which stood a baby girl was a framed Christ decorated with pink flowers—an amusing den of evil.

The booths proved stupid; none of the beautiful handicraft work encountered in Mexico, just kewpies, German toys and white doves painted with the words *"Consuelo al Alma."* Fuzzy artificial bugs with painted wings were stuck on a bamboo hat-rack contrivance. The remnants of the real indigenous artistic expression are found only in the buzzing markets—there a cascade of brilliant textiles, the bright *zacate* bags, the etched gourds.

2

In tropic uplands, the morning sunlight has a virginal, unsullied quality. The rarefied atmosphere and the relative closeness of the sun makes the light a limpid colorless liquid. Almost one can cup the hands to hold and drink pure exhilaration. The sky, too, is closer, and is made of pale blue silk. Buildings, however ancient, appear fresh and new-washed; their myriad tints, however faded, vibrate and shine.

On such a morning, I caught the bus from Guatemala to Antigua, former capital of the republic.

Down from the mountains trotted the Quiché women, white cloths coiled about their heads to ease their heavy loads. When they had no loads, they half uncoiled their turbans, letting a strip of cloth hang down their necks to protect their skin from the blazing sun. Their blouses are kimono-like, richly embroidered; the full sleeve falls a little way down their brown arms like a kimono sleeve. The striped red and white skirt is wrapped around the loins, unsewed cloth held in place by a red or yellow sash, fully a foot wide. This sash holds the stomach in tightly, accentuating the smooth curve of their hips and their unusually erect posture. All is of beautiful hand-woven material, bright colored, and of a more sophisticated, though no more civilized, design than in Mexico.

In the markets the Quiché women sit in formal erect rows, or they run along the streets under heavy burdens, their babies slung in *rebozos,* not on their backs as in Mexico, but in front of them, hammock fashion.

The men wear white "pyjamas" and occasionally checked blouses. If from the higher mountains, tiny straw hats are perched on their tangle of black hair, and a blue serge coat-like tunic falls to the knees in front and well down the calves behind.

Men and women—almost always they are carrying heavy burdens, but it in no way lessens their lightness of foot, the free agile play of their bodies. A swarm of these Indians hurrying along, swinging their arms, surprisingly erect, their bright clothes flaming against the deep green of the tropic vegetation, is like the flight of brilliant-hued birds. Ever they run, for the Quiché never walks—an everlasting springy half-trot stride. The bright-colored Indians glisten everywhere on the landscape, ever in motion. To the whole countryside, he imparts a rhythmic quality.

3

The bus passed through Mico, a dirty modern suburb, though actually founded centuries ago by Pedro de Alvarado, the reckless lieutenant of Cortez, to replace an earlier settlement he had razed.

Ancient Mico had been situated on the near-by height, looming harshly above the valleys of Jilotepeque and the Motagua. To-day its ruins can only be found with proper diligence, a few overgrown foundations.

In the sixteenth century Pedro de Alvarado crossed the Mexican frontier and advanced rapidly upon Central America. Tonatiuth, "Child of the Sun," as the Indians called him, suffered no reverses. Everywhere he was victorious. In those epic days there was no real stronghold. The Conquistadores went where they willed, ever stimulated by victory, reckless of life. They scaled the crags and plunged through fever-stricken morasses; heat and cold meant nought. Hardier supermen are not recorded in history's annals.

In the valley of Jilotepeque, Alvarado was advised by his allies of the famed town of Mico Indians, aloft on its impregnable height, held by numerous and experienced warriors. Two men alone could have held it against an army. Alvarado might easily have kept on his march, but he did not wish to manifest any hesitation to his followers, and so he gambled the fate of his star once more.

Various feints and flank attacks failed. Alvarado's Indian allies grew restless. At this juncture appeared another army, composed of Chinautla Indians, come to aid their Mixcan allies. Alvarado fell back and met this new menace on the open plains, routing the Chinautlans completely. The Mixcans, impassive on their secure heights, made no sally to aid their voluntary allies.

The Chinautlans were so incensed at the Mixcan passivity that they sent emissaries to Alvarado, offering to reveal to him an important secret. Alvarado received the envoys, accepted their presents, and was told of a subterannean cave which led from the bank of the river to the very heart of the besieged city.

While the main body went through the secret passage, Don Pedro sent "a rosary of musketeers" protected by huge shields to ascend the steep approach. A brave Spaniard—Bernardino de Arteaga—placed himself at their head. A rain of stones and poisoned arrows fell upon the legionary cordon. A rock hit poor Arteaga, who fell, both legs broken. A subordinate immediately took his place. At this moment, the main body of Spaniards, emerging unexpectedly from the cave, fell upon the Mixcan rear and slaughtered the startled defenders.

Having triumphed, Alvarado burned the city and tore down the walls. The handful of women and children, saved out of the hecatomb, were sent to the modern site of Mico to build a new town.

And thus the bright-colored Micos and Quichés became burden bearers for the conquerors, and burden bearers they have remained to this day.

4

The bus swept up over mountains. Great fleeces of vapor drifted through the thick pine forests. We dropped down over the ridge into the sunlight, past villages and coffee *fincas,* into the plaza of Antigua, second capital of Guatemala until, like the first, founded by Alvarado, it was destroyed by earthquake in 1773. In Antigua, though the heavy cracked arcades of the old plaza remain still bearing the arms of Spain, much of the older city was wrecked. The enormous viceregal palace is a mass of ruins smothered in tropical vines. The third capital to be built—the present Guatemala City— was in turn completely destroyed by earthquake in 1915. Antigua in its day was the glory of the Americas, second only to Mexico City. There occurred the real flowering of colonial culture. It harbored two universities, San Borja and Santa Tomás; there was published the first newspaper; there lived, died, and is buried the great chronicler Bernal Díaz. Bartolomé de Las Casas' valiant personality filled many pages of its history. Marroquín loaned it the brilliance of his learning and moral fervor. Belles lettres and historical writing flourished. It was the home of the notable Landivar and a galaxy of other poets.

When Thomas Gage visited Antigua at the beginning of the seventeenth century, he found it beautiful and wealthy and was impressed by its magnificent temples, its magnificent houses, its well-stocked stores. And yet that was before its apogee. According to Fuentes Guzmán, in 1686 it was divided into fifteen wards; it had many notable palaces such as that of the audiencia, the cabildo and the episcopate, the finest cathedral in all Central America, and scores of other temples and monasteries. It boasted of the great plaza, eight jails, three hospitals, twenty-two bridges, two colleges, a university, three drug stores and a multitude of sumptuous homes harboring sixty thousand inhabitants.

The main plaza of Antigua, above which tower the two slim volcanoes of Fire and Water, is surrounded still by eighteenth century palaces with great arched porticos. Nearly all the eighty huge churches are badly cracked. Some have lost their roofs; domes have caved in; they are abandoned.

The ruined walls of the church of Recolección now harbor a vast market, where come the muleteers and venders of corn and vegetables. At the gate stands a leather-clad tax-collector, with pockets in his aprons for coins. The Indians wait patiently in long lines, their heavy burdens on their heads, while each in turn argues lengthily over the amount of tax to be paid. One woman with a miserable handful of tomatoes is charged two reals, almost the price of her wares.

From all directions, down the streets, these Indian women come running toward the market. In the market itself, a great buzzing compound, they sit in orderly rows, usually grouped by villages, for the dialect varies from village to village, and most of them know only enough Spanish to sell their wares. And as marketing is not merely a process of gaining a livelihood, but also important as social intercourse, what pleasure could be derived from sitting among strangers, where no remarks would be understood?

Everywhere there are hum and movement, the acrid smoke and the stench of pork grease from the open-air restaurants, the rich odor of fresh fruit, the sweet perfume of gardenias, carnations, and honeysuckle, the heavy honey odor of over-ripe mangos, whiffs of manure and the smell of goats and mules.

To one side of the compound, the men squat on their haunches, long blue tunics touching the ground, bartering huge white piles of hulled corn on straw *petates* or gunnysacks.

I wander past the public washstands, where women are scrubbing bright clothes in brackish water, and come upon another little park with scalloped rose-colored balustrades. An elderly well-dressed gentleman, with cane and spats, is making love to a giggling little Indian girl. He watches me covertly from the corner of his eye as he tries to possess her hand.

At a doorway I sit and chat with a man carving cane-heads and idols—an industry for which the town is famous. His touch is light and deft, his imagination fertile, and the results artistic and graceful.

VIII SAINTS AND SINNERS

1

IN A LUXURIOUS BUT NOW empty niche in the choir of the once magnificent Franciscan temple of Antigua, an inscription records the name of the church sculptor, Juan Aguirre. His statue is gone, his name all but forgotten, but in colonial times his fame was heralded far beyond the frontier.

His masterpiece was the Virgin of the Coro, renowned during the classic colonial period, one of the images most venerated in the capital. So famed was this image for its beauty and miraculous qualities, that it attracted the attention and admiration of the venerable Fray Diego de Landa, apostolic bishop of far-off Yucatán, whose books still constitute a mine of information and reveal a subtle, generous, and wise mind. Fray Diego actually came all the way on foot from Yucatán to Guatemala for the express purpose of having Juan Aguirre make another image exactly like the first. The sculptor finished it in short time; the duplicate could scarcely be distinguished from the original.

Quite overjoyed, Fray Diego de Landa sealed the image in a casket, and it was carried away on the shoulders of several stalwart Indians. The rainy season overtook them on the road. Nevertheless, as the ancient historian Francisco de Florencia establishes beyond a doubt, though the downpour was frequent and heavy, not once did a single drop of water fall upon the precious casket, nor upon the Indians who carried it, nor upon the persons who accompanied it. And so, quite without mishap, the image arrived in Yucatán where it was given the name of Nuestra Señora de Izamal. And in Izamal it still abides, one of the most renowned of the Virgins of Mexico.

2

On Holy Friday of the year 1563, Francisco Marroquín, first Bishop of Guatemala, passed away. He had been a personal witness of the ruin of Antigua by earthquake, and being a man inclined toward good and charity, had alleviated suffering and was beloved by all. After his death, the people of Guatemala requested the King to send a man of similar merits. Philip II, knowing well that local society had become distinctly divided into Indians, creoles, and Spaniards, a combination requiring great governing tact, gave the matter careful consideration and finally hit upon the Bishop of Santiago de Cuba, Bernardo de Villalpando, of growing fame.

As a matter of fact, Don Bernardo was really quite a shameless man of the world, and greedy for money. He was obstinate, vain, insolent, hard to please. And he had better qualifications to be Sultan of Turkey than the Bishop of Guatemala.

He came from Cuba with a pompous cortege: dozens of pages, innumerable clerks, servants, secretaries, and— horror of horrors—many women with their respective maids. To the humility and piety of Bishop Marroquín, the sybaritism and obvious arrogance of Villalpando provided a sad contrast. The people had to receive him properly, but to themselves they said, "He will be bishop, but here we shall see things go as they should in spite of what he appears to be."

But the new bishop went his own way blithely, and interpreted canons, dispositions, precepts, papal orders, according to his own caprices. He threw out worthy monks, putting in their places clerics whom he could manipulate, mostly Genoese and Lusitanians, ignorant and talkative; without exception they used the ecclesiastical branch for luxury and carousal.

The civil government, chafing and perplexed, finally determined to intervene. The bishop held his ground. A prolonged deadlock.

Among the ladies who had accompanied his holiness from Cuba was one to whom he had displayed especial attention. Subsequently, they had a serious disagreement, and in order not to be further pestered by her, he married her off to a member of his own family. The bishop himself performed the marriage ceremony.

But after a few days, in a moment of sharp regret, the bishop remembered the sweet caresses of the lost lady and arbitrarily declared the marriage null and void.

Quite too big a fish-bone for the civil government and the leading citizens to swallow. They addressed a heated memorial to the King demanding that such goings-on be terminated. The Council of the Indies sent a complaint direct to Pius V. The Holy Father immediately sent two *breves* through the King, restricting the bishop's powers, and giving the governor of the province authority to put him in his proper place.

The royal communication reproduced all the complaints: the prelate's ambition had caused him to ill-treat the Indians. "He has in his house certain women who are not his sisters or his cousins, and one of them is eighteen years of age and not very honest. Due to her influence with said bishop, in order to get anything transacted one must treat with her nephew, giving him expensive presents." Even the bishop's theft of chickens and other petty indiscretions, which would have brought a blush to the cheek of the most hardened, were minutely enumerated.

The governor published the royal communication and the two *breves* by town crier. For weeks, in the churches, the markets and the public plazas, the one and only topic was the shameless conduct of the bishop.

Even callous Don Bernardo could not stand such wholesale criticism. On the pretext of visiting near-by towns, he hurried to Salvador. In Santa Ana, he shut himself up in a monastery cell, with the order that he be permitted to rest undisturbed. The following day, he did not come out. His servants waited patiently but after dubious consultation, they finally knocked on the door. No reply. Alarmed, they forced the lock. The bishop lay on his bed, rigid and cold, his eyes bulging, his lips glued together tightly. Rage, according to the records, had strangled him.

Says the chronicler of the time, "Reader, if you are a Christian, say a pater-noster for the soul of Bishop Villalpando. It is certain that, being a bishop, he went to purgatory; but as a sinner, perhaps he has not yet reached divine grace."

3

Augustín Micos in his tales of Antigua relates the story of the one and only victim of the Guatemalan Inquisition.

In the year 1650 there appeared in the outskirts of Antigua a mysterious personage whom the Indians baptized with the name Cumatz. Terrible was his aspect. Fright preceded him. Death followed him. Everywhere he sowed desolation.

The authorities, as well as private individuals, caused many prayers to be said. Efforts were made to exile him from the country. In vain. This strange personage fooled the authorities under their very beards, and continued to do exactly what he willed in all the towns of the Province of Sacatepéquez. Though he molested the *ladinos*, his predilect victims were the Indians—them he persecuted to the limit.

Who was this Señor Cumatz? To judge from ancient descriptions, Cumatz was a terrible illness much resembling cholera morbus. *Diagnosis:* Did you see a person attacked by spasms, all his muscles contracted, suffering insatiable thirst and a demoniacal fever? He was in the clutch of Cumatz. Such persons immediately made their testaments, called the priest, and prepared their luggage to march to the next world. *Etymology:* The word "cumatz" from the Cachiquel language, means "snake." The strange infirmity was like a serpent which coiled around the victim, broke his bones, and finally strangled him.

The effects of the epidemic were terrible. Neither

the baths of Almolongo, nor the treatment of the most famous doctors; neither the prayers to the most miraculous saints, nor the conjurations of the most learned checked it. The Indians believed God's mercy to have deserted them.

One day as an Indian came out from the Almolongo baths, a mysterious traveler detained him. Though dressed in the Franciscan habit, the stranger with his beautiful beard had such a noble and alert bearing that he seemed an inhabitant of a quite different world. His agreeable countenance was ascetic.

"Why," asked the stranger, "have your companions not invoked the aid of San Pascual Bailón against the epidemic? He is very disposed to favor you; he merely wishes to be importuned in order to do so. Go advise your people to put themselves under his protection."

"My Lord," replied the Indian, "I do not even know this saint. Even if what you tell me were true, my companions would not credit my word."

"You do not know San Pascual Bailón!" exclaimed the other. "You are mistaken. You are speaking with him at this very moment. That your companions believe your words, I will give you an infallible sign. If they seek my protection, the epidemic will cease within nine days; you will be the last of its victims."

Saying this he disappeared in a track of light and perfume.

For a few minutes the wayfarer remained frozen in thought, then shaking himself awake, he returned to Antigua and told the convent priest what had happened. The priest called the faithful together, and in a panegyric of the saint, gave his parishioners over to Bailón's protection. After a nine-day procession, sure enough, the terrible Cumatz disappeared, carrying away with him in his claws as a last victim the Indian of our story.

Ere long the Indians decided the image of San Pascual Bailón was the skeleton of death. To this day there is scarcely a Guatemalan ranch house which does not have its skeleton and its cult. Flowers are offered; candles are burned. Soon San Pascual was not the only saint thus venerated. The number of household Lares and Penates increased rapidly.

The Holy Inquisition, fearing ridiculous idolatry, decided to extirpate such superstition. An edict was issued ordering the priests of Sacatepéquez, on a given day and given hour, to enter the houses of the Indians and seize all idols and burn them in the public plaza.

The images of San Pascual predominated. A sight indeed to see the heaps of skeletons burning in the great pyres. Throngs of Indians howled in fright and sorrow because

Chamuscaba la Santa Inquisición
Al Venerable San Pascual Bailón.

Thus ended, so far as the Church was officially concerned, the cult and the brotherhood of San Pascual Bailón, the strange saint who had given such service in adversity. But that these occurrences should not be entirely forgotten and the lesson lost, the ecclesiastical authorities decided that each year, the procession of the Holy Burial should be headed by a horrible skeleton to symbolize Superstition being put to flight by true Religion.

Many people now ask the why of this skeleton. He represents the one and only victim of the Guatemalan Inquisition.

1

THE SUN IS OUT AGAIN. IN
the plaza, I sit down beside
Santiago, a soldier in blue
dungarees and bare feet. His
full features under straight
black hair are mobile, expres-
sive, smoldering. Poetry here—sensitivity. Toil has not
made the boor—some pride of race subjugation has never
stamped out.

Santiago had married young. His Nahualin, daughter
of one of the Principales of Acatenango in the mountains above Antigua, had not been easy to win. She
lived in a stout, double-thatched, white-washed house
surrounded by forty hectares of good bottom land.
Nahualin wore the most beautifully embroidered blouses
in Acatenango; her skirts were of the finest silks from
San Pedro Sacatepequez. Her body was the song of a
nightingale; her eyes were pools of night; her eyelids
were white knives.

Santiago was the seventh of a nondescript brood of
twelve children who starved in the Hondos and lived
in a shabby two-room *jacal,* and Nahualin's father,
Don Martín, decidedly opposed his court to Nahualin,
though Santiago was a sturdy young *mozo* with clear
open face and laughter that rang like the jumping
waters over the Quetzal Falls. He could read and write
—all in his favor but not enough.

Don Martín had other ideas for Nahualin. Not that

he placed too much emphasis upon worldly goods. But the Cacique, that powerful minion of the central authorities, was dead in love with Nahualin. It was not good to offend such people. They could make life happy or bitter, even for a Principal. And the Cacique was reputed to be something of a brute—a trace of white blood often turned out that way—fond of his power, yet always willing to pass out a drink and an *abrazo*— in return for the signing of queer papers which had mysterious potency over the signer, and caused troops to appear and take away cattle, even houses.

This had happened to Don Vicente, eighty-year-old Vicente, who now mumbled in the plaza, a bundle of bones and rags. Yet everybody knew that the Cacique and Don Vicente had been enemies for a decade. This sudden making up on the Cacique's part, his sudden effusive friendship—well Don Vicente should have had more sense, should have known the Cacique was up to evil.

The Cacique was cunning, no doubt of that. Cunning and ruthless. Convenient to have him for a son-in-law. Too, there would be such a glorious big wedding, dances, drinks, maybe a fight or two with machetes.

And so Nahualin was betrothed to the Cacique. She turned her shoulder on him as much as she could, afraid to show more violent disrespect. The Cacique, not unacquainted with the female heart, endured these affronts with patience. Women after all were chattels—and had her father not pledged his word of honor?

For some time now Santiago had been absent. Her father and the Cacique were pleased. They did not know that Santiago had gone to work on the Antigua road to earn money.

Santiago spent all he earned in part payment on a beautiful black and white cow, which he tied at the gate of Don Martín's thatched house. Though poor he would show Don Martín he knew the formalities of courtship, that his intentions were honorable and serious. Don Martín's eyes widened at sight of such a beautiful beast but he did not lead it into his corral; his word was pledged to the Cacique. And so the cow languished in the hot sun. Santiago refused to take it away, so there it died. Three months' toil on the roads gone for nought and still twenty gold quetzales to pay.

Love was not daunted. Don Martín, worried at the clandestine visits between Nahualin and Santiago, hastened the day of her marriage with the Cacique.

Santiago was building a humble little *jacal* on his father's stony land. The night before the wedding Nahualin disappeared. She had gone to live with Santiago—no wedding, no formality.

After that, of course, the Cacique would never have her. He went off to Antigua in a huff, vowing vengeance. Don Martín fumed. But Santiago had done no wrong and his neighbors loved him. The Cacique could have rounded him up in a forced labor *caudrillo* but that would prove only a momentary and too obvious revenge.

Time passed. The Cacique apparently forgot his pique. Don Martín relented and gave Santiago a little *milpa* where he could grow corn. The two chicks were very happy. With the years came two babies, a boy and a girl. Santiago now had cows, pigs, chickens, and prosperity peered over his *palo blanco* fences.

Odd that the Cacique had let the matter die so easily
—he used never to forget an affront.

2

Sixteen years passed. All was forgotten. The Cacique
had gone away; he had become Jefe Político—Governor
of the Department. He was now gray, but a sharper
intelligence was buried under his rolls of fat. He had
become more amiable but ever more cunning as he had
climbed in the world.

One day, Jaime, Santiago's son, was taken ill with
fever. They called in the local medicine woman, Doña
Adela. She rubbed the boy's body with an egg, gave him
hot teas and broths, pasted medicinal leaves on his temples and incanted strange songs. But he grew steadily
worse until it seemed he might die.

Jaime must be taken to the white doctor in Antigua.
And so Nahualin wrapped the child up, head and all,
in a sarape, and roped him to a chair which was tied to
Santiago's back. In this way, Santiago carried Jaime,
now a fever-stricken skeleton, to Antigua. He ran over
the trails with his heavy burden all night and most of
the next day, arriving in the arcaded plaza of Antigua,
gasping, almost dead himself. He eased his burden down
in front of the governor's palace near the entrance to
the Comandancia.

Whom should he see but the Cacique himself—governor now. The Cacique gave him an *abrazo*—a neigh-
bor from his home town. A doctor? Oh, yes. His face
beaming, the Cacique promised to help him. All would

be well. These fevers pass. Doctor Méndez was the man, wouldn't charge a friend of the governor's a centavo. Another embrace, and the Cacique went over to the Commandant, lounging in brown uniform in front of the barracks playing *naipes,* and whispered in his ear. Then he waddled off, tapping his manzanita cane, a little leer twisting his fat lips.

Santiago sat there on the old stones, mopping his brow with his bandanna, his head swimming. He leaned over to tighten the thong of his *cactli,* put his back to the chair again.

The Commandant approached him. "So you have carried this boy all the way from Acatenango! How strong you are! You are a good *mozo.* Bring the boy into the barracks. We'll see he's attended to." He gave orders to several barefoot soldiers.

They carried the boy inside, untied him, and stretched him out on a *petate* in a shady corner of the patio.

"You will make a good soldier," the Commandant told Santiago, smiling behind his black curling mustaches.

Four soldiers seized Santiago and carried him struggling into the barracks. He was ordered to put on a uniform. He refused. They tied him to a horse-ring and gave him twenty bareback lashes. Wishing to save Jaime, he put on the uniform. He was immediately given heavy fatigue duty.

No further attention was paid to Jaime. He died that afternoon in the corner of the barracks; they dumped his body into a trench in the cemetery. Santiago could not even be there—and a soldier of another regiment stole the blanket.

Now Santiago is a soldier for the Republic of Guate-

mala, squatting in the plaza of Antigua with smoldering eyes. If he deserts he will be shot. Nahualin wonders why he does not come back. She weeps far into the
night.

X HEAD OF A
TRAITOR

1

BACK TO GUATEMALA CITY.
The auto bus is a tangle,
Indians, bags, baskets covered with banana leaves,
vegetables. Chickens mess
over my shoes. Only one In-
dian is dressed in European style, a neat suit with a collar
and tie, but he wears a wide straw sombrero and is barefoot.

Suddenly rain comes hammering down. Curtains are
put up. But the roof leaks. We huddle more closely together; a puddle gathers on one of the seats. A young
mother reaches her hand into her blouse and flops out
her breast as though it were something that didn't belong to her and gives the nipple to her baby girl. The
child wets her rebozo and lap. She remains stolid and
unconcerned.

In order to make more room, I take another baby
girl on my lap. The child's name is Celestina, her hair
is done up in tight little black braids. Her black eyes are
liquid—no pupil visible—soft like a gazelle's, and she
smiles up sweetly and trustingly into my face.

Near the summit of the pass a woman hails the bus
and room is good-naturedly made for her. Four people
are now sitting on the driver's seat, which gives little
elbow room for manipulation as we slide around the
slippery curves. Time and again we find ourselves on
top of a slow-moving ox-cart with its heavy creaking

wooden wheels and white hoop-hood. Only by hair-breadth skirting of precipices do we avoid collisions.

2

My first search in Guatemala City was for an old friend, Luís Quintanilla, secretary of the Mexican Embassy; an Estridentista poet, the initiator of the short-lived little-theater movement in Mexico, founder of the Murcié-lago Theater, and a charming gentleman. I found him in, talking with Colonel Hernández, exiled for participation in the De La Huerta revolt.

Luis introduced me to Ambassador Cravioto, also a poet, a plump little fellow. Partially deaf, he tilted his head towards me, a condor-like movement suggesting shrewdness. He hears more than he pretends—not a new device in diplomatic traditions. He gave me the customary diplomatic folderol regarding the benevolence of the United States and the need for international friendship.

All the gossip was of the recent Catholic protest strike and of Arthur Geissler, the American Minister, a choleric German, naturalized American, who got along well with the large local German population, but was not so well liked by the American Colony. Every morning he played golf with the president, who deferred to him in everything.

The Catholic demonstration, a few days before my arrival, had been exciting. President Orellana, following the anti-church lead of Mexico, had deported all foreign priests. The Conservative party, stirred up by prominent Catholic women, called upon everybody in the city to protest by standing still on Central Sixth Avenue for five minutes every Thursday at four o'clock.

Sixth Avenue was jammed at the hour set. But Orellana promptly set machine guns at both ends of the Avenue and stationed troops all along Fourth and Seventh Avenues. This dampened even the most resolute spirits, and on the following Thursday (the day after my arrival), it was rumored this time the machine guns would open fire. Sixth Avenue looked like heaven before the death of Adam and Eve.

Luís took me to call upon Señor R, a Hondureñan, and other editors of *El Imparcial,* one of the largest Conservative papers. Over the door an electric sign announced, "Beauty, Justice, Liberty," ideals unpropagated since the previous Thursday, when the paper had been arbitrarily suppressed. A soldier in the doorway eyed us suspiciously as we entered. Though the paper had been suppressed, the establishment had to be kept open, to prove to the Guatemalan public that the owners had voluntarily left off publication. Señor R was now busy running from one government official to another, scraping and bowing and offering to change his policy "from 'criticism' to 'description.' "

3

Señor R spoke of his difficulties with a humorous sigh, then launched into a tale of persecution of another order.

In 1787, the poet, Rafael García Goyena of the Province of Guatemala, was put in prison. García, a hand-

some youth of gay disposition, was quite ripe to receive
the ministrations of love—Love with a capital *L*. When
about to finish his university law studies, a dark-eyed
Beatrice with moist red lips crossed his path. For the
love-lorn youth, the be-all, the start-all, and the end-all
became Beatriz Plácida Ubeda. García's father stormed
anathemas against the infatuation, and so the two
pigeons, swept away by their passion, eloped, and married according to law, then sought out a kindly curate
who sanctified their civil nuptials.

But Rafael was not yet twenty-one. His furious
father caused him to be seized and thrust into a cell of
the Escuela de Cristo. Later, without the least consideration for poor Beatriz, he sent his son off on a trip
to Havana where he hoped work and privation would
make him repent. The patron of the family, the powerful Marquis Aycinena, agreed this was the best plan;
and so, one cold November dawn, the poet was pulled
out of his cell, set on the outskirts of the city and told to
walk to the northern coast of Honduras and embark.

After many footsore days, he finally arrived at the
castle of San Felipe, a frightful Spanish stronghold
where many prisoners had wasted away their lives. He
took passage on a brigantine. On arriving at Amoya, the
zealous commandant of that port demanded García
show the passport required to pass through the royal
dominions of the King of Spain. The poet had nothing
but a letter of recommendation from Marquis Aycinena.
Pending identification, he was thrust into prison. The
unhealthy climate, the privation, the worry, soon broke
García's health. At the end of three long months the
papers arrived. These proved to be a lengthy explanation from Aycinena why he had given the traveler a

recommendation instead of passports. García was still kept in prison, hovering between life and death. Not until six months after his initial imprisonment did he get his liberty. The drastic action of his father and the Marquis of Aycinena almost deprived the ænemic belles lettres of Guatemala of the ingenious verses of García Goyena.

Poor Beatriz wept her eyes out in a convent.

4

"You see," said Señor R, "coercion exists in all ages—parents against children, governments against free men, the older generations ever against the new, death against life—an eternal principle. And too often death wins. We are lucky not to lose our heads, like the famous rebel, Field Marshal Cruz."

And Señor R recalled us another bit of history.

January 23, 1870, the gory head of Field Marshal Serapio Cruz, leader of a rebellion, was brought into Guatemala City by the loyal troops of General Antonio Solares; ironically, Solares was the godfather of the man he killed.

The federal general, known as Tata Tonino, was an elongated, brown fellow tanned by the winds and suns of Jalapa. Ignorant, brutal, nevertheless he was a docile instrument of President Cerna, a faithful tool of his master who was cunning as a fox and slippery as a snake.

The rebel, Marshal Cruz, had been fighting since the days of Dictator Carrera to overthrow the régime and impose Liberalism. He continued fighting against the succeeding Conservative governments of Presidents Galvez and Cerna. Cerna sent Solares after the rebel. The general kept doggedly on the trail of the rebels all along the sharp crests of Calonitos.

He fell upon them in Palencia, down in a valley. A brutal surprise. The rebels broke in confusion. His godson, Marshal Cruz, was unable to rally his followers. The federal soldiers ripped the rebel ranks with a hail of bullets; they hacked them to pieces with machetes. Tata Tonino had closed the exits to the valley, so the fleeing rebels had to scatter up the steep sides of the canyon—prey to the raking federal fire.

Even so, Cruz with a handful of faithful ones tried to resist. For an hour and a half, he kept up desperate opposition. Not until a ball shattered his legs, did he spur his horses up the side of the *barranca,* only to come rolling down.

General Solares was not content with mere victory; he wished to give ocular testimony to his superior, the president, that he had carried out his mission. So he cut off his godson's head, put it on a dish garnished with oak leaves and loaded it on the back of Luís Benavente, a young rebel student captured in the combat.

In those days, cutting off heads was not so common as to-day. Solares wished to make a good display, so on the outskirts of Guatemala, at the church of Candelaria, he ordered young Benavente to display his burden by holding it up to the crowd on the palm of his left hand. Benavente proceeded thus along Sixth Avenue to the Merced church. He was allowed to rest his arm for a moment; then the procession continued to the main plaza and the old cemetery, where the head was further displayed and photographed.

73

Godfather Tata Tonino did not enjoy his triumph very long. In November of the same year a broken barrel of powder beside which he was sitting caught on fire. Horribly burned, he died in great agony.

According to a more popular legend, when General Solares was sitting on the barrel of powder in the Administración de Rentas, Lucifer himself slipped up and set fire to the keg. There was an explosion, a sharp flame, for a few minutes the room was filled with smoke. When they sought the remains of Tata Tonino not a trace of him could be found. The Devil had carried him away to remind the people of the fate of all traitors and bad friends.

XI   MATTRESSES
FOR BANANAS

1

RETURNING FROM THE lower hot country of Guatemala, I had luncheon at the American Legation with Minister Arthur Geissler—an alert, practical, pleasant but occasionally choleric man. Geissler particularly wished to impress me with his influence with President Orellana (which I already knew), but he was careful to indicate that this was influence not pressure. This influence had succeeded in convincing Orellana to ratify the Washington 1923 treaties, to revise a railway concession, and other good works. After much effort, Geissler had secured an invitation from the Guatemalan Government to replace the French officers training the Guatemalan army with American officers; he was sharply resentful that a mere order of the American President was sufficient to precipitate military invasion, whereas Congress did not even consider Guatemala's pacific proposal. Geissler had also recommended the establishment of aeroplane service to Central America; this too had been ignored by the State Department; very likely this enterprise would pass into the hands of other countries. He dilated upon Mexican activities and influence and was obviously dissatisfied that he was merely a Minister while the Mexican representative was an Ambassador.

"It is not," he remarked, "just a question of sitting at a less important place at official banquets," though this, too, evidently nettled him, "but the psychology such a situation creates in the official mind. Mexico took this step just to annoy us." As an evidence of pernicious Mexican influence, Geissler pointed out the new labor law of Guatemala. Fortunately, the government had brought it to him for prior consideration; not at his request, but merely because of the confidence he enjoyed with President Orellana. The worst features had been ironed out before passage. Geissler, chewing at the wrong end of a cigar, spoke bitterly of the local Schwartz banking people who had tried to block some deal of the New York bankers which the State Department was pleased to encourage. The State Department had been obliged to warn the Guatemalan Government not to accept loans from the Schwartz interests.

The Schwartz banking interests in Guatemala are of long-standing influence. San Francisco capitalists of German extraction, they came into Guatemala at the time of Dictator Cabrera, whose revolution they financed; and under succeeding opposition administrations, in spite of their alliance with Cabrera, managed to maintain the confidence of the government. But being independent bankers they obstructed the general plan of financial control of Latin America by New York houses.

The question pressingly at issue at this time was the establishment of a national bank. Capital was needed. Mexico had offered to loan this money to Guatemala without interest. Geissler assured me that this offer would not be accepted. "President Orellana is far too wise to take such a step."

I switched our conversation to the Indians, the

Quichés, who made up the bulk of Guatemala population. Of them Geissler knew nothing.

2

Geissler secured me an interview with President Orellana.

Unfortunately, I was traveling through Guatemala
with the minimum of clothes. My hat had been through
a number of tropical rains. For the momentous occasion of interviewing the President of Guatemala I
decided to buy a new one, but could find nothing decent
in the entire capital of Guatemala and finally compro-
mised on a cap.

When I called at the presidential mansion, the captain of the guard was puzzled by me. I well knew the
rigorous Central American etiquette in regard to clothes;
nothing but a cutaway was proper. The captain of the
guard asked for my card. I discovered that I had left
my card case at the hotel. The captain, in a thorough
quandary, went off shaking his head, repeating my
name over and over in an effort to remember it.

President Orellana received me at once—a most likeable unpretentious personality. He sat on the edge of
his chair in an eager fashion.

I talked about the Quichés. He was obviously puzzled that an American should be so interested in the
Indian population. Time and again he started to tell
me about guarantees for American capital, the develop-
ment of roads and railroads, the concessions that had
been granted; the possibility of exploiting petroleum;

but I switched him back to those Quichés of the highlands that had so fired my imagination.

A bit irked, he remarked, "Yes, they are very docile, which is a great advantage; they are not rebellious as in other parts of Latin America."

I told him that down in the banana country the bananas ride as in a Pullman, on a special mattress of banana leaves, but the Indians are dumped into second-class coaches and have to sit on the floor because there are so many banana cars the proper number of passenger coaches cannot be provided. He restricted his comment to a nettled, "Yes, bananas are the yellow gold of Guatemala."

XII   MISTAKEN IDENTITY

1

WITH COLONEL HERNAN-
dez, I made the rounds of the
city to find out how the poor
people of Guatemala live and
how Geissler's labor law
worked. We went to the
slums, built by the workmen's association founded by
ex-President Cabrera. The money must have gone into
official pockets for these supposedly model homes were
shacks, unfloored, quite without toilet facilities or ven-
tilation.

A *carretero* or teamster was unloading cement from
a small, wooden-wheeled cart. Great jewels of sweat
were running off his face and open chest. A torn under-
shirt partially hid the upper part of his body. Panting,
he wiped his forehead with the back of his grimy hand,
and paused to reply to us courteously. His face had the
honest, patient, hopeful yet suffering expression of a
domestic animal. His wage was twenty pesos or forty
cents a day; but as he was in debt to his employer nearly
two thousand pesos or some forty dollars, he received
in cash only thirteen pesos (twenty-six cents) with
which to house, feed and clothe his family. Could he
quit his job? No, not unless somebody paid his debt or
he worked it off, otherwise he would be put in jail. How
long would it take at the rate of seven pesos a day to
pay off the debt? He had never really figured it out,
but thought it would take a very long time, especially

79

as every once in a while, because of sickness in his family or for other reasons he had to increase his debt, part
of which he had inherited from his father.

Next we tackled a *mozo* from the *juzgado* or police
court. He received about sixty cents a day. A street car
conductor told us he worked twelve hours a day seven
days in the week for ninety cents a day. He belonged
to Guatemala's labor aristocracy.

Our way led us past the market and up a slanting
street in the lee of the grim fortress which overlooks
Guatemala City. We came upon a farmer and his son
unloading sheaves of grass from a rickety cart. Between
them they received fifteen pesos a day, or thirty cents,
but had their own house on the hacienda and the right
to till a little plot of ground. They too were in debt—
an enormous amount, said the father, he really did not
know how much. If he quit work before this debt was
paid he would be arrested. When we suggested they were
sadly exploited, the father perhaps sincerely, perhaps
thinking us officials, waxed highly indignant. "We are
far better than most," he said surlily, turning to his
labors.

Colonel Hernández took me out to visit a Mexican
named Gómez, one of the signers of the Mexican 1917
Querétaro Constitution, now in exile, and connected
with a local labor union.

We found Señor Gómez in a dirty room with one
desk, a typewriter and a rickety chair. He proved a most
tricky, cowardly, unshaven, disagreeable type. Before
talking to me he went to the door to see if any eaves-
dropper was hanging about. He called in another labor
leader. Both were obviously shysters of the worst sort,
interested only in the few dollars they might squeeze

out of their ignorant followers, yet at the same time terribly frightened of the authorities. Gómez, particularly, feared deportation. They talked to me very cautiously. Finally Gómez, his fear getting the better of him, told me he would write out the answers to my rather pointed questions. "It will be quite a job," he said in an unctuous tone, implying he expected to be well paid for his trouble.

Next day I went back to see him. He had not written out the promised information. His evasive answers revealed he would not do so. Fear of Orellana's dictatorial government had overcome his greed.

Guatemala is not a healthy place for would-be emancipators; nor even for some with no such laudable desires, as Señor Francisco Castro, agent for an American adding machine corporation, discovered.

2

I ran into Castro in the Alhambra, the leading café. He wore a checked suit, spats, a loud tie, and his black hair was slicked down with brilliantine. He told me his troubles.

No sooner had he set foot in Guatemala than he had been arrested and dragged off to jail for a month. The amazing charge against this jelly-bean was that he was a labor leader. Mr. Geissler, the American Minister, had no jurisdiction since Castro was a South American, though representing an American company, but after much effort our Minister finally convinced the authorities that dapper Señor Castro had nothing to do with labor, and after a month's imprisonment he walked out of jail to sell his adding machines.

An attempt had been made to form a Central American Confederation of Labor. For the first year, the executive committee was to have its seat in Guatemala City. The Guatemalan representative was named—Francisco Castro.

Later I met the "real" Francisco Castro in Salvador whither he had fled to escape arrest, for whom Francisco Castro, adding machine salesman of the slick hair and spats, had gone to jail.

As for Adding Machine Castro, he considered his reputation ruined by his month in jail. He was hopping mad and decided he must achieve fame as a brave and wipe off the stigma attached to his name. A champion welter-weight prize-fighter was in town. Castro breezed up to the chap in the Alhambra café and without warning slugged him across the jaw. Fortunately for Purple Spats, the pair were separated before the prize-fighter could retaliate. Again Castro was taken to jail. This time he was merely fined. But, glory be! his picture appeared in the paper as the man who dared to hit the welter-weight champion. All the waitresses in Guatemala City—the tale is Castro's—fell desperately in love with him. With a disdainful wave of a jeweled hand, he informed me, he had but to choose—except, he said with a little frown, a certain *estupenda* in the tea-room across the street, who persisted in laughing at him.

1

OFF FOR SALVADOR! THREE o'clock in the morning. Dismally cold. Jammed into the back seat of a Studebaker, I have no room for my legs; they stick out over the door across a pile of mail sacks. We wind through the silent streets picking up various passengers, and sweep away lightly, upwards over a mountain road.

Glimpses of lights. Indians trotting, stumbling into market, heavy loads of produce on their backs, sometimes great towers of pottery. One carries several dozen bird cages with mountain canaries. More ox-carts, and even more dangerous here; they carry no lights—and loom up suddenly in the dark. Our brakes screech. The heavy carts careen towards the ditch to let us pass.

Dawn. Rose and gold over a sweep of valley.

We breakfast in a little town under a rear porch. Mashed black beans, eggs, coffee. "Twenty-five pesos— fifty cents, please." One of my companions, an Italian representing an American pickle company, has brought his own food. He never trusts to chance.

My other back-seat companion is a priest: greasy, silent, continually wiping his sweaty palm on his dirty robe. He wears a duster which he does not remove even on the hottest part of the trip.

Already heavy rains have fallen. Once we skid completely around.

At every town the police take our names and ask to see our passports.

We climb up a new mountain road slippery with mud and get stuck in a rut, at the edge of the cliff. The driver and we passengers (except the priest) carry large stones to put under the wheels. A whole hour is lost.

2

We run into a crowd of frightened Indian women clucking and chattering, running back and forth across the road—so many chickens.

"*Hay bandidos!*" they cry.

The chauffeur stops the car.

They chatter to us all at once. Bandits were holding up the car just ahead of us. The women point up the road excitedly, telling us to wait. But with a shrug, our chauffeur limbers up his gun and starts on again.

Around the second turn my heart jumps. We run full into a group of men carrying drawn pistols, gesticulating excitedly, talking loudly.

They prove to be the male folk of the party of Indian women we just passed. They have just frightened off the bandits.

We drop down into lower, barren country. Here it has not rained. But the river is high; we must run through sands and cactus for about a mile along the bank before we can find a suitable place to ford.

We whirl through villages, children run screaming out of our path, dogs run yelping. The natives have not yet become accustomed to autos. Nor have the animals —lethargically they move aside. The chauffeur fails to see a dog in the middle of the road. We run over him and he is left squealing, holding up his wounded paw pitifully.

3

About three we reach the frontier. On the Guatemalan side, a spectacled, chinless man takes our names—the twelfth time at least.

On the Salvadorian side enormous signs announce "modern roads indicate the cultural level of the community." And we hit an almost impassable road of bowlders and sand. (It has since been improved.)

Six miles further on we reach the customs. We get out stiffly, stamping, stretching. The chauffeur unstraps the baggage. I am presented with two huge balls of mud, in the centers of which are my suitcases. The officials paw through my effects and lay aside two folding steel coat-hangers, then close my baggage.

"How about putting these in, too?" I ask.

"Concealed weapons aren't allowed."

Laughing, I open out the hangers.

"How nice!" exclaim the officials and apologize. Sheepishly they replace the two "weapons."

About dark we reach the hotel in Santana—after a fifteen-hour run. I give the hotel boy half a *colón* to rediscover my suitcases. He sets to work with a pail of water, a huge brush and a rag.

The picturesque little town, set in a rich coffee region, is ruled over by tall cocoanut trees. The houses are built with many doors opening on the street, all with swinging shutters, like a saloon. It is so hot that most of the time the people sit in the open doorway. But at night, in spite of the heat, they carefully shut and bar all doors and windows.

But now, in the early evening, the people are still sitting before their houses, in bright clothes. Their soft Spanish chatter floats on the balmy caressing air—passing by the open door, one can tell that Salvador is a far more religious country than Guatemala. The parlors of the middle class homes are veritable chapels, with large altars and images. Near the plaza are open air cafés with tables sprawled over the sidewalks and under the trees, as in France and Italy.

The market, divided off into stalls by smoked brown curtains, is filthy. None of the handicraft work of Guatemala, just a dreary collection of food products and dirty eating booths. But the Indian girls are buxom and aggressive. They eye me with receptive, suggestive glances and voluptuous smiles. A word would suffice.

In order to break a large bill, I bought a package of pins without asking the price. (Evidently to buy anything in Salvador without asking the price is never done.) The proprietor, about to make change, came back to me from the till to tell me how much they were. "Do you want them?" he asked.

Music struck up in the cantinas. Hungry, I turned into a place with a sign "*Tamalería Nocturna*" and asked for tamales. I was told there were no tamales, and discovered that in all Salvador *tamalería nocturna* is a conventional name for an establishment where one may discover drinks at a small bar in front and prostitutes in the rear.

4

San Salvador is the most densely populated country on the mainland of the Western hemisphere. Villages lie close together. Traveling by auto, if one lights a cigarette in one village, he will be in the next before it is finished. The bulk of the population is Indian, most of them Pipiles (Aztec). In the outlying sections of the country they own their own *milperías* and houses, yet most of the country is in the hands of about thirty native Creole families—coffee growers, who run everything (the most perfect example in Central America of the perpetuation of the Creole overlordship tradition). Government is a petty military dictatorship; the army is trained by Spanish instructors.

In the mountains of Honduras, the Maya, Quiché, and Toltec race stocks break up and become confused. May this not explain, to some extent, the latter day political confusion of that disturbed country? Not until we get to Nicaragua do we again find more marked racial crystallization. There Toltecs predominate, divided into Choroteganos and Niquiranos. The feuds between these two groups, even to this modern day, contribute to Nicaraguan internal disorders. In Costa Rica the Indians belong to the numerically unimportant Chiba group. Confined to a few outlying and unhealthful regions, they have little social or political importance. The bulk of the population is descended from the Spanish conquerors, *Gallegos,* as contrasted to the Andalucians who settled disorderly Nicaragua. Pure Spanish blood and resultant lack of racial conflict, greatly explains the relative advancement of Costa Rica and its more liberal political traditions, in contrast to the petty super-state, super-race domination in Salvador.

The train from Santa Ana curved away through iridescent jungle, passing over a black mass of lava—not a spear of vegetation—like some ugly scar cut across the green tropics.

Many Germans drift about in Central America; one heavy none-such-meat occupies four whole spaces with his baggage stacked around him, his big feet plunked on the seat in front, reading *Die Woche*. At the head of the car, facing us, are two young lovers, who kiss and fondle each other at regular intervals. Seizing upon the lava flow as an excuse, I strike up a conversation with a plump girl and her plumper mother. The lava flow, only a few years ago, swept the railroad tracks away and destroyed many coffee *fincas*. The plump girl breaks off to buy something at a station. She buys everything. Soon she is surrounded by great purple banana buds. She buys mangos, sweets, and flowers. She buys cocoanuts of the Sitio del Ninol; the best cocoanuts in the world she tells me. I break one of the shells for her; we share the milk. She tosses the white inner meat to a beggar playing music on a hollow gourd.

XIV   "SSST...
HONEY"

1

SSSSSST

Hotel Nuevo Mundo was full. I insisted on a place. The manager finally gave me the key to Room 22. But on opening the door, I was confronted by a tall, disheveled German. The room, stacked with baggage, was a pig-pen.

I apologized. He burst into a torrent of excited German, shouting all his troubles at me, with a frenzied glare in his painfully mild blue eyes. I beat a retreat.

Downstairs the manager informed me, "Yes, but he hasn't paid his rent for three weeks. You can have the room if you want it."

Anything was better than facing the German again. I had forgotten, however, the scorching June sun pouring a blaze over the flat little city, beating the wall and pavement with heavy sledge blows of heat and drawing up nauseous stenches from the asphalt. The mountainous sleek proprietor of the Hotel Astoria offered me a windowless room at an exorbitant rate. I tried the cheaper Hotel España across the street. Again, only an inside room, but facing the sun again was worse.

What a hotel! Pulling mule's teeth to get the least thing done. Julia, a sniggering negress, agreed to wash my clothes. In my room a wash basin but no pail. My room has no lock. Everybody hunts for a padlock, nobody finds one. They forget about the matter. Half a dozen times I make my request, and lose my temper completely; the landlady appears on the scene. Sadly she informs me that Mr. Pierson, also an American, always stays at her place and leaves his door open. I ask her why her Salvadorian guests lock everything up. Much talk and much bad feeling, but at last I am provided with the padlock I covet.

"Take me to a place where I can dance." The taxi driver took me across a bridge and dipped down through adobe houses and tiled roofs out past a park to the outskirts. "The only place, sir. Public dance halls were prohibited—the first night this one has been open."

A large house, amid Chinese lanterns, far back in a garden, had a large veranda, set aside for dancing. In the shadows, curious Indians stood watching.

The place was jammed. Drinks were flowing freely. Four men to every woman. The crowd was rowdy.

I finally segregated Lola, drew her to a table. Cocktails. Lola, a beautiful mestiza, spoke a curious clipped Indian Spanish. For some time all I could understand of her talk was *"Que manzo, que manzo"* or *"que ligero,"* to express her envious approval of various good dancers.

A quarrel started on the veranda. Two men were finally separated, growling like dogs.

Lola and I danced, then we strolled through the garden under the Chinese lanterns.

The quarrel on the veranda started again. Two shots were fired.

Lola dashed in fright toward the high hedge beside the house, I after her. She paused there in the dark, pressing close to my side, trembling, eyes agape, thoroughly thrilled.

Whistles.

"The police!" cried Lola.

A big auto truck banged through the gate. Soldiers leapt out.

Lola gave a little squeal. "Oh, they will take us all to jail!" She seized my hand.

We ran along the hedge. An opening. We ducked through. Our feet sank into the plowed loam. We stumbled away in the dark. Lola's high-heeled satin slippers made going difficult. I picked her up and carried her. She was a feather.

We stood under the dark trees in the street. Lola clung close to my arm, excited, trembling. Behind us we heard shots, guttural commands, screams of women.

The soldiers loaded all the girls into the truck. The men were not arrested.

2

"Go down and get a taxi," suggested Lola. "I'll wait here."

"I know a place the police won't bother," she suggested, "clear outside of town."

We motored across town and down a graded highway to a suburb called "Mexicanos." "To the Jazz Palace," she told the chauffeur.

The road was completely dark. Soon we switched off and wound through a lane even blacker. Tropic trees leaned over the fences. Bushes jumped up uncannily. Branches rustled against the auto hood. A gruesome ride, on and on, for miles.

To all my inquiries, Lola reassured me with the proper amount of affection that everything was all right. Vividly I recalled a recent scandal of how a girl, in connivance with the chauffeur, lured her unwary victim to a dark road where he was murdered and despoiled. And here we were, miles from the city, winding in and out along a country road, apparently without houses, pitch-black, save for the pale glow of our headlights, which merely made the thick vegetation more fantastic.

At last behind a high wire gate we came to a huge funereal-looking house set among funereal trees.

"Here it is!" exclaimed Lola.

I peered at the spectral place.

The chauffeur turned around in the seat. "Closed up."

"Not a soul about," replied Lola, disappointed. She named another place. We drove on in the dark until we passed by a gayly lit pavilion set about a half a mile back from the road.

"Is this it?" I asked.

"No, that's La Chabela. I wouldn't go in there for anything. Only *bad* women go there."

We drove on, plunging into the darkness again. Another high house, closed and lugubrious.

"Well," exclaimed Lola in disgust, "no luck. Nothing to do, I guess, but go back to town."

3

On the way back, no longer alarmed, I talked with Lola. I could now understand practically everything she said. She was exactly seventeen, romantic, eager to find out all about life. Did I know her former employer, Mr. Brown, also an American? "He is no longer in Salvador; he was very good to me," she said.

"What was his business?"

She did not know. Her job was posing for nude art photographs.

Not a profession I had expected to find in Salvador.

"We can go to El Modelo," suggested Lola.

Clear across town once more. But El Modelo proved very tame—a small open air refreshment stand in the center of a public park, dismal and shivery; only three other people in the place. The floor was rough; the phonograph had no dance records. We sat and talked.

I could observe Lola better here. Her skin was a soft brown texture; and though so young, she was fully, pleasingly formed. Her liquid black eyes, slightly slanting, almond shaped—Chinese eyes; her black hair soft and luxurious. She seemed wistful, though now and then she laughed at me for no reason whatever, just out of sheer contentment. When my attention deserted her a moment, she gave a little "sssssst . . . honey" in English, and laughed again.

We motored around the park; after half an hour Lola suggested that I go to her home.

Another long taxi trip clear through town, out in another direction. I don't know why she invited me to her house, such a sad little two-room slum place, with a few wobbly sticks of furniture and several canvas cots covered with *petates*. Her mother, an apologetic woman, obviously defeated by life; her sister, a big-bodied, voluptuous, frizzy-haired girl with a heavy mouth and bright teeth, flashing easily into broad smiles.

They had been sitting in the cool doorway under gloriously brilliant stars. Hospitality now required that we all go into the stiflingly hot interior.

No electric light. Lola stuck a candle in a hole in

the floor, closed the front door and wedged an old skirt into a crack so passers-by could not look in. The mother apologized profusely because she had nothing in the house to eat or drink. At my request, Lola's sister went out and brought back beer and tamales of gelatine and boiled peas and wrapped in banana leaves instead of corn husks.

Our conversation? Why ask, reader? Humble people the world over talk little of ideas, of philosophy, of art, but of the so-called petty problems. The widow told of her husband, their home in a mountain village, the bullets of revolt, a tumor operation on her throat, mosquitoes, the heat—and if this were a novel, out of that meager conversation how easy it would be to shape a woven pattern, and through that pattern would run a fatalistic thread of people resigned to misfortune and perhaps best suited for misfortune, save for Lola, whose lithe body and quick enthusiasms might, with opportunity and education, have made her the equal or superior of many a great dancer.

When I left, Lola asked me where I lived. I had moved over to the Nuevo Mundo.

"To-morrow," she said, "I shall be there."

4

Late afternoon. I was leaning from my upstairs hotel balcony. In the street below, Lola with hesitant air was walking to and fro, as though trying to get up courage to come into the hotel. I called "ssst . . . honey."

She looked up with a happy smile, waved.

She was, I now observed in the daytime, very poorly,

though neatly, dressed. But I led her boldly into the hotel lobby and sat her down in a huge plush chair. She felt out of place, but sank into the seat with a great sigh of utter animal pleasure. Trying her best to be a grown-up lady, she chirped admiration of the horrible wall frescos. I ordered lemonade with plenty of ice, for it was a sizzling afternoon. Lola, regaining her composure, prattled on.

Lola took life as it came; her actions were weighted with no consciousness of sin. She was as natural as water. At no moment had she betrayed the least hint of calculation in her interest in me; but she had enough imagination to be alert and sensuously appreciative of everything novel.

As my thoughts strayed, a little "ssst . . . honey" brought me back again.

Presently I took her down the street, bought her some candy, and she danced away very happy.

The next afternoon she had courage enough to come into the hotel lobby and ask for me. A knock, and there she stood at the open door, the hotel boy grinning at me over her shoulder.

She greeted me with a little "sssst . . . honey" and a mock bow.

She came in on tiptoe with a little catch of her breath and then, having got her bearings, ran all around the room like a puppy dog, to see what it was all about—she poked the furniture to see if it was real, admired the ugly prints on the wall, and thought everything perfectly gorgeous. Though the best room in the hotel, it was shabby and in execrable taste with all the hybrid makeshifts of frontier regions. But to little Lola, every object was a most amazing discovery.

I ordered up cool drinks, and she sat sipping hers in a big wicker rocking chair, thoroughly pleased at being alive. Then suddenly, with a little "ssst . . . honey," she fluttered out, twinkling her fingers.

I called to her, "I'm leaving town in the morning."

A pained look crossed her face. "Where to?"

"La Unión."

She came back slowly into the room, thoroughly unhappy, started to say something, then biting her lip, remarked, "I will come to the station, Carlos."

Suddenly she threw her arms around me, gave me a hug and kiss, then with another "ssst . . . honey" she ran down the corridor. At the head of the stairs she twinkled her fingers at me again and disappeared.

1

THE UNSAVORY FRANCISCO Malespín of Salvador was on his way to Nicaragua at the head of a few brave followers to fight Gerardo Barrios and Trinidad Cabañas, two rebel compatriots whose forces had received asylum in the neighboring lake country. Malespín left his office in the hands of the vice-president, Joaquín Eufrasio Guzmán, a man of good antecedents. Malespín crossed the frontier and sniffed around for his enemies. Resistance melted before him, but Barrios and Cabañas escaped. And so Malespín left Nicaragua in flames and marched back toward Salvador.

During his absence, his enemies persuaded Guzmán to betray his friend and superior, and proclaim himself commander-in-chief and president.

Bishop Viteri, just returned to Salvador, being an intriguing fellow, to ingratiate himself with Guzmán's new order, launched upon Malespín and all his partisans and followers a bitter anathema. His pretext was Malespín's attempt to shoot two Nicaraguan priests. Declared the Bishop:

We, Doctor Jorge de Viteri y Ungo, by divine Mercy and by grace of the Holy Apostolic See, Bishop of San Salvador, Domestic Prelate of his Sanctity, Assistant to the Only Sacred Pontifical and Apostolic Delegate, etc., etc. . . . ! In view of the following information, by our order, by our Provision, and General Vicarate, and swearing that this be true that Francisco Malespín our subject, deposed from the Presidency of the Country by the legislative chambers and separated from his command of arms, has committed the horrible aggression of ordering to be shot in the city of León two priests, Manuel Crespín and another, name unknown, of whom one was saved by the intercession of several pious persons, after he was obliged nevertheless to beg pardon on his knees; and that the first was executed with the greatest ignominy without the solemnities provided by the canonical and civil law in similar cases; considering that this crime and horrible aggression demands major excommunication, which is incurred in the very act of perpetration as imposed by the sacred canons and particularly Can. 15 of the Lateran Council in the Time of Innocent II, which declares: "If any one through persuasion of the Demon puts violent hands on any cleric or monk, he shall be punished by ANATHEMA . . . ! etc. . . ."

In use of the great power of uniting and disuniting which as a pastor of this flock has been conferred upon us by Jesus Christ, although without any merit of ours; in fulfillment of our pastoral ministry we are obliged to declare and we declare excommunicated Francisco Malespín for the execrable crime of having given with contempt a blow and an order to be shot, as occurred in León, to the Presbyterian, Manuel Crespín; and also for having ordered this same thing done to the other sacerdote, which, although not carried out, the fact of merely having ordered the shooting is sufficient to cause him to fall under censure; in consequence of this we fulminate against him the terrible punishment of Anathema and we order it declared with the fright-giving apparatus which the Church is accustomed to use in such sad and unfortunate cases; and with the deepest sorrow in our heart, we separate him from the group of the faithful and we deliver him to the power of Satan for the condemnation of his flesh in order to insure by this means that the spirit of the unhappy one— who dared to put violent hands upon the followers of Christ, whom God ordered us to respect as the children of his Eyes—may be saved on the day of our Lord Jesus Christ as was accomplished by St. Paul with the incestuous ones of Corinth . . .

And in order that our terrible but laudable sentence have its proper fulfillment and reaches the attention of everybody, we command that this *auto* be inserted in an edict which shall be read and explained to the parishioners and which shall be posted in all the churches of our Bishopric, signed by us, sealed with our arms and authorized by our Chamber—Secretary and government, and that in addition it be printed, published and circulated, thus communicating it to the ecclesiastical government of the Christian Republic, for their information in case that the execrable Francisco Malespín crosses their respective dioceses. Given in fulfillment of our Pastoral Ministry in the Episcopal Palace of San Salvador on the 23rd of February, 1845.

(Signed) Jorge, Bishop of San Salvador by order of the Holy See; Jose Ignacio Zoldaña, Secretary.

2

The excommunication was accompanied by magnificent and pompous ceremony in the Salvador Cathedral, which was draped in solid black. Bishop Viteri y Ungo presented himself decked out with all the insignia allowed by his high office, accompanied by priests, assistants, and followers. The church overflowed with the public, curious to witness an act which according to all conjectures would be terror-inspiring. The bells of the church rang out their most lugubrious notes and the pious people imagined that legions of demons swarmed through all the plaza, shaking their great wings like bats. The holy ones placed upon their bosoms scapulars and blessed branches; and frightened children hid in their mother's skirts. The episcopal edict was read, and the solemn, ominous voice of the bishop declared: "Francisco Malespín is delivered into the power of Satan." The voices of all the priests responded with rancorous accent, "Is delivered into the power of Satan . . . is delivered . . . is delivered."

The bells rang even more lugubriously, the censors threw out sparks as from hell's sulphur and the great black curtains which draped the interior of the cathedral swayed with mysterious undulations—it was whispered that the beating of demons' wings caused this uncanny serpentine movement.

Too, on the twenty-third of February, an infernal mist passed over all Salvador. Terror ruled all weak hearts. Children who performed pranks saw themselves immediately toasted in the fires of the infernal regions, and mothers chided, "Look out, Malespín is coming after you." On all sides no one talked of anything else but this excommunication.

But the following day the odors of burning sulphur gradually abated; the atmosphere became more serene. Within a week the affair was hardly mentioned, and within a month the excommunication was spoken of as something quite remote—as one remembers a puppet show.

The news of these goings-on had reached Malespín in Honduras. Razing towns, executing harmless citizens, leaving brutal memories in his wake, he returned to Salvador through San Miguel, and in spite of excommunication continued his struggle to regain his lost power. The excommunication proved no obstacle—his arms were everywhere victorious.

What was more ironical, in spite of this excommunication of Malespín, the bishop fell out with the Guzmán Government, whose good graces he had so cravenly sought to curry, and he was arbitrarily deported from the country.

The good Bishop Viteri immediately re-affiliated himself with the excommunicated and "execrable" Malespín. Malespín was now the true upholder of the Catholic religion, and the bishop covered the returning general with benedictions and sang a Te Deum for the Devil's child.

XVI THE RAW TROPICS

1

LIFE IN TROPICAL COUN-
tries ceases to have dignified
significance. Dignity among
southern peoples is a protec-
tive coloring. A false note
invades it; the plumage is
too gaudy. Fierceness, brooding, alternating with aban-
don, rhythm, passion—these are the deeper qualities.
Courtesy with us is a normal attitude; with the Latin
of the hot countries it is a bright embroidery; it must
be exaggerated. It is the duality of some indestructible
hate for everything and everybody in the universe outside himself. A burning egoism forces the southerner into
a paradoxical and often insincere attentiveness toward
other egos. The greater the politeness, the more self-con-
scious the ego. A defense mechanism. The overwhelming
fecundity of these regions so overrides the individual that
the individual reacts into a super-individualism. Something similar may happen in the north when the machine
process levels us a bit more. But in the south—and this
is the best proof of the vanity of mannered dignity—
the individual is utterly careless, not merely of other
people's lives but of his own as well. Courtesy becomes
a cloak for callousness. Sharp class divisions, recoiling
from the individualistic attitude, also contribute to callousness. The pleasure-loving upper classes are quite
unconcerned about the misery of those beneath, doubly

so because they often represent a different race. Universal lack of sanitation is one of the symptoms. This lack, however, lays its finger of death not only on the lower classes but upon the whole community.

Foreign experts usually mess things up. Salvador, at fantastic cost, borrowed money from American bankers that Americans might at a fantastic price pave the streets of the capital, where much dust carried germs. The result is an American customs collector and other meddling humiliations. It is doubtful whether paving tropic streets is an unmixed blessing. In this terrifically hot land, paved streets do not contribute to coolness. As for dust, it could be laid by a thin coat of oil; and probably the inhabitants would profit, not by pouring out fabulous millions to lay down a few miles of pavement, but by planting pleasant shade trees, gardens, and making more accessible to the populace those little luxuries, swimming pools, ice, electric fans, etc., which might render heat more endurable.

In contrast to her smart paved streets, San Salvador has a *rastro,* or slaughter house, which is a foul blot on mankind. It emits a frightful stench; streams of blood and patches of flesh rot everywhere; even the fence posts are daubed up. Women come out with fresh meat dangling over their shoulders or carrying it in baskets on their heads, the red juice running down over their heads and faces. The meat is exposed to all the germs of the air. Buzzards swarm.

2

In a dirty hut beside the paved street, a drunken boy was begging his mother for money. She refused. He called her vile names. She doused him with a pail of soap-suds. He reeled away cursing. Then took to chasing all the little boys in the street, his head down like a steer. The boys, fascinated, at the same time afraid of him, would torment him, then run away screaming.

Finally, he stopped short, took out a looking glass and peering at his countenance, upbraided himself for being such a vile creature. He dropped on his knees in the middle of the street and prayed. Presently he toppled completely over, full on his face. A dog sniffed at him. A crowd gathered. Two policemen appeared on the scene and interrogated the neighbors. The mother was taken off to the police station.

Suddenly, the drunken boy sat up, shook his fist at the crowd and cursed. He struggled to his feet. One of the policemen seized his arm. The boy protested, so the officer smashed him in the face, yanked him along and smashed him again. Finally, tired of dragging him along in this fashion, he gave the boy a blow and a shove. The boy flopped into the gutter. The policeman kicked him again and again, brutally. Seeing the boy could not get up again, he laughed and went off about his business. The spectator took it all as a matter of course, not a word of protest against the policeman.

The police in every land are brutal. Everywhere their psychology and actions are: legal treatment for the law-abiding and criminal treatment for the law breakers.

No one is so quick to break the law against breakers of the law as the police. In these backward colonial countries, since the governments are dictatorships of one sort or another—and particularly is this so in Salvador, where a few rich coffee planters dominate political life—the pettiest gendarme considers the entire public as a potential law breaker and treats it as such. The military in Salvador is omnipresent and arrogant. Though soldiers are barefoot, wear blue dungarees with white braid and live in shabby blue barracks, they are sure of their importance as pawns of the military caste. The officers differ little from their ignorant, brutal, feudal confreres in Mexico, the rest of Central America and much of South America. The city of Salvador is overshadowed by an enormous feudal fort, with grim watch towers and rifle holes, where the most reliable troops are stationed. Set in the heart of the city, it dominates the entire metropolis. This edifice is no more feudal in appearance than the barracks situated on Fourth Avenue in the heart of New York City; but in the latter case, not the barracks but buildings devoted to other civil enterprises loom along the skyline. In Salvador, militarism next to coffee-growing is the leading business. The fort and the cathedral—these are the main contours of Central American life.

1

THE FOLLOWING MORNING
en route for the port of La
Unión—an all day trip from
the capital. One of my chair-
car companions was Mr. Pierson, an employee of the Bald-
win Locomotive Works, the man who always left his
room unlocked at the Hotel España, and a young couple, Mr. and Mrs. Carson. Carson, consulting engineer for the International Railway, was a typical corporation employee, sharp-mannered from a sense of importance; but Mrs. Carson, dark, tall, supple in her thin
purple dress, was much more companionable than her
husband and furnished vivid proof for the universal foreign belief that American women are more cultured,
more gracious, more intellectually alert than their hus-
bands.

Sausages of Coatépec . . . Pineapples . . . Oranges
. . . La Unión . . .

A tiny port, a half-built church, grass-grown streets
slanting to the smooth harbor. Palms sway gracefully
over the red roofs. At night, plaza music soothes away
the heat. . . . The townspeople make the customary
rounds, men one way, women the other. Between selec-
tions, when the music stops, the promenade stops also.
The girls are very voluptuous—much negro blood—a
flirtatious, happy, languorous type . . . quick flashes of
eyes, a daring coquetry which seems to say—"All or

nothing"; for him with courage no test too great.

I strolled with Pierson and an Italian traveler from the hotel. The Italian strode straight ahead, jolting violently against the women coming from the opposite direction. Not an inch would he budge for anybody. His credo, stated in Italian-English was "treat da people firm, show da people der place, keep'm off da sidewalk when da white man pass."

Pierson, a colossal man with colossal paunch, had the right to live in one of the Company houses, but could not get along with the Chinese cook, who, he said, was worth seventy thousand dollars in his own name, yet still worked at the railroad house. Visiting managers and high officials received marvelous food; to regular employees, though allowed enough money to serve the best, he served only scraps—he had enriched himself in this way. Pierson long rowed with the "yellow-pig-tail" but at last had to give up the struggle and pay for his own room and board in the hotel, bad though both were.

"In spite of this dirt and this heat I'm a damn sight happier here in La Unión than in the United States. My wife, though, came down once, squealed and took the next boat right back. She wouldn't ever come again." Pierson chuckled.

"How about malaria?" I inquired.

"I always keep a case of whisky on hand—get it down duty free. Drink plenty of whisky and you won't ever have a touch of malaria."

2

Mr. Carson and his wife were going to Tegucigalpa, the capital of Honduras, to arrange for the extension of the Nicaragua Railway line around the Gulf of Fonseca through Honduras to La Unión. They were leaving in the company launch at seven the following morning, with special permission to avoid the island customs port, Amapala, and go directly to the mainland San Lorenzo. If I could get similar permission from the La Unión commandant, Carson offered to take me along. I went up to the barracks about eight o'clock that night. Troops were lined up at attention. The commandant was giving them hell. His aide said it would be impossible to see him. I mentioned Mr. Carson; I had to leave on the railway launch early in the morning. Immediately the aide's attitude changed to deference. "Come back in half an hour." When I returned, the commandant was eating in his office. I apologized for the intrusion, but immediately he rose from the table, bowed and stamped my passport. In Central America it pays to have good relations with a powerful American company.

The following morning my *mozo* shoved my suitcase aboard the half-past six train which runs down to the company pier. Peons, naked to the waist, were already carrying the trunks of Mr. Carson aboard the launch. Their bronze backs glistened in the early light. Off for a five-hour ride across the enormous Gulf of Fonseca. The captain of our little launch seemed, at first, a taciturn machinist intent only on his duties; his greasy cap was drawn low over sullen eyes. He looked and acted flabby; the edge of him was gone—the fate of many foreigners who live long under these hot suns.

With just a little prodding the captain's taciturnity fell away completely; his life-story poured out.

Brought to Salvador as a baby by his parents, who owned a large hacienda, he had never seen the United States, of which he was a citizen; but he was exceedingly proud of his country, despising Salvador to the depths of his soul. Proud he was, too, of his Pennsylvania Dutch stock; some of his ancestors had come over on the *Mayflower*.

Married to a native woman, he had separated from her. With a sad shake of his head, "All the people here are too clever, too damned clever. Take my wife—she twisted around and squirmed around and talked and talked until she got her way always—and her ways were not my ways. They are sensuous and tricky, these people. They flow through your fingers like water. You never pin them. Things aren't clear cut. Sun and shade mix, no sharp line. But our minds work differently. Our bodies work differently. It's their land, and they beat you. Hate them and they beat you. Love them and they beat you worse. My wife beat me. Her ways were not my ways, and her ways were the ways of those about her. She beat me. She had her way, so soft, so feline, so smooth, so weak—but she had her way."

He had grown daughters and a son, the latter a bookkeeper. "None of my children care a tinker's damn for me. She won them all over. They belong to her, to her land, to her race, to her way of thinking. I am just an outsider. I'm all alone now; no one loves me. I do my job. I eat. I sleep. That's all. I have no one. I'm a good workman, one of the best. But can I get ahead here? I am an American; I have always been a stranger in this land though I have lived here all my life. When my father died, I had to shift for myself. The estate had gone to pieces. I worked as a blacksmith, and now, after all these years, I earn only six pesos a day. They send down machinists from the States who don't know half what I do, and they get fifteen dollars a day."

"Why don't you go to the States?" I asked.

"Ah, I'm too old now, I wouldn't fit in there either. I'm all alone now." Glumly he picked up an oil-can and began oiling the engine.

XVIII AN ANCIENT ERUPTION

1

THE BAY OF FONSECA IS grandiose, majestic. It shimmered under the hot sun, miles and miles of blue expanse broken by tropical islands. Three countries. Salvador, Honduras, and Nicaragua, border on its shores. It is the Pacific hub of Central America—one of the greatest ports of the world, one of the prizes of empire. Behind us was the Volcán de la Unión, and still farther in the distance, the tall, slim cone of San Miguel. Far to the right lay the Island and Volcano Coseguïna, hazy in the sharp sunlight.

Eighteen hundred and thirty-five looms in the annals of Central America. Coseguïna erupted. The President of Guatemala at the time was Dr. José Mariano Galvez, still hailed as a brilliant statesman and a wise ruler. Salvador was racked with revolutions after President Martín's downfall. Colonel Francisco Ferrera, following a severe struggle, exercised supreme authority in Honduras. In Nicaragua, Dr. José Núñez had seized power; in Costa Rica Rafael Gallegos was scheming against President General Morazán. Such was the political world.

The terraqueous world was in no calmer state. On January 20, 1835, throughout all Central America, from the bowels of the earth were heard strange rumblings. These subterranean noises struck terror throughout the countryside. During the night of the twenty-second, the atmosphere filled with a fine powder. At daybreak the horizon was dark, an obscurity which gradually deepened into blackness.

Cosegüina had erupted with a violence that frightened the inhabitants from end to end of the Central American Isthmus. The rain of ashes fell over a diameter of fifteen hundred miles; they reached as far north as Vera Cruz, Mexico, south, into the upper portions of Colombia, west to Jamaica, and over vast stretches of both oceans.

A captain of a vessel who passed along the coast a few days after, said that for one hundred and fifty miles, he moved through floating pumice, scarcely anywhere seeing any water.

In León, Nicaragua, the nearest large city, the people believed the day of final judgment had arrived. The priests passed through the streets and houses administering extreme unction and comforting thousands of unhappy persons. For a hundred leagues the people groped, dumb with horror, through the thick darkness, bearing crosses on their shoulders and vines on their heads, in penitential abasement and dismay, believing the day of doom had come. In León, as a last resort, every saint, without exception, lest he be offended, was taken from his niche into the air—but still the ashes fell. The paint on the Virgin's face was blackened by the thousands of candles, and people wailed that she had contracted smallpox. People embraced each other, saying eternal good-by; everywhere, weeping, cries, lamentations. At last, with superb faith, President Núñez, not knowing the reason for the strange phenomenon, ordered the church bells rung and cannons fired to conjure the calamity away; and sure enough as the hours passed the tempest calmed.

The commandant of La Unión in Salvador made a picturesque report of the occurrence:

On the twentieth day of this month, which dawned serene as usual, there was seen to the southeast of this town at eight o'clock in the morning a dense cloud, pyramidal in form, which, preceded by a dull noise, lifted up until it covered the sun, and at this height and at ten in the morning it veered toward the north and south; then lightning and thundering commenced as occurs only in the winter time. This cloud extended over the whole hemisphere; and by twelve, the earth was cloaked in the most horrible obscurity so that the nearest objects could not be discerned.

The lugubrious braying of the animals, the birds of all species who came in flocks to seek asylum among men, the terror with which these were possessed, the general weeping of women and children, and the uncertainty of so rare a phenomenon, beat down the spirit of the most robust, making them fear all sorts of calamities; and even more so, when at four in the afternoon earthquakes began, keeping the ground in continual undulation, intensifying minute by minute.

This was followed by a rain of burning sand, which continued until eight of the same day. Whereupon there commenced to fall a fine but heavy powder-like dust. The thunder and lightning of the atmosphere . . . lasted until the twenty-first; and at eight minutes after three in the afternoon there was an earthquake so strong and continuous that many of the men walking in the penitential procession fell down. The blackness lasted forty-three hours, making it necessary for every one to

go. about with lighted candles and even then scarcely
permitting any one to see anything. On the twenty-
second it was a little lighter, although the sun could not
be seen. In the early morning hours of the twenty-third,
continuous thundering was heard of the loudest sort, as
though artillery was being fired. With this new happen-
ing, the rain of dust continued from the dawn of this
day until ten o'clock, when an opaque light painted
everything with the saddest outlines.

The ground in this town, which had always been un-
even because of the great quantity of stones, was now
flat because of the great amount of fine dust which had
fallen. This same dust had made men, women, and children so unrecognizable they did not know each other
except by the sound of their voices and other traits.
Houses and trees were indistinguishable for the dust.
The people walked about, giving everything an aspect
even more terrible; and though this was melancholy
enough, the fear became worse because of the blackness with which we were again submerged after ten
o'clock as on the previous day. The general agitation,
which had grown calmer, now increased; but it was
extremely dangerous to leave the city, for the wild
animals had abandoned the forests and were prowl-
ing the highways and the towns. Nevertheless both in
Conchagua and here in La Unión, the fright possessing
the townspeople was so great that over half of them
left on foot, deserting their homes, persuaded that they
would never be able to return to them; for the complete destruction of this town was expected, so they
fled, terrorized, seeking security in the mountains.

At half-past two and at three in the morning of the
twenty-fourth, the moon and a few stars could be seen
as through a curtain. The day was clear although the
sun was invisible, for the dust which had already cov-

ered this entire pueblo and its environs five inches deep, still continued to fall.

The twenty-fifth and twenty-sixth were like the twenty-fourth though with frequent earthquakes, but of short duration. On the first day of these events, on the twentieth, in agreement with the council and mayor of this town, a commission to investigate this phenomenon set out; and in effect left at nine in the morning in a canoe; the mayor, the citizen Marcelino Argüello, the alderman Vicente Romero, and the citizen Juan Perry. They reached the entrance to the port whereupon it grew so dark that they could not see where the eruption came from and were obliged to return here, arriving at six in the afternoon after the greatest efforts to get back, not only because of the obscurity but because of the wind which blew with much force so that they were unable to orient themselves exactly; but they had the good fortune to arrive at the coast half a league from this town and came the rest of the distance by land.

Four trustworthy persons who had come from the island, El Tigre, situated about eight leagues east of this settlement . . . assured us that there it rained pumice stone about the size of a *garbanzo* increasing in size until stones of the size of a hen's egg fell. The earthquakes there were much stronger than here and everybody was so nearly suffocated that the commandant and the rest of the inhabitants fearing the island would sink, embarked and remained in the water, though without knowing which direction to take. . . .

The people have been suffering from catarrhal infections, headaches, and infections of the throat and chest, without doubt the result of the dust. Many of these are gravely ill, and yesterday a child died with symptoms of *esquilencia*. The cattle all about are dying, five in this town have already perished. Dead birds lie in great heaps on the road. Most of the aquatic birds are also dying and those who came from El Tigre say that hundreds of birds of every species were floating dead upon the waters. The rain of dust continued until the twenty-seventh.

La Unión, 25 January 1835
M. ROMERO

2

Behind us lay this same El Tigre, which centuries ago was used as headquarters by the English pirates. We passed fairly close to the port of Amapala, a low town simmering at the base of a mountain, then by mangy Zacatillo. In the distance loomed Conchagua and Mian-güera. We passed between Sirena, a small island, and Garoba, brown and bare. On the left, lay Inglasera, Con-chagüita, and Pirigayo. Las Almeas was covered by tall obscene-looking *Guarumo* trees with scraggly boughs and bare trunks; black with buzzards, for this island is used as a cemetery. Next came the Isla de los Pájaros, around which circled and fluttered and cried swarms of gray *tijerías*. The Island of Pinüela has been usurped by red birds—*chupamieles* and *papamieles*. Here and there on some of the islands, a few inhabitants cultivate milpas of sadly burned corn patches scattered on the side of the harsh mountains.

Circling one of these islands, we secured a view of the high Sierras of Honduras—fantastic, like crenelated leaves. They looked as if still striving to be mountains; their outline might well have been cut out of cardboard without rhyme or reason by a little child. They are raw, nascent, showing by formation and contour how recent their geological formation. Little of the brusqueness of their first volcanic upheaval has been worn away. Yet glaciers once scraped the higher levels and left scratches on Ometépec in Lake Nicaragua, still further south.

Close to shore, twisted roots of mangrove trees rose up from salt water into dense tropical tangles. Long-bodied cranes moved heavily past us, gulls circled, pink herons stood along the shore. We heard the call of macaws. Hour after hour we chugged on and on under the blazing sun.

We had lunch. Mr. Carson talked of the United Fruit Company, fifteen millions invested in Puerto Cortés. He had lived for a time on an hacienda in the Honduras lowlands. The Hondureñans were different, he claimed, from the rest of the Central Americans. Half Indian and half negro, only slightly Spanish, their violence had more of a negro than an Indian character.

He switched to Mexico. The present government, he declared, bitterly, was out and out Bolshevik. Here in Central America this Mexican influence was manifesting itself in the railway shops—agitators, discontent—all spite work against the United States on the part of the Mexican government.

"Why should Mexico feel spiteful?"

"I don't know," he replied, "they owe everything to us."

"And what does Central America owe to us?"

"They couldn't do without us."

I thought of Salvador's paved streets, staggering debt, American customs officials, marines in looted Nicaragua, banana rule in Honduras and Costa Rica—nowhere had I seen any American preoccupation, except by a few charitable foundations, to perform any service which did not pay big profits.

"Mexican influence," gesticulated Carson, "must be stopped in Central America at any cost, before it's too late." He said this with such vehemence, his spoon fell off his paper plate into the wide Gulf of Fonseca. Mrs. Carson reminded him it was a silver spoon and shouldn't have been lost.

3

San Lorenzo, where we landed among beautiful spider-lilies, is no more than a few mud houses on a sweltering shore. The hotel has four dirt-floor rooms without furniture or windows. Travelers hasten on to the highlands because at this point yellow fever is endemic. Carson had telegraphed from La Unión for an auto to take us up to the capital, about a six-hour run. The government had ordered the local commandant to accompany us.

We rode through the lowlands, near abandoned, over-grown henequen fields, deserted during the last revolution. We stopped in Perspire for coffee. Twilight fell upon us in Sabana Grande. Behind us, racing up the valley, advanced a driving rain. The chauffeur put up curtains, covered our baggage with oilcloth, but by dark the rain caught up. It rattled on the hood for hours. We swung through the night. Not until we dropped over the ridge into the valley where nestled Tegucigalpa, the capital, at the foot of tall Pecacho hill, did the air turn warm again. The valley was a sea of fireflies which heaved towards us in waves of light as we dropped down the ridges; then valley, fireflies, and the lights of the town were blotted out by misty drizzle.

Even so, after finding a room, I could not resist walking about the town. Tegucigalpa dips up hill and down hill. From the high garden on the slope of Pecacho it drops down to the more level center; from here there is a second abrupt drop to the river. More of the town, low and flat, stretches on beyond the river. On the sharp river slope stands the presidential mansion. Its circular entrance faces the upper part of town, its postern is a grim curving rampart, thirty feet high, sheer from the river bank.

Observed as we came through the countryside, Honduras was more poverty-stricken than any part of Central America I had yet seen. The country is so broken up, so mountainous; population is so sparse. The people live isolated in rude huts with a few animals and little cornfields. Tegucigalpa is set on the high crest of the country like a commanding fortress. Far more accessible, for a capital, would have been Comayagua, center of a rich agricultural region, in a broad valley which opens out in two directions towards the Pacific and the Atlantic. But Tegucigalpa is strategically better from a military standpoint; and here in this eternal fortress of despair, like medieval barons constantly defying their own subjects, the governments of Honduras have barred themselves against their little world, defying for a brief day, an inevitable doom.

Here the military rulers try to hold together the country in political unity. The mixture of the blood, Spanish, Indian, negro, contributes to a brutal sort of disorder; Honduras has been the least stable of all the Central American countries; 1926 saw forty days of bloody combat in its streets; the dead lay around unburied.

1

HONDURAS IS THE KINGDOM par excellence of the banana companies; the United Fruit Company, the Cuyamel Fruit Company (now united), and the Standard Fruit Company, located in the ports of Tela and Trujillo, Puerto Cortés and Ceiba, each with its private or leased railroad tapping the banana hinterland. The powerful United Fruit Company is in possession also of the Tropical Radio Corporation.

The financial position of these companies is remarkable. They function in Honduras, contributing scarcely a penny to the government revenues. Every article used on the plantations or the railroads, and in the company stores, is brought in duty free. To the customs income and certain taxes known as *"especiales"* the companies' contribution ought to be more than half; but because of the terms of the concessions this is remitted. Of the entire theoretical income of the government, about thirty percent is uncollected because of the untaxable character of the fruit companies' interests. Of the moneys actually collected by the government, about seventy-five percent is "earmarked" to pay up on the internal debt. In other words, not only do the companies fail to pay appreciable taxes but three-fourths of the national income flows back into their coffers, to pay off loans at exorbitant rates contracted in moments of revolutionary stress.

Not only does this make the country's financial position untenable, but it kills all local enterprises. Thus the United Fruit Company owns stores all over the north coast. It sells goods brought in its own banana freighters, which go loaded to the United States and would otherwise return empty. It brings in the goods duty free. It ships the goods into the interior on its own railroad, in cars that would otherwise go back to the fields empty, and sells them in company stores, not merely to the employees but to any one who wishes to buy. These stores sell every conceivable article, and as a result no native business, which must pay duties and has no such facilities, can compete. Hondureñans are obliged to become poorly paid employees of the banana company, in positions inferior to imported Jamaica negroes.

Not many years ago in Tegucigalpa an American citizen, Franklin S. Morales, used to be the bartender at the Hotel Pratt, where I was now staying. Subsequently he left Honduras and went to New Jersey where he engaged in democratic politics, and as a reward for his services was named Minister to Honduras. Morales proceeded to ingratiate himself with the President Rafael López Gutiérrez, and Morales' brother engaged in various lucrative businesses. Came the Honduras election in 1923. The Liberal party was completely split—three candidates, Bonilla, Carías, and Colindres; Carías was the Conservative Nationalist candidate. No one received a majority; the election was thrown into Congress. Congress was dilatory in choosing the successor.

The reason—Morales had whispered in the ear of his good friend López Gutiérrez that it would be much better if he continued in office, and promised State Department support. In return for this aid, Morales insisted López Gutiérrez dismiss from his cabinet his two strongest men, Lajos and Huete, the very ones who would have made this dictatorial policy possible, but who were hostile to Morales and his dubious schemes.

Congress adjourned; López Gutiérrez declared himself dictator. But Morales was unable to convince the State Department to support his favorite. Washington actually withdrew recognition—an open invitation for revolution. The forces of Carías, who had received the largest number of votes, finally occupied the hills surrounding Tegucigalpa—Ell Baruche, Cepile, Juanalainas, and El Pecacho. American Marines landed and held the radio station above Tegucigalpa. Ammunition and supplies slipped from the Marines to the Carías troops; the Marines participated in his victory. One of the fruit companies had already donated an aeroplane.

After forty days of sanguinary street battle Carías was victorious. But, after all the military actions had been completed, after the most destructive operations and great bloodshed, after permitting the Marines to assist Carías and insure his victory, the State Department informed him that under no circumstances could he be president. The factions were called arbitrarily aboard the *Milwaukee* in the Gulf of Fonseca; and there the United States empowered General Vicente Tosta as provisional president to call new elections. The State Department, instead of permitting a free plebescite, refused to let Carías run, and pushed in a docile puppet, Paz Bahona.

In other words, the United States waited three months, while Honduras was rent asunder; then when the matter had been settled, intervened. Sumner Wells,

suddenly sent down to make peace, forced the accept-
ance of Tosta's name on the *Milwaukee,* and the signing
of a treaty between the various factions. The result was
a post war led by General Gregorio Ferrera. Lawrence
Dennis, of later Nicaraguan fame, came upon the scene
as Minister; he was followed by Summerlin of Mexican
fame. Carías, chafing at being pushed out of the scene,
threatened to take the presidency by force. Summerlin
indicated his displeasure, and Carías desisted. We invoked the Washington treaties of 1923 against Carías;
but in Nicaragua permitted the leader of a national revolt, José María Moncada, to become president, while
Emiliano Chamorro, with whom we had a quarrel, and
who had also staged a coup d'état, was not even permitted to run.

Theoretically we have a set policy in Central America
—"no government established by force will be permitted." Actually our policy has been dominated by
ignorance, opportunism, or self-interest—usually the
last. Nor is self-interest always national self-interest, but
the self-interest of special concessionaries, banking
houses, large corporations, and even the self-interest
of diplomatic representatives, promoting private deals.

2

The auto for the north coast left Tegucigalpa at three
A.M. Even in summertime in the tropics, early morning
mountain hours are piercingly cold, and we stamped
the street lustily while the chauffeur strapped on our
baggage. Impossible to get anything to warm our stom-
achs at such an hour. As we climbed out of the valley the

chill breeze swept through the car. We drew our coat
lapels about our ears.

Dawn crept over the mountains. Now and then, as
the sun came up, we occasionally caught the warmth
from its yellow level rays, abrupt glints of light on the
stones, pale gold on the road, and silver threads unwind-
ing from tinseled leaves. Then, a miasma rose from
the canyon walls; a dismal mist blanketed everything.

Gradually the day brightened. We dropped down toward Comayagua, a town founded in 1537 by Montejo.
Hours of descent into the vast valley, the road in terrible condition. Most of the bridges consisted of two
heavy beams with rough branches nailed across them;
many of these were broken down; we had to make
wide detours.

A one-armed colonel, just appointed Commandant in
a small frontier town, and his wife and baby rode with
us. The colonel had lost his left forearm in the latest
revolution. This had made him cocky. He gave peremptory orders to everybody, about everything. He told the
chauffeur how to strap on the baggage, how to avoid the
ruts; he told his wife how to feed the baby. His joy
in life was his pistol. He toyed with it constantly. Now
and again, quite without warning, he would take a pot
shot at some roadside object. At every stop he sent a
telegram to the War Minister. The whole family had
an eye infection. The colonel wore blue glasses. His wife
wore yellow glasses. The baby was a miserable squalling
creature, covered with sores, apparently scrofulous. The
colonel was dirty. His wife and child were dirtier.

In Comayagua the little Commandant insisted on taking me under his wing. After lunch, he dragged me all
over the place, introducing me to various storekeepers

to whom he explained over and over again how his fore-arm had been shattered by a dum-dum bullet and had to be amputated. He bought a quarter of a bottle of Murine for his eyes and various rounds of whisky.

3

Such strutting colonels make Honduras politics, of which the following is an example:

Back in the fifties, General Trinidad Cabañas was an honorable politician, brave in battle, but not such a good head. His bravery served to commit him to an unusual number of foolishnesses; his honorableness made him stiff and obstinate. As long as Don Trinidad kept his honor polished in idleness or fought with his own shadow, things went very well; but when he had need of a little talent, a little judgment, a little political astute-ness—Don Trinidad was like a chicken trying to swim. And so, in spite of his boldness, he was given many a good trouncing on the field of battle and retired from conflict, flesh sliced by the lead of his enemies.

In politics, Cabañas was an obstinate Liberal who hammered out a hard and set course, without under-standing what "liberal" means. He was a fanatical Unionist, believing the only great cause in the world to be the union of Central America, though it is doubtful if he had any idea what real union signified. But union-ism was the alpha and omega of his existence.

Through sheer stubbornness he became president. In Guatemala Mariano Paredes turned over the presidency to Carrera, an arch Conservative. Carrera, as soon as he had consolidated his internal position, sought means to

boot out Liberal Cabañas. Cabañas, anticipating Carrera's plans, allied himself with the Guatemalan General José Dolores Nufio, and with the acquiescence of
Salvador he crossed through that country into Chiquimula, Guatemala, announcing he would soon reach
Guatemala City.

Carrera sent Vicente Cerna with orders to "go and
frighten these upstarts. Trinidad Cabañas does not need
to think that I, in person, intend to be bothered by long
marches."

Cerna soon forced Cabañas and Nufio to retire. Not
content, Carrera stirred up a revolution against Cabañas; and ere long the Liberal Honduras president was
thrown out. In 1856 he was succeeded by General Santos Guardiola.

Guardiola's administration was active. He made firm
friendships with all who stood in with Carrera, and
those who stood in with Carrera stood in with the whole
world. During Guardiola's administration, the islands in
the bay of Honduras and part of the Mosquito Coast
controlled by England, were reincorporated into the
national patrimony (through Carrera's friendship with
"my colleague," Queen Victoria). The one shadow on
Guardiola's control was the filibusterer Walker, disem-
barking on Honduras soil—his third expedition. But
Walker was trapped and shot down, six rifle balls
through his chest.

Guardiola believed Honduras was, at last and for
all time, on its way to peace and prosperity.

But at the very moment when Guardiola felt most
secure, assassination cut him short, January 11, 1862.
Guardiola was in Comayagua. The chief of this plaza
was Colonel Pable Agurcia, in whom the president had

the utmost confidence. The chief of the presidential guard was Colonel Chapetón of Tegucigalpa, a man thoroughly loyal and submissive. The guard itself was composed of Olanchano Indians who had long fought beside Guardiola and whom they worshiped as a father. The president considered himself surrounded by loyal friends.

But Agurcia did not merit this confidence. He plotted to kill Guardiola. His principal obstacle lay in Colonel Chapetón and the Olanchanos, who would not betray their chief for all the gold in the world. Among Agurcia's satellites was the evil-faced Aparicio. Obeying Agurcia's orders, this creature insulted Chapetón on a side-street and shot him down before he could defend himself. Chapetón was carried into a hospital room seriously wounded, Aparicio was arrested. Agurcia took advantage of the moment to put one of his own henchmen in charge of Chapetón's command. Guardiola thought of nothing but caring for his wounded subaltern. As night fell, Agurcia, on various pretexts, substituted many of the Olanchanos of the guard with some of his own soldiers prepared for the proposed assassination.

At nine o'clock Guardiola gave his last order, worked until midnight, then shut himself up in his room. At five in the morning, Aparicio, released by Agurcia, presented himself before the substitute presidential guard, immediately gained access to the president's habitation and hammered on his bedroom door.

"Señor President, get up, the main barracks have revolted," shouted Aparicio. "Señor President, your presence is needed."

General Guardiola jumped from his bed in his nightclothes and opened the door. Aparicio lifted his double-barreled carbine and pulled the trigger. Though the bullets pierced Guardiola's body, he threw himself upon the assassin, seizing the carbine by the bayonet. Aparicio abandoned the weapon, dashing off in fright. General Guardiola, wounded in the lower part of the abdomen, fell down dead.

Confusion ruled the next few hours. The assassins named as their head, Francisco Montes, chief of the Liberal party. Popular wrath promptly threw him out. Victoriano Castellanos, vice-president elect, who had been in El Salvador, hurried back and in spite of his age and apparent feebleness, showed a vigor which prevented the anarchy threatening the Republic. Agurcia, Aparicio, and the rest of the plotters were rounded up and shot.

XX AUTO, TRAIN AND SAIL-BOAT

1

FOR HOURS WE ZIGZAGGED right up the face of the cliffs above Comayagua; the road is a marvelous piece of engineering. Below us, at one point, we saw a broken machine that had plunged over one of the declivities. The colonel explained that during the last revolution General Méndez, with three aides, had come hurtling over this mountain road, his auto full of guns and ammunition. At a turn they had hopped into the abyss. All had been killed. The colonel laughed heartily at the story—a Honduras sense of humor I did not quite appreciate—for each of our own sharp turns was hair-raising.

One of our passengers Don Manuel, a coast storekeeper, riding in the front seat with the chauffeur, kept the door constantly open; "because of the heat," he had explained at first, but later admitted, "in order to be ready to jump."

At another turn, where we stopped to get a view of the panorama, I discovered one of my suitcases, a ball of mud, dangling a few inches from the ground; the rope holding it had been deliberately cut, probably in Comayagua by some one hoping it would soon fall off.

Below us stretched the gigantic sweep of Comayagua valley—the most open region, except the coast lowlands, of all the topsy-turvy expanse of Honduras. Back in the 'fifties that energetic American diplomat, Mr. E. G. Squier, climbed up the volcano of Conchagua to get a bird's-eye view of all this region; and through the valley of Comayagua visioned the possibility of an interoceanic railway. It still remains to be built.

Over the divide, through meadows of scrub pine; then we dropped down—for hours. Towards the end of the day we reached the shores of Lake Yojoa. Here at a rickety landing place, a shabby soldier examined our passports. From a woman in a smoky kitchen, we obtained food to be eaten on the launch as we crossed the lake.

The colonel, his wife and baby and Manuel, the storekeeper, and myself put all of our supplies into one pot and spread out newspapers on the deck for a tablecloth. I had bought several cans of salmon and some cheese. The colonel, without waiting for anybody else, gouged into the salmon. He stuffed fish and bread into his mouth and gulped them down, the oil dripping from his mouth over the papers. He ate like a ravenous animal and when he had finished, wiped his hand on his own black tangled hair and on his uniform.

His needs partially sated, he told us again of his heroic exploits—the details of his charge upon Comayagua town, when he had lost his forearm, a story we now knew by heart. Before reaching Comayagua his troops had had to pass around this same lake, for the enemy controlled the launches—six days of terrific toil through jungle and marsh and precipice.

Easy to believe. This enormous body of water was completely surrounded by mountains, heavily forested to the water's edge; tangled jungles overrun with lianas and gourds. Not a human habitation was in sight, just these wooded heights, solemn, majestic, untouched by man's hand.

We had embarked at sunset, and so for an hour had the pearly light on the water and the changing colors of mountains and forest, as the sun lowered—a stupendous pyrotechnic of color. Ducks winged past us. A flock of geese honked overhead. I stood upon the upper deck, facing the heavy breeze which rushed past zestfully after our many hours of stifling heat.

Quite dark when we arrived at the opposite shore, to be picked up by another car. The vegetation at the head of the lake had been semi-tropical; here we plunged into the densest jungle; the trees and massed vines walled the sides of the road, closed tight about us. Only occasionally did we get glimpses of the night sky. Enormous uncanny stretches of bamboo, weird masses of vines, distorted trees with great protruding flanks and expanses of white shiny bark. A warm moist stench, the stench of rotting things, of perfumed flowers, of fecundity.

Time and again the chauffeur had to get out and open gates, for the way lay through private coffee fincas. Mysterious fluttering black and white wings came out of the dense forest and disappeared. Cows got in our way, eyes uncanny green from the head-light reflection; red were the strange flaming eyes of the *cocullos*.

2

At Punterillos, we tumbled out, scarcely able to walk.

The colonel disappeared towards the station, where he intended sleeping out with his wife and child. Very foolish, he said, to pay for the hotel room for the few hours until the train left early in the morning.

At the hotel, a miserable wooden contraption above a store, three of us were assigned to one small room, with screened doors and windows.

I sat awhile drinking lemonade with a German wood-merchant—a jerky sort of conversation; it was too hot to think. He was shaking his head dismally over the possibility of future trouble. "The red Indian army in the north has never been dispersed since the last revolution. The country is divided between the followers of Paz Bahona, Tosta, and Carías. There is hard feeling, too, with Guatemala over the boundary. Anything is likely to happen."

The wood-merchant was a great bearded burly fellow, yet he drooped with that washed-out sunken posture of body and mien which affects all white men living in these regions. Now and then he interspersed into his conversation these words: *"Cada cabeza es un mundo"* (every head is a world) which seemed to sum up his entire philosophy about life; and was a picture of his sullen introspection, the frustration which sooner or later overtakes the average white resident; his incapability of ever really penetrating the ways and thought of these alien people. This little phrase permitted him to shy off from any discussion. Each man had his ideas about things, why bother about arguing—a fatalistic attitude, a belief in the ultimate inability of human beings to understand each other.

I stood on the upstairs balcony. The tropic moon flooded the miserable little settlement with an orange glow of ineffable beauty. The limitless expanse of the jungle glistened like a restless silver sea.

Fortunately the doors were screened, but even so the mosquitoes were bad, and after the eighteen hours of travel I had reached a stage of weariness which prevents sound sleep. Before dawn, came a terrible whistle, awaking us all in fright, splitting our eardrums. It lasted several minutes—the customary warning to get up and take the train. I walked bare-foot across the floor in my B.V.D.'s to take a splash at the basin. Even at four o'clock in the morning the candle which I held in my hand revealed the perspiration marks of my feet on the board floor.

The train proved to be a *mixto*, no first-class coach until San Pedro. Here the riff-raff of the *boca costa* region was dumped into the second-class coaches, pure blooded negroes with frizzly hair, mixed breeds of all descriptions, whites, Indians, Spaniards; an American, his wife and two babies, down from the silver mines in San Rosario.

Fortunately, the dirty colonel, his wife, and now mosquito-bitten baby could find no seat next to me nor even in the same car. After settling my belongings I folded my coat on the seat, and went outside again to try to buy food. When I came back I found a native sitting right on top of my coat. My nerves snapped. I yanked him out by the collar. About to make some pertinent remark regarding the event, he looked at my angry face, his mouth closed and without a word he walked into the next car.

In San Pedro, where the train stopped for two hours, the colonel seized hold of me again. I sat him down in the hotel barroom (run by a lean Yankee soured on life), while I went up to a room to get rid of some of the grime of travel. We went out again headed for the telegraph office where the colonel sent his usual wire, but only after a furious argument because he was required to buy official blanks instead of receiving them gratis. In the smaller places, the clerks had paid for them personally rather than offend his royal nibs.

3

We dragged and jerked along at the rate of about five miles an hour. The stops and starts smashed one back against the seat or flung one in the lap of the passenger in front. At every siding we halted to load bananas.

The American from the San Rosario mine and his wife and children had been in the country about three years. An isolated life, but it had its advantages. He was provided with a free house, free light, free ice, and could buy American goods at cost.

He told an amusing story about a teamster at the mines, who had come into the house one morning when the electric heater was going. The teamster walked around and around the apparatus and stretched out his hands to the glow, completely mystified, then naïvely asked, "Can I get one of these stoves to take with me on the road? It sure would be nice to be able to keep warm on some of these cold winter nights."

We shunted into Puerto Cortés over a long bridge across the arm of the bay. This bridge is famous in the annals of Honduras, for here the great Lee Christmas, an American, wiped out a whole rebel army. Lee Christmas, a railway engineer, in some jam with the law in the States, came adventuring to Honduras. Utterly reckless, he took part in every armed fracas, and for many years was the power behind the throne. His great opportunity came when he offered to destroy a rebel army in Puerto Cortés single-handed. The only way out of the town, located on a spit of sand, was across the railway bridge. Lee Christmas waited in an engine around a curve in the jungle till the whole army was on the bridge. Then, steam up, he drove upon them, wiping the entire force out of existence.

This amazing man had fourteen known wives. Ultimately the name "Christmas" in Honduras is likely to become as common as "Smith" in the United States.

In Puerto Cortés little black boys fought to carry our baggage. A tiny pickaninny trying to yank my suitcase away from a big black fellow, shouted, "If Ah was youh size, Ah'd go and do some real wohk."

In Puerto Cortés I encountered the most comfortable hotel in Honduras, which is not saying much, and a cool room—a godsend for the port was stifling and the blazing sun on white wall and corrugated tin—part of banana enterprise—was a blinding glare. A pretty little mulatto girl showed me up to my room and carefully pointed out all the advantages of the place.

My remark was, "I seem to have all the comforts of home, except a wife."

"Oh, that's mos' easy to find here, sah," and she went off giggling.

I had heard a Cuyamel fruit boat was leaving for Puerto Barrios, Guatemala, this same afternoon. In Central America if one misses a boat there is no telling how long one may have to wait for the next. Without stopping to eat, I rushed out to see the Guatemalan Consul.

"No boat!" he informed me laconically. "Might not be one for a week except the small gasoline coast launch

—very uncomfortable, rough riding. Why not take passage in the sailboat of my friend Señor Francisco Cárdenas. He is not only a gentleman but an educated man. The boat leaves this afternoon at five. You will find him at the Pensión España."

The sailboat seemed the best bet, and since it was already three o'clock I rushed out to reserve passage, then to the Comandancia to have my passport stamped and secure an embarkation permit. A tall Jamaican who "only wohks foh gentlemen, suh," carried my baggage through the town to the harbor front. I clambered across the parrot- and female-littered deck of a Mexican tramp steamer, loaded with mules, to the low lying *cubierta* of Don Francisco's schooner *La Esperanza,* where my baggage was dumped. The Jamaican had given my portable typewriter to a little pickaninny to carry. When I paid the Jamaican, the little pickaninny asked him for *pisto,* or small change, but the tall Jamaican turned on him surlily and said, "Ah, gwan home and wash youh face." I gave the little chap some loose coins, and he went off, sticking his tongue out at my assistant.

Since five in the morning I had not eaten. A bath seemed more important in San Pedro; and a boat more important in Puerto Cortés; I hurried back to town again for food. So dilatory were they in my hotel that I went on up to the ramshackle Hotel Lefebre, managed by two Irishmen. I asked for ham and eggs. "Eggs are rarer than gold nuggets, be jabers," protested one of the proprietors. So I contented myself with ham and potatoes.

"What kind of ham would it be you are after having?"

"What kind of ham is there?"

"Be jabers, now I come to think of it, we have only one kind, sugar-cured ham from Virginia that'll make your mouth water, like the sight of fine looking legs."

It did make my mouth water. But just as the dish was put before me, one of the sailors from the sailboat dashed in. He had been looking high and low, all over town for me.

"The boat is leaving. Come along." The clock on the wall said four-fifteen.

"The wind has shifted," he explained; "we have to slip out at once."

I seized a piece of bread and made a ham sandwich, which I ate on the run to the boat, where I landed breathless, half nauseated from so much hurry in the beating sun.

4

All night long the little two-masted schooner of Don Francisco (or Don Pancho, as he soon became) ran before the stiff breeze and scattering rain from Puerto Cortés to Puerto Barrios, the long and terribly hot coast of Central America.

It had been a relief to get out of the dirty yellow houses and the heat of Puerto Cortés and feel the cool salt air sweeping past. At the orders of the willowy blond English captain "from the Islands" the Standing-Mutt and Flying-Jeff were hoisted, and we tacked away from the low dirty shore of Honduras, fief of the Standard Fruit Company of New Orleans. We swung full into the breeze before the bar. The captain shouted, "Hoist that top sail, ease up the jib." The heat-dancing shore, the warehouses, fell away into a silver haze, the waves spanked against the prow, a shark's fin sliced through the water. We bowled along at a lively gait.

The crew was mongrel and nondescript. Hard to tell what language they spoke. A few scattered words of English, Spanish, French, Indian, Dutch, the almost unintelligible Caribbean sailor's patois.

BARON
BANANA

1

WE STOOD NEAR THE STEER-
ing wheel getting acquainted,
three of us ducking the sweep
of the mainsail boom, I, Don
Pancho, and Doña Isabella,
the latter my one and only
fellow passenger, a lean, middle-aged Guatemalan
woman, addicted to corn-husk cigarettes and gold-circle
earrings, on her way to see her sick daughter.

As for Don Pancho, the words of the Guatemalan
Consul proved in no way exaggerated. Fate had cast him
in Honduras—except when he is careening in his two-
master against the Caribbean gales from Colón to Belize
with petty loads of corn, beans, and vegetables. But it
was not until we were bowling well along the coast, sitting in front of coffee and rolls, spread out in the lee
of the hatchway of the tiny cabin, that I discovered the
truth of the second half of the Consul's remark, "Don
Pancho is not only a gentleman but an educated man."

The boom still creaked over our heads, the water
washed against the sides of the boat. Don Pancho and I
skipped airily over Spanish history and literature and
found common interests in the fact that five years before, when on a walking tour through Catalonia, I had
stumbled upon his native village.

"Central America is going black," was his thesis.
Every year more negroes from Jamaica and British
Honduras come flooding into the banana fields; and he

painted a mournful picture of degeneracy from the mixing of negro, Indian, and the flotsam and jetsam of the *boca costa* region—a jumble of broken, backward people festering in the hot banana ports where drink and disease and promiscuity and the immoralities of a dozen dislocated races stalk like black specters through the hot restless nights, devouring men endlessly. "Lands of doom," he characterized the region.

"Bringing civilization to the tropics! You Americans go to pieces like the rest," was his verdict. "You believe in democracy. We Spaniards never made that mistake. We came as conquerors, and to this day we have remained as conquerors. We brought culture and cruelty from Pedro de Alvarado to Gil Gonzales down to the present. The rôle of the white man is not to mix, not to democratize, but to rule, to direct, to create; and these people are just the raw materials."

"If you use shoddy material, your cloak is shoddy," I ventured. "Are human beings ever just raw material— except perhaps the welder of the Be-All and End-All?"

"Benevolent dictatorship," was Don Pancho's quick-clipped creed.

Never would he sink to the standards of the half-caste people among whom he had been thrown. He walked with sure chin-up tread; his habits were temperate, only an occasional glass of cognac. The lures of the cheap women and the gambling dens of the banana ports had never snared him. I tried to get his personal motives in life. Did they reduce just to making money in a two-master? Where had he read his books? Why had he landed in this out of the way part of the world?

Don Pancho was one of those rare adventurers who never forget the laws of conduct, self-preservation, and race-integrity. Of a middle-class family, his life had been patch-worked. Jilted by a sweetheart in the early twenties he had suddenly thrown up his prospering drug-store business to travel with a theater troupe. Later he had won grace in Toledo when the King had come through and had been appointed pharmacist in Capo de Oro, right on the equator. There he'd learned the ways of the blacks.

"They should be kept naked with loin-cloths, only," was his decision. "They are good animals with too beautiful bodies for clothes. There is nothing more ridiculous than a well-dressed negro. And the women—now their firm ample flesh seems ready to burst through the satin skin—like ripe fruit! But when they are clothed—a travesty!"

Don Pancho did not hold out long in Capo de Oro. He wrote a satirical poem about the pompous governor who had erected an enormous statue of himself in the harbor entrance. Don Pancho was promptly thrown into a dungeon. A negro boy, who had served him loyally, connived his escape and smuggled him out of jail on to a Portuguese tramp freighter loaded with ivory and cocoanuts. Don Pancho had landed in Lisbon, where like Espronceda he threw away his last penny so as not to enter such a magnificent city with so little money. He then shipped as a common sailor on a boat to Central America and had skipped off in Puerto Cortés.

Did he long to return?

No, he would never go back. He had made a niche for himself here. He liked the adventure of trading in petty cargoes, trafficking with custom officials, the repeated danger of storms, the contact with the outlandish types that drifted into the banana ports from every corner of the world. The business gave him security plus variety, spiced with occasional adventure.

And on long still nights when *La Esperanza* lay becalmed beneath the burning tropic stars, he sat by the lit "nigger" in the wheel box, smoking, and gazing out toward the moon-blanched, palm-waving shores beyond the silver path of the sea, working out his sententious philosophy, thinking—thinking of the girl who had jilted him before he went storming off with the traveling troupe—an old hate and pain and desire that had never died, and that may have accounted for much of his arrogance toward the people of the "lands of doom," may have explained his self-restraint, his ability to live by his own lights—a bit aloof, observing, registering irony, weighing events in the balance of some capable judgment forged early in life.

2

Night fell swift and cool, the "nigger" was lit in the wheel box; phosphorescence quivered through the black waters; and I lay me down in a piece of sailcloth to stare up at the dagger-like tropical stars until fitful rain from drifting clouds grew heavier; the sky clouded completely over and finally the wet drove me down into the tiny stuffy cabin where sprawled four nondescript barefoot sailors, Don Pancho, and the now-vomiting Doña Isabella. I finally went to sleep, water from the deck dripping near my left ear, and an occasional gigantic cockroach scuttling over my neck.

Rose and mauve dawn on the beautiful Amatique Gulf! A purple sea shading to violet, a dim, slate-gray shore keying up to deep jungle green and red tiles and silver glints of sheet iron. And then, the sun, snarling like a yellow dragon over the Espirito Santo Mountains.

While we rode at anchor near the United Fruit Company pier, waiting for the leisurely port officials to finish their *desayuno* and let us go ashore, Don Pancho again bewailed the evils of the lands where Fate had cast him. He repeated this intently, yet in that half absent-minded way of his, as though, in spite of his apparent sinuous surety of himself, there was at the bottom of all this whirl of races and habits, this cultural break-up, some perplexing enigma, some secret source of vitality which concerned him profoundly.

We finally went through the customs with no trouble save a pair of brass knuckles which Don Pancho carried in his suitcases for emergencies, and which the official confiscated until such time as Don Pancho would be leaving Guatemala again; and save for a gigantic cockroach which to my embarrassment scurried over my clothes and out of sight when the lid of my suitcase was opened.

An officious clerk in the Hotel Grace, in reply to my demand for a good room, replied, "They're all good rooms—in winter!" But he gave me one on the cooler side of the building facing the veranda which overlooked the sea through fronds of enormous palm trees.

Puerto Barrios and its inhabitants, I soon saw as I strolled around the shabby town, could easily account for Don Pancho's sentiments of superiority and his eloquence anent the glories of Spain. Here in Puerto Barrios are the unmasked crudities of the raging fever of modern times to wrench forth raw materials. In Puerto Barrios, Baron Banana rules supreme, and he rules roughshod

with little regard for the beauty or happiness of his people. Although to the Baron, Banana goes by the aristocratic cognomen of *musa sapientum,* and President
Orellana called him "Guatemala's Golden Prince," he is
the most plebeian of the whole family of *plátanos.* The
Spanish, with satiric flair, have given him the phallic
label, "Fig of Adam." But abroad in the United States,
Baron Banana struts in frock. Fruit salads at banquets,
banana-split sundaes in mauve-lighted Park Avenue tea-
rooms, banana brandy for jaded Village bobs, dances to
the tune of "Yes, we have no bananas," attest to the importance that this single tropic fruit—one of hundreds
—has acquired in the diet and imagination of the United
States. Bananas and more bananas!

The United Fruit Company and its lesser competitors
can hardly keep pace. Their engineers go slashing
through the jungles; their railroads reach iron fingers
out and out; their yellow clapboard buildings, hotels,
bunk houses, stores, offices, hospitals, warehouses, spring
up like mountainous fungi beside a hundred streams
and marshes, in the heart of vast mangrove forests, and
on a dozen glowering shores. The big green stems of fruit
are cut from the tall, broad-leafed, plump-trunked
trees, loaded on mattresses in the open cars—roofed-over
"reefers" through which tropic breezes may sweep—
and are run down to a dozen ports, banana fronds dragging and rustling endlessly over the sleepers of the track
—down to Puerto Barrios, on the older maps not even
mentioned. Puerto Barrios, boom banana port, epit-
omizes the haste and cruelty and bleeding rawness of the
process. Back in the jungles, the smallpox yellow, the
screech of trains—all the drive and jangle of the banana
industry—shrinks in the face of vegetations so vast. The

ceibas, the guayacáns, the flaming *palos de sope* soar up
and over the handiwork of human beings. The constant
nerve-racking struggle to push back the monstrous
trees, to clear out the jungles with their reeking enervat-
ing perfumes, poisonous insects, dangerous beasts, terrible fevers—this struggle is tragic yet puny in its relative
inadequacy. But in Puerto Barrios the conglomerate
ugliness of raw-product exploitation is spewed forth into
the glaring torrid sunlight.

Here the yellow buildings are not so overshadowed by
the jungle. They squat brazenly on the golden, heat-
hammered sands by the deep blue, brooding ocean. That
first morning when we left *La Esperanza* and put the
irritating immigration, customs, and police officials behind us, then straggled through the blazing heat between seared lawns to find refuge on the wide piazzas of
Captain Grace's Hotel, the Government of Guatemala
apparently had suddenly ceased to exist. Only Baron
Banana, ordering his reefers in the train-yards, oversee-
ing the typewriters clicking in the smallpox yellow
buildings, accepting company *fichas* in the stores. The
only open evidence of the Governmental Center's interest in Baron Banana's exportation of "yellow gold"
was the dilapidated blue barracks in the rear of the town
whence at intervals came the cocky snarl of bugles and
drums whose rhythm and melody repeatedly broke down
into Indian surliness—the bafflement of the highlander
at the terrors of the hot country, his amazement and
resentment at the restless energy of the blond beasts
from the north, at the throb of this constant belching
forth of bananas, more bananas, the constant buzz of
this dirty port on the edge of tropic seas, dazzling seas

in the day, but at night softly flaming with phosphorescence and starlight.

Yes, Puerto Barrios is an achievement in ugliness in a natural setting of beauty. Puerto Barrios is the only place I know where people stick water-closets in their front yards. In the cool of the day, I often wandered out through the hodge-podge town, built on a pestiferous marsh, reeking with spilled petroleum, out along the twisted paths where are massed in utter promiscuity the atrocious blue and yellow shacks of negroes and Indians and Chinese. Boards and gunnysacking, banana and palm tree leaves, river cane, sheet iron and rags have gone into the making. Picking my way through the slime and excrement and swarms of naked, mud-smeared children—white, yellow, black; kinky-haired, straight-haired, curly-haired; round-eyed, pig-eyed, slant-eyed— I came out on the walk fronting the foot-high breakwater over which the waves sometimes come flooding into the low shacks, and there saw the curve of the shore and the line of tall taut cocoanut palms broken by an interminable row of spider-leg piers stretching out to cubbyhole water-closets set about four feet above high tide. *This* is Puerto Barrios' highest word in esthetics.

Here in the muck of Baron Banana's postern, human life swarmed meaningless—so many maggots squirming. Yet not without sun, not without color, not without joy. A group thumping the marimba, "Yes, we have no bananas." A half-dressed couple behind a slide window dancing the rumba lasciviously. A gargantuan negro pair enormously paunched, screamingly overdressed; he, in white spats, patents, waistcoat, and derby hat; she, in white satin, and carrying a pink sunshade. In a corner under a mango tree, a Belizian weaving a double-rhomboid fish trap out of river cane, "Don't be so good this here cane, sah, as honest-to-god bamboo, but c'n catch any fish mahn a pound. Some weeks Ah makes goin' on fifteen quid, yas, sah." At a turn, a Chinaman, shirt-tail out, staring forlornly at the sea, beyond the water-closets. And here, crossing the footbridge of a little creek, shaded by bread-fruit trees—which half make life on muck not too onerous—the town broke down into Indian *jacales* with thatched roofs. In this rag-tail port Baron Banana has dumped the lost sons of five continents, made them his groveling subjects—that Waldorf and Plaza salads may be. Here are huge rag-tail negroes from Jamaica, never looking for a job, but for a "posishun" or "emplawment, sah," mysterious orientals smoking long pipes; alert Japanese; white girls, ex-prostitutes or dopes, now content to marry the black-skin or yellow-skin trash of the world; broken beach combers, vagabonds, the taciturn Indians from the highlands, sailors of every breed, within and without the law. Marimbas quiver through the hot night air; piano players rattle jazz in the cantinas and gambling joints; a hundred cast-offs of the world carouse and fumble black women, who laugh coarsely.

XXII　THE SONG
OF THE
CARVERS
OF GODS

1

"SAY, BO, IS THERE IVER A
chance yez 've a ten cent
rraveled rrope end in your
trrousers?"

In such wise in front of a smallpox yellow building
of the United Fruit Company beside the tropic sea on a
sweltering night in Puerto Barrios did Jim indicate to
me his pressing need for a cup of coffee. He snatched
the ten cents from my hand and vanished. Half an hour
later I met him in the grassy path between Captain
Grace's Hotel and the Negro-Chinese-Indian quarters.

"Say, an' it's some quinine I'm arrfter needing bad.
Last night I slept on the open porch o' them Chinese
buggers, an' Jasus the fever's got me fer fair. I'm shakin'
like an aspen leaf. But the yellow bellies 're the only
decent folk when it comes to lettin' a guy slape."

Jim was an attractive wastrel. Stocky, curly-haired,
blue-eyed, with knotted, freckled arms, sleeves rolled to
the elbow, revealing the blue tattooing of a nude woman
rising from evanescent smoke—or it may have been a
sea. A rollicking dare-devil who took to adventure like
a duck to water and never worried about the morrow.
His big arms and beefy hands showed he knew how to
work when the notion struck him. His twinkling blue
eyes and easy brogue had a way of catching hold of the
heart-strings as he told some magnificent figment of the

imagination. To-night it was his girl wife in Mobile, up there waiting for him to get back—"an' she without a cent." On his last trip across the pond, he had run into the girl in Dublin, married her, brought her back to the States and settled her in Mobile. Then he'd gotten a job in the Central American lines as an A.B.—"able-bodied seaman." So his story went.

A good graft these Central American lines. Every trip, he smuggled in pistols and cartridges at a handsome profit. But his last trip he'd run into a plain-clothes dick who had given him the "fale overr. Begorrah, an' I slugged the guy fer fairr, right on the pier coming off the boat, laid him out cold as a dog's nose. That's what got me in Dutch. Thurrty days in the cooler, mind yez, forrty of us in one o' them squash cells—*bartolinas* they calls 'em—sweating like pigs and eatin' stinkin' rice and beans. Well, I'm lightin' out in the mornin' on the *Landsdowne,* if these cops'll only lave me alone for another night. Jasus, yez never'd glimmer what it manes slapin' out in these rains. The waterr comes down like steel spikes, it does. A guy might as well be on the holy cross, he might. But fer all that I kapes clean. Twice a week the Mex kid and I hoof it up the river to wash our clothes." He motioned toward a lad hovering under a near-by bread-fruit tree. "But it's the slapin' out that's hard here. One night I dozes off in one of them 'reefers' —that's what they're afterr callin' them banana cars. I wakes up next mornin' thirty miles up country in a banana plantation. Holy Crripes!

" 'What yez doin' here?' they asked me. 'You'd better make tracks.'

"I caught the passenger on the fly. Jasus. What a funny ladders the cars have in this countrry. One foot went plumb through—hit the whale box or begorrah little Jim'd 've been prrayin' the Good Lord for a wooden stump an' a tin-cup."

With quinine and fifty cents in his pockets, Jim went whistling off with his Mexican "pardner"—with whom he couldn't even talk—down to the jazz-crashing points of nigger-town.

2

From Puerto Barrios I rode second-class up to Quiriguá, jammed in with the sweating bodies—vast families of the dark-skinned sprawling over the backless wooden benches. Bananas travel laid out carefully on fiber and leaf mattresses, the people, like pigs on the spit-covered floor, sweltering at a dozen stations while the train leisurely loads bananas.

Quiriguá is a shop center for the banana country. More smallpox yellow up above along sweeping green lawns and a neat concrete hospital run by a malaria specialist. Not a room was vacant in the company hotel, in charge of a grumpy ex-Catholic priest. At the hospital, too, I was told, "Full up, come back at ten and if no one is dragged up in number 4, our emergency room, with a broken head, I'll chance putting you up." It was suggested I try the next village, Los Amates. So I toiled under the sun for two and a half miles along the tracks running through the jungles and the plantations. Los Amates is a straggling thatched-roof Indian pueblo. More smallpox yellow on the company store, but no place to sleep except in the "two houses"—the most pretentious clapboard edifices in the town (also painted smallpox yellow)—where the employees of the company on Saturday nights bestow money and maudlin caresses on mulatto and Indian girls—more toil of the tropics and the frontier. I was forced to sleep that night on a chair on the porch of the company hotel, lulled to repose by a mosquito symphony. Accommodations can't keep pace with company expansion.

But not my interest in Baron Banana had dragged me to Quiriguá to discover that he has none of the traditional feudal *noblesse oblige;* the next morning I caught a banana train out to the ruins—early remnants of Maya Quiché culture, vying with the destroyed cities of Copán and Palenque, Chichén Itzá, Uxmal, Mayapan, and a hundred others scattered from Yucatán and Campeche down through Chiapas and Guatemala to Honduras. Dropping from the reefer, I avoided the usual traveled path and cut straight through the banana fields, steaming sickeningly with the odor of over-ripe fruit, to a half-obliterated track through the jungle by the side of a tiny stream gurgling invisible beneath mammoth leaves. A hundred creatures—lizards, insects, snakes—started from under my feet. Macaws and parakeets screamed from the depths. Overhead was a solid lacing of branches and vines, enormous cedars, sapotas, cacaos, dragon trees, rubber trees, with fluted trunks. From the branches streamed long parasites of brilliant hues. In every cleft and trunk, aerial vegetation had sunk its roots and flung forth its flaming color. Parasite on parasite—not so unlike the human order. Long wisps of steam curled up, sucked forth by the terrific heat. Nauseatingly powerful perfumes were wafted over me in serried waves. The vegetation had a poisonous emanation, a cruel animal quality, frightening and menacing. I hurried on to the small Lagoon of the Idols, the scene, perhaps, of ancient ablutions, rituals, and sacrifices, and reached a wide open space reclaimed from the wilderness.

Quiriguá is not so obviously impressive as the ruins of Teotihuacán, Mitla, or Chichén Itzá, yet this open space between prominent shattered platforms—thanks to the lofty carved monoliths standing in gigantic solemnity—retains the atmosphere of ancient grandeur. I found a little difficulty in re-creating for myself pictures of the pageants and ceremonies of olden times, the great processions of nobles and sacerdotes wearing elaborate robes woven of the emerald and red feathers of the quetzal, that glorious bird, now emblem of the Guatemalan people, that in the beginning, after the great flood, sprang forth as a symbol of power and beauty—"a flying water lily"—from the crest of a mammoth guayacán tree.

The old stones of Quiriguá tell of the ancient emotional and intellectual striving after god and the mysteries, the seeking for Nirvana. The faces depicted on the various columns and monoliths reveal high intelligence plus brutal will. Here is one; flat, bold forehead, flat broad nose, large round protruding eyes, square ears, massive protruding lower lip; esthetically, simplicity of representation, calm almost bitter realism, set off by grotesque background and formalized carvings of toads, lizards and tigers.

I found myself rushing from stone to stone in a fever of discovery, from the great frightening turtle to the legless, handless woman, to the huge stone twelve feet in diameter, with its snarling tiger and fringe of six emblematic figures above a base of small circles. I hurried up the platforms over crumbling stairs. The old teocalli have fallen; the old thrones have vanished; there remain but broken fragments, mysterious niches, carved lintels, great door slabs. Descending ancient steps, I became absorbed in a representation of human fertility, a woman with features more delicate, nose thinner, the ears not square but formed by three concentric circles; and all about her the engraving of the beautiful leaves of the *conte*. Capably she supports a child by a single thumb and stares forth with the same calm command that the artist imparted to her two thousand years before.

3

My haste had been injudicious. Suddenly I discovered myself on the verge of sunstroke. I managed to get to shade and in my need for air ripped off my shirt, heedless of the myriad insects.

Not a leaf moved; the sun blazed and shimmered. I lay there unable even to lift my hand to fan myself with my sun-helmet. Supreme admiration welled in me then for those young engineers of the United Fruit Company who carry their surveying outfits under the beating sun and hack their way foot by foot through marsh and jungle, defying venomous animals and dangerous diseases; an admiration for the genius that drove railroads through such a country of fever and heat. Likewise, supreme admiration for those older carvers of stone who cleared this site beside the Motagua River and cast up these symbols of power and hope.

In easy stages I again crossed the wide open field past the tall monoliths with their black-faced heads towards the banana railroad, stopping to rest once where some person, better acclimated than myself, had found energy to build for the comfort of wayside travelers, a little palm-leaf *champa* on high ground away from the jungle and its reptiles. And so I left the capital of an ancient empire behind me. A gasoline motor hurtled me back to the smallpox yellow town of Quiriguá where the newer Baron Banana lords it over a newer empire, riding his iron steed of modern progress, breaking the jungle with his iron fingers.

The scene shifts. A New York cabaret. Elegance, luxury, jewels. "Life has no sores. . . ." And then—a note out of the jungle. Jazz! "Yes, we have no bananas to-day." (Marimbas of Puerto Barrios' heartache.) But through the smoke of my cigarette I am just romantic enough to see the face of maternity, that child supported by one strong thumb, that calm assurance of motherhood carved in stone, those great bold eyes that have gazed on the world through the storms of two thousand years—and just realistic enough to remember a row of water-closets against a sunset sky over a purple sea, a row of water-closets breaking the noble line of feathery palms; just realistic enough to ask, "Why are the carvers of Gods breaking their hearts on jazz-time in the mire of Puerto Barrios?"

BALUM VOTAN

ONE OF THE GREAT HEROES of past epochs who passed through Quiriguá was Balum Votán.

Balum Votán was an engineer of bell towers, who during his best years studied the various possibilities of his fecund profession; also he was an excellent engineer of roads and highways. Conserved almost as the day it was built, stretches the beautiful road which he planned and executed between Cuidad Real of Chiapas and Yucatán. As an engineer of bridges he acquired fame, although in the centuries that have elapsed these have all been destroyed by floods. As an agronomist he established and wrote about the latest methods of cultivating corn. He invented the use of chocolate as a drink. He discovered that the *tepescuintles* could be eaten. He established fisheries in which he raised trout and salmon, fat as rabbits.

When Balum Votán reached thirty years he was a magnificently built man, skin bronzed and burned by the winds and the sun and the sea. The fire of his glance from his large black eyes seemed to burn through and through whatever they gazed upon. He kept his nails trimmed and clean, his hair properly cut. He wore a Pharaoh-like beard, which made him look older than he really was; but he never cut it off because it gave him a majestic and sacerdotal appearance.

Balum dressed precisely. Yet he had no desire to fall beneath the yoke of matrimony. His philosophical temperament induced him to resort to the enjoyment of various feminine entertainments, the echoes of which were generously bruited abroad. These diversions, according to reports, did not precisely diminish the population of the Maya dynasty. But superior to the formulas and the scruples of his epoch, he guarded his solitary state jealously.

Through a powerful comprehension of life superior to the criterion of his contemporaries, he never told about his past. He gave it to be understood that he had been born in distant lands, very distant, on the other side of the sea. But in spite of his reticence, the historical truth has come out and the inscription of his birth was seen not so very long ago in Sonora near the place where were inscribed many centuries later the baptism of Alvaro Obregón and Plutarco Elías Calles.

But for Balum, the region of Sonora was too small a frame for ambition; he went on to Puebla where he was highly esteemed for his knowledge of engineering and his handsome person.

A necromancer of this epoch predicted that the great flood would be repeated and that instead of raining forty days and forty nights it would rain twice as long. The panic was enormous. It was decided to call upon an engineer to plan for a tower which could be constructed as an asylum for the people until the great flood passed. The expense of the tower and its construction was borne by popular subscriptions raised by a commission working on the case. Balum did not have to be begged to undertake the task. He closed himself up in his house with a square, a compass, a supply of pencils and several well-planed pine tables. He sketched the bold lines and planned a tower different from that cylindrical Babel. Balum planned his edifice to be pyramidal and in truth it resulted pyramidal. Still in this twentieth century can be seen the work of this Votán, which to-day is called with great injustice the pyramid of Cholula instead of the tower of Balum Votán.

2

But everything in life does not have to be a tower and so, his task concluded, our engineer decided to wander over the earth. He went into the regions of Tabasco and finally arrived at the confines of Nicaragua. He studied the relative advantages of all the various localities, and picking the best, he gathered the dispersed tribes together. Selecting a group of individuals whom he baptized with the generic name of Votanites, he founded his empire. As he planned, so he did. On the eighteenth of January, 324, a bagatelle of 1600 years ago, Balum Votán and his Votanites laid the first stones of the kingdom of Mitlán, a city later on designated by the historians as Xibalbay. His empire included the regions which to-day are known as Yucatán, Chiapas, Guatemala, Salvador, Honduras and Nicaragua.

Having laid out his capital he founded other cities to the number of twenty, the most flourishing being Huehuetlán, Palenke, Zacatlán, Utatlán and Copán. His work can be considered titanic and comparable to the labors worked in Greece by Hercules. Hercules has been made much of by the historians because of his connection with Jupiter, but poor Balum Votán has been looked upon as little less than a bum. According to some historians Balum made friends with the Canaanites, who had come from the remote land of Canaan on a pleasure trip. They were spending their summer on the islands of Cuba when our hero came to know them. He loaded their boats and brought them to the domains of Xibalbay, where those good men carried on a marvelous cultural labor—they were as industrious as bees. Under the wise direction of Balum they were able to realize the praiseworthy and enduring works which have since become immortal. Those gentlemen of the period, for the first time in America, made an exact calendar, more exact indeed than the Gregorian. This calendar had no days of the saints. The only practical advantage that it possesses over free coco-cola calendars is that it determines for us the exact day and the year of the foundation of Nat Chan.

3

High up in the mountains south of Zacapa—a town on the way from Puerto Barrios to Guatemala—near the river Tepoctum lies Esquipulas. It now dozes in forgotten isolation, but in the sixteenth century, before railroads, Esquipulas was an indigenous center of the ecclesiastic province, Chiquimula de la Sierra, through which passed travelers and merchants on their way to and from the provincial capital and the north coast, and where came fifty thousand pilgrims for the annual fiesta.

The parish of Esquipulas had been founded in the fifteenth century by Fray Gómez Fernández de Córdoba, Provisor of the Bishop of Guatemala, Cristobal Morales, Fernández called upon Quirio Castaño, the most famous artificer of the day, to sculpt a Christ for the new Esquipulas church. The indigenes, the first catechists of the new parish, donated cotton to pay the hundred tostones demanded by the artist. Castaño set to work industriously, making the figure a dark tint, not exactly black, to indicate the blood of death and please the brown-skin natives. Upon the face he stamped a suffering expression meant to wring all hearts, and evidently did so, despite its rather clumsy proportions, and what now seems a bit ridiculous—its long female hair, decked with angels with cotton-wool wings. Soon word flew about that this Christ was the most miraculous on earth, and did not content Himself merely with the cure of nervous affections as did the Virgin of Lourdes; He surpassed all rational limits; His miracles were really miraculous. His fame passed beyond the frontiers to Comayagua, San Salvador, far Chiapas, even to Mexico. Within less than a year after the making of the image, the peregrinations became interminable.

Juan García, a native of Havana, found himself in Mexico, with a wife and more children than means of subsistence. Hearing of the wonders performed by the Lord of Esquipulas, he promptly set out for the far shrine.

After long arduous travel, he arrived before the image. He told it of his troubles, his poverty, his sufferings, how in spite of all his labor his family suffered horribly. He poured out the full vase of his misery. Relieved of the burden of his brooding, he returned to Mexico, taking back as souvenir to his wife three large stones from the adjacent river.

Juan García told her of the exhausting hardships of his trip and said: "As a souvenir, I have brought you these three stones from the river Tepoctum."

Opening out the cloth in which he carried the stones he found—three gold nuggets, *"tetuntes"* as the Indians call them. And so his suffering was ended. His family was provided with clothes and lived happily for many long years.

The news of Juan García's good fortune spread like wildfire; nothing could have been more efficacious to move pious hearts and simple souls than gold nuggets. Year after year long files of the faithful journeyed to prostrate themselves before the prodigious Lord. Day by day the number of worshipers increased. The blind came and went away seeing, the dumb came and went away talking. Ulcers and sores were healed. Every ailment found radical cure. Ill-fortune turned its back. In the moments of disaster and suffering, of fires and ship-wrecks, distressed wayfarers, facing calamity, by merely calling upon the intercession of Christ of Esquipulas, put an end to all misfortune, warded off all dangers.

4

About this time, from the remote region of Peru, came the illustrious Pedro Pardo de Figueroa to serve as seventeenth Bishop of Guatemala. His health was bad, his body broken, his soul sick and sullen. But in spite of ill-health, he immediately pulled wires to elevate the cathedral of Guatemala to the category of an Archbishopric. Success crowned his efforts; he became the first Archbishop of Guatemala.

These preliminaries over, the Archbishop turned his attention to his own health and sought out the famous Christ of Esquipulas in person. One beautiful November morning, escorted by his guards, he set forth with his family. The trip was long and hard, the prelate suffered atrociously. At the worst moments, he felt it really was not worth while to seek alleviation, nor even worth while to be one of the elect of Our Lord. But little by little, the leagues between the capital and Esquipulas were overcome. One happy day he arrived at the modest church sanctified by the many sufferers.

The illustrious father prayed interminably before the holy image; he prayed and prayed, and as his prayers prolonged themselves, he felt in his whole organism a positive well-being. When he rose from the spot, people saw his face brightly animated; a smile substituted the wrinkles of bitterness which had furrowed it for so many years.

"For the glory of this image," said the Archbishop, "I shall build a magnificent temple that will at least be some partial expression of my great gratitude."

From that date on, he did not rest until he had contracted for architects and had embarked upon a plan truly sumptuous. He even removed his headquarters to this distant precinct of Chiquimula to oversee the work, to be ever within sight of the ambitious undertaking.

The worries and cares of his vast diocese frequently called him away and caused him to lose much time; nevertheless he kept on with the project. Sixteen years hurried by. The last years of his life, Pardo de Figueroa passed fairly tranquilly in the beautiful valley, watching the massive white walls and arcades rise. It was built for the centuries with walls twelve feet thick. Four corner belfry towers rise in four stages. The lower one has but an oval side-window; the second is pierced by a narrow niche-window flanked by pilasters; the third

has two lower and wider windows on each side; the
upper stage is octagonal with a single arched window
and is capped by an almost conical dome. Toward the
rear rises a large tiled dome and lantern.

The whole edifice is set on a broad platform surrounded by a fence of masonry and wrought iron between pillars, to which leads a broad flight of steps.

Within are red tiles, and numerous pictures, a
cenacalo, and one of a group of ranchers lassoing Christ
in the best local *vaquero* style.

Towards 1751, feeling himself weary in body because
of his age, he prepared to die before the image he adored
so greatly. February 1st, he felt his strength leaving him;
the time had come for him to appear before the Creator.
On the second (the date of the celebration of the Virgen
de la Candelaria), the Archbishop of Guatemala
breathed his last among his family and the priests who
had surrounded him to hear his last command. The following day, he was interred at the foot of the image.
The Franciscans, in accordance with his instructions,
finished building the temple, at a total cost of three
million dollars. Castaño's image of Christ was put in its
proper and permanent place; and below, the remains of
the Archbishop.

To-day the pilgrimages to the Jesus of Esquipulas have
a commercial, rather than a pious tint; nevertheless the
humble and the simple of spirit still go there to implore
the intervention of this Christ. Even in this century of
radios, telephones and aeroplanes which destroy distances, the lowly peasants of Guatemala undertake endless arduous pilgrimages on foot and muleback up into
the high Sierra to render homage to the great white
shrine, enormous even in so vast a setting.

XXIV   THE LA-
CANDONES

1

AMONG THE INDIANS WHO
longest resisted Spanish domination were the Lacandónes
and the Puchutlas. On more
than one occasion, in Tabasco,
the Spaniards had attempted
to wreak vengeance upon these people in the most bar-
barous fashion; but the Lacandones lived a very primitive life; their houses were very simple—of straw and
wood—no great loss if destroyed. Too, their towns were
very scattered, their headquarters were in the inaccessible central island of the Lake of Petén, and they spent
most of their time in the forest in small groups ever disposed to injure the invaders; it was very difficult to
chastise them.

To this day the northern province of Petén is wild
and inaccessible, though late in colonial times a good
road was constructed from Guatemala to Yucatán. But
for the Guatemalans of the capital, even to-day, it is
about as well known as Java or Beluchistan. It still re-
quires two weeks of difficult travel by river and horse-
back to reach it. Only in recent years has Petén been
brought nearer by the explorations for petroleum and
the scientific investigations of the Mayan Society.

The pacified districts of Vera Paz complained constantly to their Captain General of the injuries perpe-
trated by these Indians. So many were the complaints
laid before the Council of the Indies that in 1556 a

Royal edict authorized the Captain General of Guatemala to war without quarter on the rebellious tribes. Other urgent matters however delayed the carrying out of the crown disposition; and in March, 1558, a new and more severe order was issued. But now the Captain General, Rodriguez de Quezada, was in such bad health he could not take the field, and again the war against the Lacandónes was postponed. Rodriguez died, and the President of the Audiencia, Pedro Ramírez de Quinónez, a man of advanced age but of eager spirit, took charge of public affairs.

January 4, 1559, a few months after taking office, the royal orders concerning the Lacandón expedition were read to the accompaniment of trumpets throughout the colony.

The Dominican friars, deeply interested in the spiritual redemption of the Indians, lifted their hands to heaven in fright.

"How is it possible that His Majesty the King could have forgotten his own recommendations of persuasion and kindness in the treatment of the Indians and thus without notice ordered that these tribes be subdued through extermination?"

Their protests notwithstanding, the expedition was fitted out. Ramírez enflamed the populace to carry the war into the Indian territory; all the leading families of the capital aided and engaged in the expedition, which in due course set out from Guatemala City, the Spaniards at the head and Indian allies behind, with great supplies of food, great quantities of bows and arrows, lances, shields, helmets, coats of mail, trumpets, drums, flags, enormous calabashes containing drinking water. Even small brigantines were transported in pieces to be put up rapidly if it became necessary to cross lakes and rivers. All the way, the army marched to warlike music.

The expedition went first to Comitán where another body of men, similarly equipped, was waiting them. In this far town of the Chiapanecas, the two armed groups presented themselves before the Bishop. He blessed their banners, gave absolution to the soldiers; Ramírez reviewed them.

Then they crossed over the mountains. The Chiapanecan allies went ahead and cleared a road. After two weeks of arduous advance, they reached the shore of Lake Petén, opposite the Lacandón island stronghold.

Canoes came to meet them, offering friendship. The Spaniards asked for transport to the island, but the natives brought only eleven canoes, saying they had no more.

The Spaniards did not fall into the trap, but set up a brigantine and sailed full tilt for the island, where they occupied the city easily, captured the Cacique and head sacerdote, looted and burned the houses.

The army returned to the mainland and proceeded towards Topiltépec. Now, marching more carelessly, the Spaniards were attacked in a narrow pass by eighty Lacandónes. Many of the expeditionary force were wounded by the rain of arrows and Topiltépec when finally reached was completely abandoned. The Spaniards pushed on to Puchutla, another lake town, and constructed boats, since the brigantine had been abandoned. The Indians launched thousands of canoes against them, but the superior arms of the Spaniards turned the tables—the enemy was put to flight. Puchutla was also found abandoned. Ramírez thereupon declared the campaign ended and returned to Guatemala with a hundred and fifty captives. These soon fled from the city, back to their old haunts.

Some of the Spaniards were rewarded, some recommended for promotion and some merely wasted good paper petitioning in vain for recompense. The Chiapanecan allies were rewarded by having their tribute lightened; and those who participated directly were given, in addition to the booty carried off, swords and pikes, weapons which were shortly taken away from them as being improper arms for Indians.

One Indian, unable to lay his hands on any booty but afraid to face a shrewish wife without something tangible to show for his long absence, filled a basket (*chiquihuite*) full of pebbles and covered it over with a cloth. On his arrival home, his wife was overjoyed at the sight of what she thought to be treasure. But on examining the contents she became so furious that she hurled the pebbles at the head of her spouse. Blessed is matrimony!

The Lacandónes rebuilt their simple homes and continued to harass the inhabitants of settled Vera Paz. The costly expedition brought no permanent returns at all.

2

A century later, another expedition undertaken against the Lacandónes resulted in the building of the road mentioned before between Guatemala and Yucatán. The population of Petén, during the entire previous century, had been augmented by the proud and warlike Mayas who had fled from Yucatán rather than submit to the Conquistadores. Joining with the Lacandónes they added to the general recalcitrancy of the region.

And so in 1692 Barrios Leal, Governor of Guatemala, decided to subdue Petén once more. He would head the expedition himself, which (following Crown instructions) would attempt to convert as well as coerce the Indians. A corps of priests accompanied the troops, and the famous historian Jiménez, whose noted history gives the details of these expeditions. The invasion penetrated by four routes, one from Ococingo, another by Huehuetenango, the third by Vera Paz and the fourth from Yucatán.

The last was led by Martín de Ursua y Arismendi, of Mérida in Yucatán, who had the concession from the King to build a road through Chichén Itzá to Guatemala.

Yet this ambitious second invasion, striking toward the Lacandón country from four directions, was also doomed to failure. The rainy season came sooner and heavier than usual; the rivers rose dangerously; the enemy proved warlike and aggressive, inflicting a series of annihilating defeats. Leal returned determined, however, to set in motion another expedition. But in the midst of preparations he died from the privations of the first.

His successor, Sánchez de Berrospe, continued the undertaking. But before the new Governor could set out, charges were brought against him.

In the meantime, Martín of Mérida, working on his own, undaunted by lack of coöperation from Guatemala, descended from the Lake Itzá region, overcoming natural obstacles, opening a road as he went, which has endured for over three hundred years.

Arriving at the north shore of the Lake, he built boats to transport his troops and his war supplies. This work was constantly retarded by the Indians, but he defended himself vigorously and continued indefatigably. At last, in 1697, his troops embarked and sailed directly toward the island capital.

King Canec led his Indian warriors out in small boats to oppose them. Martín's soldiers carried large shields for defense against the arrows, and were under orders not to discharge their guns.

Not until reaching shore did the Spaniards fire upon the city. They leapt out of their boats up to the waists in water and redoubled their attack, firing volley after volley. The city resisted for two hours, before the inhabitants fled. Martín took possession in the name of his Sovereign, ran up the Spanish flag on the highest building, burnt the Indian temples, threw the stone idols into the water.

Martín avoided all unnecessary hostility, gradually the Indians returned to the island, being received with kindness and deference and promised their condition would be improved, that pure religion should animate their soul. Even King Canec, accompanied by the high sacerdote, finally presented himself.

In conquering Petén the Spaniards had finally penetrated the last and strongest refuge of the highest civilization of the new world. Captain Martín de Ursua y Arismendi returned to Yucatán, leaving the first permanent colony of Europeans in Petén, a priest, a surgeon, mechanics and fourteen families.

The Council of the Indies gave Martín Ursua the title of Castilla and an *encomienda* of Indians with an income of four thousand ducats a year, about the same income as that of the present military governor of Petén.

1

QUETZALTENANGO, THE SEC-
ond largest city in Guatemala, is set in the high Quiché
Sierras. From Muluá the road
winds up through beautiful
mountains, here and there
gashed by the new rail line of the German Electric
Company.

Along the road dog-trot the picturesque Quiché Indians in bright clothes. Many carried heavy loads, to
which were attached little legs, so that they could be
easily set down and taken up again. These loads were
held on the back by broad bands across the foreheads.
So accustomed are these people to run with loads that
sometimes in lieu of anything else they fill their crates
with heavy stones.

Near here, on the flank of Santa María, was fought
a decisive battle between Alvarado's little force and
12,000 Quichés. Over the head of Tecum, the Quiché
commander, hovered a gigantic quetzal, which savagely
attacked Alvarado. A lance was driven through the bird,
and as it fluttered dead to the ground Tecum also fell
lifeless at the feet of his enemy. The Quiché runners,
both men and women, were branded on cheek and thigh
and sold as slaves at public auction, one-fifth of their
price going to the King of Spain.

We swung into Quetzaltenango, under the shadow of
tall Cerro Quemado, at dusk. The streets angle and circle

in every direction, up hill and down, flanked by houses of light brown lava quarried at the volcanoes.

Quetzaltenango is eight thousand feet above the sea, and though late June, it was bitingly cold; soon a heavy fog rolled over town and plaza, blotting out the ornate cathedral where Liberal Vice-President Flores, during the last days of the Central American Union, took refuge from political enemies, only to be, though clinging to the high altar, torn limb from limb by a fanatic mob of women, egged on by the priests to violate their own holy sanctum.

Next day the sun shone and the town was gay with color, for Quetzaltenango, the Tzakahá of the ancients, is the trading center of the Quiché handicrafts. No lovelier woven and embroidered stuffs are made anywhere in the world. The market blazes and scintillates and cascades with them. On every hand one is startled by the Chinese sounding Quiché chatter; Spanish is almost a foreign tongue.

Here the glitter of the well-imposed superstate is definitely lost. This is a realm in itself. Guatemala is not one piece, however well its parts may dove-tail! It is composed of distinct racial and economic units. Read the following startling, though exaggerated, page from *Manuel Aladaña,* by Rafael Arévalo Martínez:

Returning to my house after my first convalescent outing, I brought back a sad, exact, clear picture of this tropical country. Guatemala was, in the physical order, the country of malaria; and in the moral order, the country of tyranny. Endemic fevers debilitate the population. On every side one saw pale faces stamped with weakness and suffering. Three-fourths of the country were lowlands in which malaria ruled as a despotic lord, destroying bodies and souls. From the provinces to the metropolises flowed a macabre procession of agonizing ones seeking quinine injections. . . . Guatemala—was a Job stretched out beneath a sun of fire. Only the sane ones, five thousand feet above the sea, redeemed the nation from malaria. And it is for this reason that from there, the Highlands, descended our rulers. I suddenly had the clear vision that our physical ill was the father of our moral ill; we have tyrants because we are a sick people. Presently I remembered another factor; our ethnic characteristics. The million Indians weighting down the country. This enormous burden hung from the feet of the agonizing Job and dragged him toward the abyss . . . I saw the swift picture of Guatemala as a lamentable country with three lowlands; the first lowland consisted of eighty thousand square kilometers —of the hundred thousand making up the country—less than five thousand feet above sea level. This low altitude, which in temperate zones affords the best conditions for life, was here, mortal. The second lowland was the million Indians. The third lowland was a million slaves, whose ignorance, lack of culture, and poverty made them the proper basis for the erection of a despotism. . . . In addition to these conditions characteristic of tropical regions, and among which one must not forget the terrible heat that consumes with slow fire and stupefies thought and will, there was the procession of terrible evils, cause of degeneracy. In first rank were Alcohol and Syphilis . . . But why enumerate them?

There are four Guatemalas—distinct, separate, semi-autonomous; the banana country; the coffee kingdom; Indian Guatemala (not so devoid of hope or future as Arévalo Martínez believes) and wild jungle Petén, home of chicle, hardwoods, fevers and wild animals. Guatemala is a four-leaf clover—but each leaf has its own characteristics.

I had just crossed the kingdom of Kaiser Koffee. I had just been through the domain of Baron Banana.

2

Here in the highlands, the Indian integrity was noticeable. Here was a civilization within a civilization. Dress, custom, speech, psychology register the change. The bright mantles, or *tilmalli,* the scarlet sash, or *maxtatli,* the sandals, or *cactli,* the Scotch plaid effect of the trousers, the jaunty ribbon-decked hats—attest to the persistence, beauty and exotic character of the Quiché civilization, which has survived conquest, continued conscription, and the constant pressure of alien forces. Votán, "the God of the *teponastle* drum," still thunders; the *huëhuës,* or patriarchs, still render weighty decisions. Recently, on the lofty Santa María cone, three German hikers discovered in a rocky chapel native idols for the worship of the God of the Mountain. These they impiously overturned, whereupon the Indians hashed the offenders into mince-meat. The Indian soldiers of Quetzaltenango refused to arrest the culprits, so the Commandant of the lowland Department of Retlahuleu was obliged to come up in person to exact punishment. The old gods have not died.

The villages retain much political autonomy. In Nahuala Santa Catarina, San Tomás Chicastenango and elsewhere graver affairs are still submitted to the Junta de Notables, composed of "Principales." There are towns where the bride still walks with her *huipil* sewed to the shirt of her husband; hereabouts are lovers who still use the powdered bone of Zihüapate to provoke the affection of the disdainful object of their passion.

Here the foreign *fincas* no longer rule. The Indians possess their own cornfields—*milperías*. The character imparted by picturesque old-time industries survives: San Pedro Sacatepequez, famous for its beautiful cotton and silk sashes; San Tomás Chicastenango, cotton weaving; Joyabaj, pasturing, fruit, peanuts, salt and weaving; San Migüel Usupantán, straw sombreros, mats, sunshades and brooms; Palín, sweets and candied fruits; San Cristobal, pottery, fire-works, and those marimbas that slither their tunes in a hundred towns on hot tropic nights. Totonicapán, famed for its weaving and pottery, is made up of twenty-six thousand descendants of the Tlaxcaltecans, brought four centuries ago by Pedro de Alvarado, the conqueror, from the Mexican uplands, to subdue Central America.

Rafael Arévalo Martínez sees these million Indians as one of the pestilent "lowlands" of Guatemala, the basis of its traditional tyrannies; but the Quiché civilization is one of the four great powers of Guatemala and perhaps its only human beauty. These colorful people remind me of their own legend of the national emblem, that emerald and scarlet quetzal which sprang forth after the great flood—"a flying water lily"—from the crest of a mammoth guayacán tree as a symbol of perfection. Time and again these Highlands—Los Altos—have sought independence; and it is from here, as Arévalo Martínez admits, that the powerful leaders of the country have descended. Los Altos stands fortress-like and serene above the hectic modernity, the raw-product scrambles of the hot land and their mortal pestilences, superior even to the aristocratic coffee coast.

True, the superstate has definitely delineated their sphere. Even the markets, those meccas of Indian life, have none of the buzzing Mexican hodge-podge, none of the raw surging fecundity that floods up and over one in a thousand clashing sounds and colors. The women sit in orderly rows before their baskets and mats of produce neatly arranged. The folk from each village sit together, orderly, different, defined. Sounds and colors are not lacking, indeed they are omnipresent; but they are blended into a more sophisticated pattern, touched with grace of more conscious form. The Indian fabric is better preserved, more integrated, more complete than in most of Mexico.

On every hand the Quiché highlanders flow into the lowlands bringing their quaint Oriental-sounding speech, their free-limbed grace. They are never idle, never walking, always running with swinging arms and springy tread and lithe bodies, erect as soldiers, their babies slung in vivid shawls, sometimes nursing them as they trot with their wares to market. There came to me the abiding impression that all Guatemala is running, a moving kaleidoscope of brightness; and so strong has been this feeling that at night even the mountains beneath the drifting moonlight clouds seemed to be running, and the houses too, up the tilted streets and over the angled hills, running toward some unknown goal. Often I heard the endless passing of sandaled feet, like an echo of the dip and turn of those old religious dances, the Xahob Tun, and the ludicrous hips of the *huëhuë-chos*, when the unspoiled heart, through rhythm and laughter and grotesqueness, leapt toward the mysteries.

The law of the highlands is the law of the Quiché, the law of ancient mysteries, of smoking mountains, blue placid lakes and sweeping stars—it is the law that runs lightly with sure tread and far-flung gaze.

3

These, then, are the four kingdoms of Guatemala, each distinct, more or less mutually exclusive. Here is the four-leaf clover of which the central Government is the stem. Guatemala City, with its affected modernizations, its aristocratic cachet, clashes in spirit with the banana country, the coffee country, the Indian highlands, and the Petén; Guatemala City, in a land of jungles and mountains and raw-product production, in a land of Indians and peons and imported negroes, is anomalous. It is not even a distributing center. From the ports foreign goods are shipped direct to the plantations and the fincas, or they are shunted up to Quetzaltenango for the highlands. Petén gets its outside necessities through Belitz. Thus Baron Banana and Kaiser Koffee, and the Quiché highlanders, and the Chicle and Rubber Knights rule over units economically autonomous, at times even politically autonomous. Guatemala City is a bright parasite on the larger tree of nationality, something of a prostitute tricked out from the modern bargain-counters, a necessary evil, a center of the vague tradition of national order, and of Central American international unity, a place more of militarists and politicians than of organic culture. Its tentacles are good barracks, a military system, machine guns, and *ladino* intrigue. Guatemala City is a clearing-house, adjusting accounts

with Bananas, Coffee, Indianism, Petén and the outside
world, particularly with the growing pressure of the
United States, and ever hoping some time to become
the leader of all Central America.

Actually, it is the fortress of the conflicting bureau-
cratic interests, the militarists, the politically-minded
ladino class maintaining their grip on the four outlying
regions. From this center, with its suave international
contacts, the government jockeys for power and afflu-
ence, striving for patriotic and selfish ends to tie the
country into a unity denied by the political, racial and
economic facts. The Jefes Políticos are sent out to the
Departments; blue-overalled, barefoot soldiers play
cards for cartridges in a hundred barracks from Livingston to San José; the coffee and banana plantations pay
their taxes and necessary graft; the Petén finds its labor
sequestration facilitated by the border line with Mexico,
and the protecting shadow of the central government
too remote to be directly meddlesome, hence obeys.
Guatemala City has no real economic roots. It is the
place where politicians, militarists, corrupted journalists,
and civilizers, drawn together by mutual cosmopoli-
tanism and modern-world contact, pluck the clover and
twirl the stem.

Once the capital, and particularly Antigua, had its
chief *raison d'être* as the cultural fountainhead of Central America. In the olden days it harbored men a credit
to any nation—Francisco Marroquín, the great builder;
the philosophers Pedro Zapiain, Miguel Tranceschs, and
the illustrious Antonio Lundo y Goicoechea; the notable
historians Antonio de Remesal, Francisco Vásquez,
Francisco Ximenes, Francisco Fuentes y Guzmán, Domingo Juarros; the brilliant poets Rafael García Goyena,

Rafael Landivar and Matías de Córdoba. But the glory of learning and art has fled. If it exists anywhere in the Isthmus it is in San José, Costa Rica, where more tolerant and enlightened governments have kept abreast of modern times and have fostered a spirit of freedom that has rarely existed in Guatemala. Before the old glories of scholarship and literature are reborn, a new order must arise; but it will not be born in the capital but up in Los Altos.

There, where over the mountains and down the valleys and across the sweltering plains is heard the long echo of the running feet of the burden bearers, running toward some unknown goal.

XXVI   OFF FOR SANDINO

1

MY SECOND TRIP TO CEN-
tral America was made for
the specific purpose of interviewing General Augusto
Cesar Sandino, rebel chief in
Nicaragua, combating American marines.

On a January afternoon—after traveling from Mexico City to Honduras over the same route as before, I
rode out of Tegucigalpa, the capital of Honduras, for
the camp of Sandino, the terrible "bandit" said to respect no American's life or property.

After making proper connections in Mexico and
Guatemala, the thread of Sandino's underground with
the outside world led to Salvador and Doctor José de
Jesús Zamora, President of the Nicaragua Autonomist
Association, a block and a half from the Nuevo Mundo
Hotel.

He was a young, well-dressed physician, slightly lame,
—a quick, nervous, independent type. He greeted me
professionally. I handed him my letter of introduction
from Mexico. He gave a startled exclamation. Hurriedly looking out the open door of his office to see
if any one was hovering about, he said to me *sotto voce*:

"I am constantly watched. Wait until I have dispatched this patient," he nodded his head toward an
Indian woman, "and then we'll be quite alone, without
distractions."

I sat there in his cool office, the perspiration running down my face. The hot sun striking half way into his office, painted the red tiles scarlet. Presently he called me in.

Obviously he was more interested in propaganda than medicine. Papers were stacked high on all sides. A few instruments were scattered about carelessly. Medicines stood tipsy on their shelves.

He came to the point immediately. "I have a messenger who goes back and forth from here to Sandino's encampment; he will take you. The only thing is we are very badly off for funds; it may be some little time until we can raise enough to get him to Tegucigalpa."

"I am willing to pay his expenses."

"That's hardly fair," protested the Doctor. "We can hold a meeting of the Nicaraguans to-night, and I'm sure we can raise at least enough to get him to La Unión, perhaps further. We also wish to send some quinine and other medical supplies. Anyway you'll have to stay here in the capital about three days. The launch from La Unión to Honduras leaves only twice a week. I'll find out exact details.

"Now for the rest of your plans. I'll give you letters for Froylán Turcios, Sandino's representative in Tegucigalpa. Come back here to-morrow noon. Better you come here than I go to your hotel; here I am a physician; if I go there, my acts may arouse suspicions. Also think of a plan to hide all your letters when you travel. You may be searched. This government and that of Honduras are opposing Sandino at the behest of the United States."

From his office I went to the *Diario del Salvador* with a letter for Señor M. M. was a short, heavy-set fellow, with a two days' growth of beard. More curt than the doctor, he was equally serviceable and immediately wrote out a letter for Turcios, Sandino's representative in Tegucigalpa.

"Turcios if he desires can see that you get there. It's dangerous, though, doubly so for you—an American."

2

Zamora again took a quick look around to see if police were lurking, then pulled me in and introduced me to the messenger, a General Rivas—a tough customer, with a heavy blunt nose and flat face. At first glance, I felt he was a man without principles of any sort. A brutal irresponsibility ruled him. Zamora, however, seemed to trust him greatly.

"You will have to start back immediately," declared Zamora.

General Rivas complained. "It's a hard trip; I'm played out; my kidneys—"

"I understand," said Zamora, "but we have to do what we can for the cause, each of us."

General Rivas complained of lack of funds. "I need four *colones* for my room here . . . I need a girl, and something for *copitas*. I'm not a fish, I have to drink."

"We'll fix all that up," promised Zamora, patting him on the shoulder. They discussed the things Rivas should take to Sandino's camp—quinine, flash-lights, etc.

Rivas and I went out separately, then rejoined in the plaza. I took him over to have a drink, and he talked of his previous trips to the camp, but in such a loud voice I had to caution him.

"It's a hard trip," he declared.

"That doesn't matter."

"Many a night you'll have to sleep on the ground. Some days there'll be scarcely anything to eat. We can't burden ourselves with food. Times, too, when we won't be able to get horses; that means going on foot; some nights we can push over a woman, some times not."

"Minor worries," I assured him. "The main thing is to get there."

"We'll do that, if you are willing to face the music. Once over the Nicaraguan border, Sandino will send an escort for you. There may be aeroplanes and bombing; it would be nice if you saw a good fight.

"By the way, a good business—I know where the skull of Lieutenant B. is. We can dig it up, then we'll get a signed statement from Sandino that this is B.'s skull. You can take it back to the States and sell it to his family. I bet they'd give you five thousand dollars for it, at least five thousand."

"We can discuss that later," I suggested dryly, beginning to get the man's full measure. "Tell me something about Sandino."

"He's on El Chipote, with five thousand men. It's a model camp, and he's got a perfect system of fox holes. It's impregnable, I tell you. The soldiers receive no pay, only rations and clothes. Some are pretty ragged because they can't get clothes through. They have planted corn, and beans and tobacco. Plenty of women have come up to sew, grind the corn and cook—of their own free will. And all the peasants round about bring the army food. There's no forced requisitioning, no need for it. As soon as you step into Nuevo Segovia you'll be in Sandino's camp. All the town officials are for Sandino. In Jalapa the mayor treated me like a prince. There's no booze either. Any soldier found with booze is shot. I like my drink, but I suppose it is a good thing in camp to forbid it. Sandino keeps perfect discipline."

He switched the subject. "Say, this traveling back and forth is a grind, I get nothing out of it. I like women and I like to drink."

"Well, we can see to that."

"Say, I can get you a nice girl. Wouldn't you like to take her along with you? We oughtn't to go alone. We can take them as far as Tegucigalpa."

"Have your girls while we're here, but you and I go alone."

"Down this street, after eleven. Leave it to me." He winked.

On the way out of the cantina, Rivas introduced me to a greasy-looking Nicaraguan. "I'm taking Beals to Sandino's camp."

The man shook hands, eying me suspiciously and passed on. Rivas remarked, "He's collecting funds for hospital supplies for Sandino."

"Well, none of them will ever reach Sandino. That man is a cheap grafter. What is more, I warned you, don't tell any one, not a soul, where we are going."

"Oh, that man won't say anything."

"No one, except you and Doctor Zamora, is to know my plans."

Rivas promised to keep his mouth shut.

"Hereafter, we won't even mention Sandino's name to each other; he shall be simply—el Jefe."

Again Rivas agreed. We separated.

Towards sundown he came back with three flasks of quinine, asking me to put them in my baggage, and begging me for ten dollars.

3

The night before we left, Zamora came to my hotel with the letters he had promised.

"How have you decided to conceal your documents?" he asked.

I showed him a large official envelope, covered red with seals bearing the American eagle for which I had utilized a twenty-dollar gold piece. I had to put all my letters for Turcios and Sandino into this envelope and had addressed it to His Excellency, Minister Arthur Summerlin, Tegucigalpa, Honduras.

Zamora grinned. "Central American governments are servile. Here in Salvador, on the request of the American Minister, the newspapers have been officially ordered to cease printing news about Sandino. The American Minister tried to get me expelled from the country because I put a letter of the Association of Nicaraguan Independence into Charles Lindbergh's hands recounting the violation of Nicaraguan sovereignty by the marines and urging Lindbergh not to permit his flight to be used as a cat's-paw for imperialistic chestnuts. You know, too, the Government here is under the thumb of W. W. Renwick, Customs Collector and virtually financial dictator . . ."

"Yes, I had heard some of these things—street pavements, loans—"

"And what will you do with my two letters?"

"I'll have to take a chance on them, I guess."

"Put them in a book, or something, probably they won't be discovered."

XXVII MY DIPLO-MATIC LETTER

1

Zamora came to the station to see us off.

Just before the train pulled out, he pulled me aside. "One of your fellow passengers in the chair-car, is Dr. X, a spy of President Díaz of Nicaragua. Watch out for him."

"Is he shadowing us?"

"I don't know. Make that fool Rivas keep his mouth shut."

I called Rivas and warned him.

"Yes, he's a spy." Rivas promised to be careful.

But time and time again, I had to caution the magpie.

A few stations down the line, he pulled me out of the chair-car. "Come on down the train to second-class. I want you to meet my wife."

"Your wife! You told me she was in Cuba?"

"I have got a wife in Cuba, but as I'm not there—you understand—"

Singularly displeased that he had disobeyed instructions, I followed him along the train. He introduced me to Magarita, a low-class mestiza girl of buxom proportions, with stringy hair. She was clad in a cheap and not too clean gingham dress.

Nothing to do now but to make the best of it. Wiser

to have the girl for a friend, so I bought her a pineapple and some wayside nicknacks.

Presently I worried about Rivas for another reason. He complained of being sick—malaria. At intervals he shook like an aspen leaf; his face had turned sallow and sunken.

In La Unión I went to the hotel. Rivas went off to sleep at the home of his new wife's aunt.

2

The next morning, I found Rivas' "wife" already waiting at the boat-landing to embark. She was worried that Rivas did not appear.

I too became worried.

Magarita raced off, came back, clucked around generally, attracting much unnecessary attention. I had a premonition of trouble and sent two small boys scurrying to hunt for Rivas.

Finally he came tearing down the pier, his worn brown suitcase flying at the end of one long arm.

"I had quite a little trouble with my papers, had to go over to the Nicaraguan Counsul and get a new passport. Guess it's all right now."

"How do you feel?"

"Much better—took some quinine."

We rushed our passports in through a little wicket to be examined and paid our embarkation fee. The officials noticed that I paid for Rivas and his wife.

For some time, I had observed a soldier with a gun always standing near us. The moment came for the baggage examination. A police officer came over to me, to

Rivas and his wife, and ordered us to go alone into the customs room. The door closed behind us.

Confronting us were the head customs official, the chief of police and a dozen subordinates.

"Search everything carefully," ordered the Chief. "Take off their shoes. And the girl—take her to another room. Have her thoroughly searched. Don't fail to examine a single stitch of her clothing." Afterwards we learned that they denuded her completely.

"This is an outrage," I protested. "I demand an American consul be present."

"Take everything out of your pockets," commanded the Chief.

I pulled things out of my pockets, keeping as watchful an eye on my effects as I could in the confusion of so many mauling agents.

A dwarf, pock-marked soldier thrust his dirty paw into my side trousers pocket. Angered, I swept my arm back with all the force I could muster. He spun half across the room and fell backwards over a suitcase. "Keep your damn dirty hands out of my pocket," I blazed.

The fellow got up glowering.

The Chief motioned the fellow aside and said to me, "Clean everything out of your pockets if you don't want us to do it."

"There's nothing here but money. It's my purse and some loose bills."

"Put them on top of that trunk," ordered the Chief. I obeyed.

In Rivas' coat, an official came across a letter. Before he could read it, Rivas snatched it from his hands and tore off the signature, rolling it to a pellet between his palms.

"The key to everything!" cried the customs head. "Grab him."

The police seized Rivas' arms. But he jerked away and managed to swallow the pellet.

"Why did you let him do that?" wrangled the Chief. "Idiots!"

The officials now went through everything with a fine-tooth comb. They examined the notes of my trip, confiscated them. Every book was gone over leaf by leaf. Everything, every piece of clothing was turned inside out, even the seams were examined.

Finally they came upon Zamora's letters, one addressed to Froylán Turcios, the other "To the Chief of the Libertarian Army."

"For whom is this one?" demanded the official. "The Salvadorian law does not permit you to take sealed letters out of the country."

"All right, I'll unseal it."

"Not now. The authorities mail them, and in Honduras you pay quadruple postage."

"Why not let me open them? You can read the contents."

"No. Who's this for?" he said, continuing to stare at the envelope bearing no name.

"It's none of your business. But I'll open it if you wish."

"We'll keep it."

"I demand this outrage be stopped."

Rivas chimed in; I signaled him to keep his mouth shut.

"Where shall we send this letter?" demanded the Chief.

"Send it to Froylán Turcios, Tegucigalpa," I replied and wrote the address on it.

They took off my shoes. Again I protested violently and refused to assist them or lift my feet from the floor.

The shoes were finally removed forcibly, but not until I had trod viciously on one set of brown fingers.

I noticed, sadly also, that my suitcases were being pawed over anew by a pair of dirty claws, freshly stained with orange juice.

Finally the envelope with the seals, addressed to Summerlin, was discovered. The Chief picked it up, turned it over and over in his hand.

My heart jumped. I visioned it being mailed to Minister Summerlin. He would have a queer surprise—letters for Sandino.

"We'll respect *this*," said the Chief, handing it to me with a certain deference . . .

I acquired new arrogance. "You had better respect it," I blustered. "It's about time you appreciated exactly with whom you are dealing."

"Put his things back," ordered the Chief to his men. His manner had completely changed. The search was stopped. My things were hastily put back. The officials now treated me respectfully, almost apologetically. Could a sealed letter to an American Minister work such miracles? What a glimpse of official Central American servility!

But when I looked around for my money, the loose bills—some seven dollars—had disappeared.

XXVIII ARREST

1

WE STEPPED OFF THE launch at the landing stage in Amapala, island port of Honduras. An official shouted out General Rivas' name.

More troubles!

Rivas stepped forward.

"You are under arrest."

"My name next," I thought. But all the passengers, including myself, were ushered into the customs room.

A chance came for a few whispered words with Margarita. "He says he will get off right away because the Port Commandant is a good Mason. If not to-day, then to-morrow. He will join you in Tegucigalpa. But you must give us some money."

I slipped her a twenty-dollar bill.

2

After a night trip up from San Lorenzo to Tegucigalpa, I lodged at the Hotel Roma, to the proprietor of which, Venditti, I had a confidential letter. The following morning, I hunted up Froylán Turcios. His office proved a combination book-store, editorial headquarters, and parlor. After a few minutes' wait, he appeared clad in a sweater and cap, a middle-aged man of charming simplicity; just a hint of politician along with the poet. Under President Bonillas he had served as a Secretary of

State. He published (until the authorities suppressed it at the request of Minister Summerlin) the periodical *Ariel* which he had converted into a pro-Sandino organ. (The name "Ariel" is taken from Rodo's book *Ariel* which symbolizes Latin America, Caliban symbolizing the United States.)

Turcios glanced over my letters of introduction. He knew my name and work. The letters carried double weight.

"We won't need to waste words," he said. "Go back to your hotel and I will prepare your credentials."

"Fine."

"I'll put you in touch with the underground. We have Indian runners who carry correspondence to and fro. Even so, things happen. Just the other night, the authorities caught one and beat him up frightfully. I am under constant surveillance, but fortunately my house has three doors and it keeps them busy watching me. In order not to arouse suspicion, we had better have as little contact as possible."

I told him about General Rivas.

"Frankly," replied Turcios, "you are well rid of him. It is to be hoped he doesn't show up. He uses his Masonic credentials to coerce people. He has often tried to get money out of me. As a fact, Sandino has never received him. But the chap has indefatigable energy. Likely as not he'll pop up."

Some days later the press carried the news that Rivas had been deported to Tempisque, the Nicaraguan Gulf port in the Bay of Fonseca, and turned over to the Nicaraguan authorities. Promptly he told them of my plans; these were communicated to the marines; the Honduras authorities and Minister Summerlin were warned by wire. But by then I was well along my way.

I lunched with Eugenia Torres, a Mexican elocutionist whom I had met in the bus the night before. She told me that the Honduras Minister of Education, on whom she had called that morning, had ordered her point-blank not to recite several patriotic poems of Froylán Turcios, the Sandino representative, "because we are on very good terms with the Americans just now."

On very good terms—the bait being the semi-promise of a loan (which never materialized) on the strength of which the government was busy giving away concessions to American companies. Most of the Honduras army was massed on the Nicaraguan frontier to prevent supplies from reaching Sandino. Any one passing in either direction was searched and correspondence confiscated. The press of Tegucigalpa printed only unfavorable and abbreviated news concerning Sandino—orders of the government. A Nicaraguan poet who published a poem to Sandino cooled his heels for a month in jail.

At a near-by table sat General Tosta, the ex-president imposed upon the country by the United States—a youngish, plump, alert individual, but whom I wouldn't have trusted alone in the dark.

After lunch I returned to Turcios' house to read the complete file of *Ariel* on Sandino. My passport to Sandino stated frankly, that though an American, I was worthy of every confidence. My picture was affixed to the margin.

"The sooner you get on your way, the better."

I agreed. "Things over yonder are going to get hotter very soon. When I left Mexico two thousand more marines were headed for Nicaragua. I want to get to Chipote before they attack."

"I am unable to secure horses yet, but I shall try again this evening. I won't go to your hotel, but will get word to you. I am concerned for your safety and am thinking of sending you with an exiled Nicaraguan General, anxious to join Sandino. He knows the country and his people."

Shortly, there appeared a very tall, thin, dark type, obviously intense, nervous and arrogant—General Santos Siqueiros. While a mere boy he had been mixed up in the Mena revolt in Nicaragua, then in the last revolution in Honduras, becoming Commandant of the banana port of Tela. When the revolt failed, Siqueiros had been shipped to Guatemala in an American battleship. After fifteen years of exile from Nicaragua, he was now burning to throw in his lot with Sandino. Unfortunately he was an object of suspicion to the present Honduras government, so that this side the Nicaragua border his company increased the possibility of official interference.

3

The next day I saw Turcios again. Still no horses. A religious festival in a nearby town had drawn every available mount out of the city. Turcios told me he had commissioned Siqueiros to find some at any cost.

"Tell him to buy them if necessary."

Every minute's delay increased our future risk in Nicaragua.

Turcios and I walked up to the high park above Tegucigalpa on the side of the historic hill—a civic embellishment which Turcios himself effected when Minister under Bonillas.

We talked literature, politics or this and that. He told me about his sister who had recently died, a poetess also, whom he grieved for greatly. "She was my confidante and inspiration, and our love was greater than of this earth."

At home again, he brought out some new books on Latin America. "You see, I am a very foolish bookseller. I only keep books which I think worth-while—in every literature. And I try to make my magazine *Ariel* not only a Sandino organ, but a guide to·the best new books."

Siqueiros entered. "I've secured horses for to-morrow morning at five. We can't leave earlier without being challenged by the city guards."

"From where shall we leave?"

"Your hotel is too conspicuous. Tosta is there, and many government people. Sleep with me at the Hotel Unión to-night. It's run by a Nicaraguan patriot, pro-Sandino."

4

At the Hotel Roma, I advised Venditti I was going out on a finca in the direction of Cedros, quite away from the route I expected to take. "When you are going to Pisa, say you are going to Siena."

"With whom?" he asked.

"Emilio Hernández," I invented.

"Hernández . . . Hernández," he repeated. "I don't know him. Who is he?"

"A rancher, a chap I met on my previous trip."

"Queer, I don't know him," puzzled Venditti, and tried to get details out of me.

I interrupted, "Please keep my things until I get back —in about a week. And another matter—if anybody asks you where I've gone, tell him I've gone out in the country for a few days and I will be back soon. There's a certain General whom I met in La Unión; I don't want to renew his acquaintance."

"Anything you say," promised Venditti, eyeing me queerly.

An Indian girl came up from the Hotel Unión; I gave her the few belongings I meant to take with me.

General Siqueiros and I lodged in a little back room near the corral, where we would not meet other guests and from which we could slip out through a back gate.

That night when our door had been barred, in the little back room, by the guttering candle, Siqueiros in an impassioned voice read from a personal manuscript dealing with his revolutionary experiences; how he had been arrested in Salvador by the authorities for propaganda against Chamorro; how he had been molested in Guatemala; now lone passages of flaming eloquence about Nicaraguan liberty. He read on and on, drunk with the sound of his own voice, until an ungodly hour, oblivious to the fact that we had to be up before dawn.

1

WE AROSE BEFORE FIVE. No horses appeared. Seven o'clock rolled around—still no horses. Eight o'clock. What could be the matter? Siqueiros stormed out to investigate.

While I sat waiting, an Honduras General came into my room, an elderly, alert gentleman, with long sinuous hands, dressed in spotless homespun linens.

"The hotel keeper," he explained, "says you are going to Sandino's camp. I was formerly Chief of Police of Tegucigalpa. Came the revolution, and I was ruined. My store was sacked and burned. But our chance is coming again. Soon! I have offered to raise six hundred men for Sandino, each with his rifle and machete. Sandino answered [and the General showed me the letter], 'I have enough men in El Chipote. Save your forces until the marines land in Honduras.'"

It was noon before the horses came, brought by a pock-marked Indian rancher, Don Simón.

Don Simón, owner of the horses and our guide, wore a red sash and a huge conical sombrero. With a leer and a hiccough, for he was a bit overseas with *pradero*—(firewater) he shrugged. "One hour is as good as another."

We cantered out of the city, Siqueiros nervous becáuse we were leaving in broad daylight. "The authorities suspect me, and if they see us fitted out for country travel with our *maletas* [the packs behind our saddles] they may imagine us bent on mischief."

The words were no sooner out of his mouth, than we met the Chief of Police himself.

"Where to?" called the official.

"Back to Jacaleapa," replied Siqueiros (Jacaleapa was his home) and we rode on.

"Bad, very bad," muttered Siqueiros. "He may telegraph ahead."

We followed the hill road alongside Turcios' park, but passed a military guard without being accosted.

"Now I breathe easier," said Siqueiros.

Up and up went the road, a steady climb out of the mountain-ringed valley of Tegucigalpa.

At a wayside store we bought oranges and crackers from an old crone. Don Simón had his bottle of fiery *"agua"* to swig.

2

Late in the afternoon this side San Jacinto Peak, beyond which is the world-famed Rosario silver mine, leaden clouds piled round the mountain crests, hiding the mighty pine-clad ridges towards which we were riding. Soon a mist blanketed us—piercing cold, and the trees quivered fantastically. The mist turned to drizzle. The wet branches swished into our faces. It was growing dark.

We spurred against the hail-storm sweeping down upon us, head and sombreros low trying to brunt the cutting drive of the tempest.

A few rods, and Siqueiros shouted, "We can't go on, I doubt if there's another house on the mountain."

We turned back to a wattle-woven hut we had passed. The wind howled forlornly through it.

We stacked our saddles and blankets in a corner and Don Simón took the horses off to *pasta*. We stamped and cursed, beating our arms about our frozen bodies. The woman of the place leisurely spread out a cold supper of tortillas, cheese, and oranges. Having no charcoal she could make no fire. We ate standing up, stamping our feet. Don Simón sullenly refused to eat. That meant spending money. Instead he stuck to his bottle.

Night fell. The woman lit carbide lanterns. Presently, a young teamster, in a torn, cream-colored sarape came in, his arms about a young girl, and asked for lodging. They had descended the mountain through the storm. Dripping and miserable they sat mute on a bench in a dark corner.

The two of them went out under the open *ramada*, and lay down under the one thin sarape locked in each other's arms for warmth. For us, the woman of the house swept out a little lean-to and spread out boards for us to sleep on. I huddled in a corner in my red blanket. By the dim light of the carbide lamp, Siqueiros wrote a letter to his wife, with her family in Salvador. The letter finished, he again read me part of his diary. I marveled—as I have often done—at the Latin indifference to discomfort, the ability to function on an elevated mental plane in the most unpropitious moments. The rhetorical periods of his voice tuned in with the drive of the rain on the roof, with the wind which wailed through the cracks of the lean-to in icy gusts. My feet were frozen, my teeth chattering, but Siqueiros read on and on.

3

At three A.M. after a little sleep, we lit the carbide lamp, and stumbled out into a mist thicker than curd. Stepping over the young pair—to whom for warmth were now added a pig and several dogs—we shook Simón awake to get the horses ready.

Up over precipitous mountains. The way was slushy, slithering off into the abyss, overhead great trees. With each gust of wind the trees sent showers of water on our defenseless heads; the big drops pattered on my hat, trickled down my back. We crossed the divide under the crown of San Jacinto and descended a steep trail.

Sun-up. A feeble warmth stole over the world. Gold threads unwound from rock to rock; silver threads wound from glistening leaf to glistening leaf. The valley was a lavender lake from which emerged a few green tufts—the crests of mammoth trees. We were dropping down to the San Rosario mine. Came the far faint stamp of the smelters.

Gradually shreds of mist shivered loose from the billowy valley. Veils of mist drifted up the mountain slopes, tangling among the trees.

Tiled and sheet-iron roofs were perched here and there on the steep flanks of the mountain. Roads twisted in and out. Far below, a little town clambered on two sides of a narrow stream. Now and then, up the road came groups of Indian women, now and then a man or two. Little of the cascading Quiché color, yet here a scarlet kerchief, there a purple sash.

We reached the first houses. Workmen were headed for the shafts, their lunches slung over their shoulders in fiber bags. One stopped, looked intently at Siqueiros, addressed him.

"My general," he said deferentially, "do you remember me?"

"Oh, Pancho, to be sure!" exclaimed Siqueiros. And they chatted over a past campaign.

"Whenever you take the field again, I'm with you," said Pancho. And he took a side path toward a shaft.

4

Near a large building on stilts to the side of the mountain stood a tiny cabin. We tied our horses to a watering tank and clambered to the door. Three girls welcomed us and pulled out wooden boxes for seats. One of the girls was busily cooking breakfast over a brazier; her two friends had just dropped in—they were mestizan, naïve, provincial, yet half wild and wicked. They talked boldly. One had picked up a steady man, but wasn't averse to having a little fun. The other, red garters and rolled stockings, hoped also to find a miner with steady pay, willing to keep her. Siqueiros brazenly promised her to take her to Tegucigalpa on his way back, where he would give her a job as ticket-taker in a little vaudeville show he was starting.

Eggs, ranchero style with green chili, and hot coffee made a good breakfast.

Outside I made the discovery that the color of my red poncho was not fast; little bloody streams were running down the horse's legs; my coat-tail was pinky.

Haunches sliding, we dropped down past the mine into San Jacinto, a tangle of houses and orchards.

Approaching the town, Siqueiros called to me, "Keep close to my side, so I can speak with you. There is a military guard here. All comers must pass over a narrow wooden bridge across the stream—you can see it from here. On the other side are the barracks. All travelers are supposed to show papers. Stick my letters into your saddlebags, down deep. When we cross the bridge, give your horse the spur and talk loudly to me in English. If they think you are an American, they may believe you belong to the mine and won't bother us."

We clattered down along the stones towards the town. At the narrow bridge, we spurred, raising a rattle between its flimsy hand rails.

The guard, who sat with his rifle on the barrack steps, stirred as he heard hoof-beats, rose, started towards us. I shouted in English to Siqueiros—"You must hunt me up a good horse, that saddle—" Hearing English, the guard sat down again, watching us desultorily.

We whipped up the steep slope leaving Simón somewhere far behind.

"We'll get out of this town damn quick," remarked Siqueiros. "Too dangerous. Make your horse travel."

We took the crest at a canter and made out along a rocky lane.

"I've simply got to buy cigarettes," I told Siqueiros, and called to a woman in a store to bring me out several packages of King Bees. Siqueiros asked for the best road toward Morselí. She gave him directions, then added sharply—

"You are Sandinistas."

"How so?" asked Siqueiros.

"Many have come through here, many refugees too, driven out of their homes by the marines. I've hidden numbers of them and have given them clothes."

"You do well," said Siqueiros. "Come," he ordered, and we made off.

"May God go with you," called the woman.

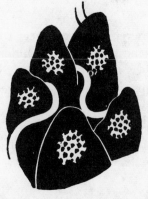

1

ON OVER PRECIPITOUS
mountains down into dust-
choking valleys, an interminable trail under the blister-
ing sun. We ate lunch in a
smoky palm-thatched hut,
surrounded by a circle of naked brown children in vary-
ing stages of ill-health, amid mangy dogs, heaps of corn
and beans and dangling strings of red peppers, dried
meat and rawhide thongs.

On again. Sun. Dancing heat waves. Dust. Cactus.
Drowsiness. The sweat of the horses. Heavy odor of
pollen. The creak of saddle leather. Gleam of crags.

Sundown. Morselí. An uneventful village with a wide
dusty unadorned plaza, wedged in between mountain
and hill.

We found lodging with Don José, one of the head
men of the village, a friend of Siqueiros.

Don Simón went off with the horses, sullenly as usual,
refusing to look at anything to eat.

"Simón is a damn *cachureco*," remarked Siqueiros,
using the stock phrase for a Conservative. "And so con-
founded tight! He's a rich man, yet here for the few
lousy dollars we give him he drags all the way to Danlí,
and won't spend a penny on food. He expects us to buy
it for him."

Our host's house, fronting the plaza, had two rooms,
one a big *sala* with sisal hammocks slung from the high

beams, the other a cubbyhole without windows, which we were given for the night. In it were two beds, covered with *petates*, for the heat makes mattresses impossible.

By the light of an *ocote* torch we had supper in the house of two elderly fleshy widows, funereal-looking in black *tápalos* over black hair.

The exposure of the previous night, the hail-storm, the cold wind, had given me the grippe. My very bones ached. Fever was burning me.

In the plaza store I bought a pint of the local sugarcane *aguardiente*. It burnt the esophagus right out of me. Nevertheless, it warmed me through, and I lay down on the *petate*. The bed was hopping with fleas. In spite of them, in spite of fever, my weariness made me sleepy.

Siqueiros insisted on reading his proposed book. To myself, I commented irritably, "Damn foolish to have brought it along; if we were searched, it would give us away completely." But the fire of conversation was ever in him. I drowsed off to his rhetorical periods.

Suddenly—shots!

"What in hell!" cried Siqueiros, throwing down the manuscript. "That's my pistol." On arriving at the house, he had handed it over to his host—Honduras etiquette. "Some trouble has broken out. I may lose it. And I've got so few shells." He listened intently.

He called through the flimsy door, "What's happened, Don José?"

Silence.

"Don José, what's happened?" Siqueiros repeated in a soothing voice.

"Nothing," replied Don José, resentfully.

Siqueiros pulled on his shoes and went out. Low-toned conversation. Siqueiros returned.

"What was the matter?" I demanded.

"Ignacio, that fool kid of José's, has an enemy in town, so he swiped the pistol and went looking for him. Fortunately, he couldn't find him, which made him so angry he had to let off steam, so he shot in the air. It might have been worse. If he had killed his fellow with my pistol, we'd have been in a devil of a mess."

2

Midnight. We crept out by a side door, shook Don Simón, who was sleeping under the open *ramada*. Grumbling, he went for the horses. We made up our *maletas*.

Outside of town, we followed the wrong road for several miles. Siqueiros had to ride clear back to Morselí to ask directions. A pistol shot from the last junction signaled me to return. When I finally arrived, he had gone on ahead along the right road, occasionally pointing his flashlight back for me to follow.

The trail was treacherous, very volcanic. We had to ride with our flashlights ever playing before us. Even so, the feeble uncanny light accentuated the bumps and hollows. It was difficult going.

Long before daybreak, we stumbled into another settlement and tried to get food. We hammered on a dozen doors. Barking dogs. Sullen replies—"No food."

Up a new trail climbing into mountains—ridge on ridge among the pines, then open meadows. A long grassy stretch, even in the dark, we risked taking at a gallop. A number of times my horse skidded, dizzily, but saved himself. Dawn found us dragging down into a little *casería* on the edge of a bald knoll.

Here, too, we were refused food. Sometimes mere cantankerousness, but often there is no food. The people are so miserably poor, they think themselves lucky to have even a little coffee to drink.

Siqueiros asked about troops. Two days before guards had been stationed at the passes. They had searched everybody. Other soldiers were working on the trail.

"A risk," Siqueiros told me, "but there is no other way to go."

Up and up the ridges we climbed. In a steep narrow pass we found evidence of recent repairing of the trail. Rocky ledges had been hewed down. Crushed stone filled in where rivulets had cut it away. As we progressed higher, the trail became more uncertain. Great fallen trunks forced us to make detours. We arrived among huge pines at a little clearing and a neat wooden house, boarded up, though chickens were round about. We had met no soldiers. "It's clear sailing from here on," said Siqueiros.

Muttering complaints, Simón reeled after us ever more dizzily.

"The fool will fall off and crack his pate," said Siqueiros.

1

IN JACALEAPA WE RESTED IN the house of a Liberal Honduras General, Señor Carmona. His home was stripped of furniture and decorations. Doors and windows were half hacked to pieces, mute evidence of partisan politics.

General Carmona, round-bellied and jovial, apologized for the decline of his star which made it impossible to treat us more hospitably. A big meal was set for us under the arcades of his colonial house, looking out over orchard and fields to the river.

Simón knocked oranges off the trees in the yard rather than buy himself some food, until finally General Carmona told the servants to take him some tortillas and meat. Thereupon, Simón lay down with his feet in the sun and his head in the shade, eyeing us.

When we were ready to start for Danlí, Simón flatly refused to move unless we paid him extra. "Never," declared Siqueiros. General Carmona would borrow new horses for us in town. Simón departed without even a farewell.

As we rode toward Danlí, Siqueiros told me that from now on I should speak only in English, not a word in Spanish; he would pose as my interpreter. My mission was purchasing coffee *fincas*.

And so, to roadside acquaintances, Siqueiros boasted of the good job he had with me, that I was paying him

a ridiculously large salary—just like Gringos; to all of
which I listened, mum as an oyster. We met up with
the customary rich man of the community, proprietor
of most of the land about. He looked at me unpleas-
antly, for he himself was trying to get hold of every
disposable acre. His slink-eyed secretary, for half a mile,
kept firing questions at me in Spanish, then went off
contemptuously.

On the gentle upper slope of a meadow the white
town of Danlí loomed unexpectedly. A white church
stood out in the dusk, catching the late light of the
sun. Half a mile away, we branched off from the main
road, crossed the meadow, and entered into the town
from one side, unobtrusively. Turning several street
corners flanked by adobe and thatched houses, Siqueiros
stopped before the rail fence of a small cabin. We led
our horses to the rear into a large orchard.

Here lived a black-bearded Nicaraguan, who had fled
from Ocotal, abandoning his home, to escape the battles
between Sandino and the marines. For a living he now
cultivated a little patch of ground and carved saints,
which he subsequently painted, gilded, and peddled.

Siqueiros told his wife to lock up our papers, letters,
and the pistol. "We'll pay our respects to the Commandant," said Siqueiros. "Wisest to go without any in-
criminating evidence."

"Why leave the pistol?"

"I have no permit. He might use that as a pretext to
give us trouble. We ought to go to see him; as I am of
the opposite party, I don't want any unnecessary suspicions aroused. If I take you there and explain your
coffee-buying mission, he will think my presence here
quite natural."

2

The Commandant was lounging in his doorway picking his teeth and rubbing his huge paunch.

Siqueiros explained our presence. The Commandant stared indifferently into space. When we started to leave, he asked in a flat, disinterested tone: "Which way do you expect to go from here?"

"Toward Teupacentl," said Siqueiros, naming a town inland, in the opposite direction from the frontier. "We may look in at the mines, too."

"Come back to-morrow if you are here," grunted the Commandant, turning on his heel and going inside to a waiting supper table.

We went back to the bearded carver of saints, whose wife served us supper in the outhouse—a combination kitchen and dining room. We ate in the dark, save for the charcoal gleams flickering fitfully around the terra-cotta pots and casting grotesques on the wattle-woven walls.

We paid for the meal and Siqueiros added, "Can we stay here for the night?"

The bearded carver of saints mumbled excuses. "No room."

"Well, let us sleep outside here under the *ramada*."

Our host mumbled other excuses. It was obvious that we were no longer welcome.

Siqueiros gave me a sign. We cinched the girths of our horses.

"Many thanks, my dear compatriot," Siqueiros called sarcastically, as he swung into the saddle.

The bearded carver came to the fence, now quite apologetic. "Perhaps," he started to say, "I could fix you up a *petate* out there—"

But Siqueiros spurred off into the dark. "Go to Hell," was his reply. To me—"I won't sleep in a place where I'm not entirely welcome. Trouble might come of it. But where in the name of the blessed saints shall we go now? It's late." He thought a moment. "Come, I have a good place, only I didn't want to use it unless absolutely necessary. A widow I know runs a little store. She's a Liberal, absolutely to be trusted. The Conservatives killed her husband, and she's very bitter. As she is a woman, the authorities are not particularly suspicious of her. Let us go there." Then he added: "The women of Honduras are wonderful. They are loyal to the end. If they believe in anything, or have suffered from their political enemies, there is nothing they will not do for a friend."

1

OUR NEXT LINK WAS A
Señor Enrique Yánez. "We
must hunt him up this very
night," declared Siqueiros.

We finally located his place,
a large corner building; all
the front doors were open; a stream of yellow light
poured into the dark street.

"Damn it, his place is next door to the Commandant!
Watch your step." We reconnoitered the side street,
which ran up to the hillside and dwindled off into the
rocks and heather.

We came back to the lit house. In the front room a
group of five people sat in cane-bottom chairs in a close
circle. We could see a small table, a huge mirror and a
wicker settee.

"This is bad," muttered Siqueiros, "everybody can
spot us." We walked in.

"Señor Yánez?" we inquired.

"Your servitor," was the conventional response from
a tall man with a steel-gray pompadour.

Siqueiros spoke rapidly in a low voice. "We have
letters for you. Take us inside."

Yánez caught his cue, the others present immediately
vanished. He led us to a dark arcade opening on the
back orchard.

"A light, please," he called to a servant.

A feeble oil lamp was set on the table. I handed Yánez our letters.

"Excuse me." He went back into the front room to read them by electric light.

"This is difficult," he announced. "The situation in Danlí has changed overnight. The Government used to wink at our activities. Now the Commandant watches me like a hawk. The frontier is closed. Dangerous even to hire horses. To get through you may have to go several days east." He explained a possible route.

"But that will add five days' travel. We have to get through in the least possible time."

"I'm giving you my best advice. I am a personal friend of Sandino. Everything I have is at that man's disposal. But I tell you things are difficult here. Formerly we sent people through the Ordóñez hacienda, right on the frontier; but that's sewed up . . . Isidro," he called.

A barefoot Indian came forward.

"Isidro is my most trusted *mozo*. He runs through with mail for Sandino and carries it on down to Turcios. He has just made the trip."

In a dialect which I could hardly understand, he corroborated Yánez' words.

"What is the best way?" queried Siqueiros.

"If you go on foot, we can take the customary route through the Ordóñez property."

"We can't go on foot," decreed Siqueiros. "We may need horses on the Nicaraguan side."

The Indian suggested much the same detour as had Yánez.

"He can take you himself; he's absolutely trustworthy," declared Yánez. "Only he's pretty played out; he ought to have three or four days' rest. How about it, Isidro, could you set out again?"

The man looked at Yánez with doglike eyes and heaved a big sigh. "Yes, Master."

"What is absolutely the shortest route, regardless of risk?" asked Siqueiros.

Yánez told him.

"And does your man know this route also?"

"He can take you."

Siqueiros questioned the Indian, who now seemed less assured. He stammered. Siqueiros grilled him. "Can you get us through without too great risks?" he demanded again.

Before the Indian could reply, a strange thing happened. Siqueiros rose, put his hand on his gun, and in sharp cutting phrases, said to Yánez, "I want the straight goods. No man is going to double-cross me, do you understand, Señor Yánez? I know how to look out for myself; and the man who is treacherous dies the instant he arouses the slightest suspicion. Get me straight, I'm not a man to be trifled with. This is a life and death matter; and if I'm put in a trap, some one is going to pay the price. If I die, some one dies with me."

Yánez paled. He stammered. "I told you, I am a friend, a personal friend of Sandino's. And—"

"All right. I take your word. Now get us a guide who knows the route we've chosen, the direct, quickest route, however dangerous, a man who knows it absolutely—foot by foot, inch by inch. No hesitation and no doubting. Can you get such a man?"

"Yes," replied Yánez meekly.

"And right away?"

"I'll have him here inside of half an hour."

"Very well, in half an hour, we'll be back. But mind you, no crooked business or you will know who is going to pay. By the time we come back, have the front doors closed and be ready. When you hear three taps, open the side door in the lane. Let us out that way . . . No more words . . ."

We slipped out into the lane. "This way, up the hill," said Siqueiros.

We walked across the dark hill, then by a back street to the widow's house.

2

Siqueiros, still angry, was breathing heavily.

"What's the matter?"

"I don't trust that man."

"He seemed all right to me."

"You don't know Latins well enough," replied Siqueiros. "Where were your eyes?"

"I don't understand."

"Didn't you see Yánez nudge the Indian when I asked him whether he knew the route we wished to go?"

Were we walking into a trap? To me Yánez had seemed sincere enough, only not encouraging as to our prospects, a little doubtful of our success. It might be essential honesty. Perhaps Yánez had turned or had gotten cold feet. But there was Turcios' letter; and I remembered Turcios' words, "Yánez is a man you can trust implicitly."

Was it possible that Yánez, after all, was playing a double rôle—perhaps facilitating the transmission of correspondence, and at the same time keeping the authorities informed?

I thought over every incident. I was willing to swear that Yánez was absolutely straight.

Why then had he nudged the Indian? Perhaps because the Indian was slow-witted. Siqueiros had a most inquisitorial way. His questions may have frightened such a simple-minded person. I suggested this to Siqueiros.

"I don't trust Yánez," he replied doggedly.

"Then why did you ask him to get a guide? In that case he wins anyway."

"Not necessarily," replied Siqueiros. "He already knows our plans. We can't get in any deeper. But if he gets the guide as he promises, that will show he wishes to please us. The guide we can size up for ourselves."

1

WE REACHED THE WIDOW'S
house. In the garden Siqueiros
turned to me grimly. "I'm
going to let you walk into the
trap alone."

"What do you mean?"

"You are going to Yánez'
place by yourself. You are an
American. Nothing will be done to you, even if you
should be arrested. But as for me, I'm a Nicaraguan. I
can be maltreated, imprisoned, deported. The authorities, already suspicious of me, would welcome any pretext to make trouble. Yánez will understand by my not
coming that if he tries any monkey-business, I intend to
carry out my threat. He'll be damn careful not to do
anything underhanded. For that very reason I think
you'll be quite safe. However, if you don't want to . . ."

"I'm quite willing to go alone. I'm not afraid. I think
Yánez is on the level."

"The proof of the pudding is in the eating. If the
guide is O.K., we start to-morrow."

"Why to-morrow?" I asked. "The sooner we get out
of here the better. Time is precious. Dangers may multiply."

"First, we're tired. We need a few hours' rest. You
are sick. Second, we can't thrust our heads in the lion's
mouth without being sure his jaws are propped apart
so that he can't bite. The next jump is our most danger-

ous lap before we get to the firing line in Nicaragua. On what we do now hinges everything else. Better not go off half cocked. True, we should get out of Danlí, but the dangers on ahead may be far greater than the risk we run here. Third, if Yánez has anything up his sleeve he's bound to show his hand within the next twenty-four hours. Don't tell him where we are stopping. If no one knows that, it may give us a little elbow-room. Fourth, we have to conceal our documents properly."

I knocked three times on Yánez' heavy side gate and was instantly admitted into the pitch-dark garden and stumbled to the rear porch.

"Here's the guide," announced Yánez.

He presented me to Mariano, an Indian boy of about twenty-one, much more intelligent than Isidro, with alert black eyes, a serious cast to his face but a ready smile—quite likeable.

"The General didn't come?" Yánez asked me with a little frown. "Why not? We could have settled everything right now."

I said Siqueiros was not feeling well.

"You see I have complied with my word," said Yánez with an aggrieved air.

I quizzed the guide.

He replied frankly, "To get by, you'll have to go on foot. Hiring horses here will instantly arouse suspicion. And to get past the frontier guards is virtually impossible. We'd be too easily spotted."

"As for the suspicion here in Danlí, we have already called on the Commandant. It is far more logical that we should go mounted to buy coffee *fincas,* rather than on foot. Would it help to travel at night?"

Mariano replied thoughtfully.

"Perhaps. By traveling at night we would avoid preliminary suspicions along the road. We could get to the frontier just before daybreak to look over the ground."

The boy inspired confidence in me. "Good, I'm going to tell the General. Come with me."

2

I left Mariano by a little fountain two blocks away from the widow's store. Siqueiros was pacing to and fro in the garden.

"I'm sure the guide is O.K."

"We'll see," said Siqueiros.

We went out to Mariano. Siqueiros turned his flashlight on the boy's face and person and questioned him rapidly.

"I think you are right," Siqueiros said to me in English. "This chap knows what he is talking about." In Spanish, he said, "Come, we mustn't stand here; it will excite suspicion."

We walked towards the widow's store.

"Here is where we stay," said Siqueiros to Mariano. "Hire three horses. Have them saddled in the rear of the store, not later than seven-thirty P.M. to-morrow. Be careful. We can't afford to arouse suspicion. If any one asks questions, say that the horses are for a coffee-buyer and his assistant; say we are going into the interior."

We rolled up in our blankets on tables in the rear of the widow's store.

Next day, we sewed our papers in a heavy burlap sack, to be used as a saddle-blanket.

Early in the afternoon it began to rain. Siqueiros had a rain-coat but I had none; worse, my blanket ran red. No store in the village having any rain-coat, I bought some wide black oilcloth, cut a hole in the middle, and slipped it over my head.

1

THE GRIPPE HAD NAILED ME to the cross. My bones were cracking with fever.

But at eight o'clock we set out into a driving storm. We wove in and out through the back alleys of Danlí and took the open meadow to the southeast trail we sought at a full gallop. Dogs barked. Doors opened. Light surged across our path, vanished as we passed by—many a mind wondering what travelers could be riding so hard on such a road at such an hour in such a storm.

Up over a ridge, down into a slot of a valley. Flashlights in hand, we slid sickeningly along edges of cliffs veiled in inky nothingness.

My oilskins and my fever kept me burning hot, but my knees grew wetter and wetter. The water ran down inside my puttees, my feet froze.

Near eleven, the rain slackening, we stopped to swallow some whiskey against the exposure.

We were uneasy. The sound of our own horses' hoofs and the crackle of oilskins echoed and magnified into an army of pursuit behind us in the unknown dark where fireflies lit a thousand watch fires. By eleven-thirty a thin moon followed over my left shoulder, slinking behind us through the tangled branches and clouds like a famished mountain-cat. Over all the world a vagueness of indirection—neither beginning nor ending, a going on through a shifting topsy-turvy world, a giddy progress. Horses' hoofs, oilskins squeaking, saddles rubbing, now and then a clang of spur, a muffled call, one to the other.

By midnight, wind and rain again—great sluices of rain.

Hoofs chugged in mud.

A wayside cabin. We woke the inmates with shouts, for here lived an Indian friend of Mariano. He was sleeping under the front *ramada* on a *petate*. The gnarled trunk of his naked body rose out of a red blanket. We asked about troop movements. Bronze arms over bronze chest, gleaming gold under Siqueiros' flashlight, he answered:

"Until two days ago, there were no troops on this trail, but they are expected to-morrow—near the frontier."

We galloped out of the yard. A pig squealed. A clothes-line caught me under the chin and knocked me out of the saddle.

I landed heavily, half strangled, on sharp rocks.

Slushy shoes in stirrups again; aching back to the saddle; stiff cold fingers on the bridle; spurs cruel to the flanks. We leapt into the dark and the rain again.

Our arrival at the crucial frontier point we decided to time for daybreak—as Mariano had suggested.

In spite of rain, we had made good time and could afford about two hours' rest in front of an abandoned Indian hut, under the *ramada*. Two hours of weary tossing, nerves taut. I writhed in my damp clothes, in my rain-soaked blanket; feverishly warm, yet shiver-

ing with cold. At the end of the two hours, I shook
Siqueiros awake, glad to be off.

Gallop. Up and down. Up and down. Centipede hours
over ridges, on into inky valleys, here past cultivated
fields, there through long cactus lanes. Now dense
woods, now driving rain, now uncanny patter from
densely massed jungle leaves, now the moon padding
along behind us, making low clouds into humped camel
trains far across the desert mist of unknown canyons.

A gray quiver. The morning star beckoned us through
tangled jungle tracks known only by our guide. Dawn
greeted us at the pebbly ford of silver river, walled in
by silver trees under a plated sky. Between worlds. Night
to dawn, and silver shaking beauty over an unknown
scene. Silence. Not even the call of birds.

The wind moved fresh, nuzzled against the skin like
a cold snout. A breath of moisture. The sour sweet odor
of the jungle rot. A glow . . . Level rays . . . Threads
of gold. A yellow sheen. The endless on-going lifted to
sudden song. Now the birds—early birds—shouting joy.

Beyond on a little hill above an enormous twisted
matapalo tree, we approached a thatched Indian cabin
still in morning shadow. A spiral of blue smoke drifted
up. An old woman in a dirty dress squinted at us resentfully from sleepy eyes.

"When did the troops go up to Escuapa?"

"They passed here two days ago and came back yesterday. The road is clear."

We were relieved. We stretched in our saddles.

"How about some coffee?" called Siqueiros to the old
crone.

"Haven't anything," she replied surlily.

"That's Honduras hospitality for you," muttered Siqueiros. "Not wise to wait here anyhow."

We proceeded cautiously. . . .

Eight o'clock, Escuapa. A straggling line of Indian shacks on a razor-back ridge, sloping off into jungle depths. No troops. The sun tobogganing gleefully down a mangy mountain.

We drank steaming coffee from carved gourd bowls and munched parched corn, given to us—sullenly. We went on. Presently we met Sandino couriers. Everybody on the trail was Sandinista. The trail was full of Sandinistas, coming and going.

In the shaggy mountains just beyond there would be no Honduras troops. We had passed our first obstacle. Ahead of us, an open road to Nicaragua. An open road to the war zone. Indeed, we could hear the dull boom of cannons over miles of virgin mountain.

"Where is Sandino?"

"In his mountain fortress, El Chipote, American aeroplanes bombing overhead, American cannon mounted on opposing heights, American troops gnawing little by little into the mountain fastness, slowly encircling El Chipote, to cut off the Sandino *reténes,* or outposts. A general attack expected any moment."

We dismounted and clambered in on foot, up and up into the perpendicular Dipilto Range, handhold over handhold, right against the sky. A mystery how the horses and mules ever made it. For hours we toiled along the very edge of colossal cliffs on a trail no better than a thread. But in the steaming struggle of that ascent under a burning sun, despite the previous night's exposure and my lack of sleep, the grippe was burned out of me—clean.

We made a meal of tortillas and cheese on a mighty shoulder of mountain—Nicaragua and Honduras dropping down and away on either side.

Great ravines and ever that tiny thread of a trail, slippery with pine-needles. At first, breathless going. Gradually I grew accustomed to it. Loss of sleep and the hot sun made me drowse in the saddle. Time and again my body jerked half out of the saddle—a gruesome awakening to find myself staring down some fearful cliff along which the horses moved placidly. On and on. Hour after hour.

Then down, down, jog and jolt, zig-zag, zig-zag, sliding of haunches on shingle, the twist and scrape around shelves of yellow sun-baked rock.

1

Even before crossing into Nicaragua, we had met General Torres, a Sandino officer, taking his family, cattle, asses, household goods, and concubines to safety, a large cavalcade winding its way down through the pine-woods.

He was bursting with stories of marine atrocities—the looting of the hacienda El Hule, pillaging, brutalities to women, an old grandmother dragged with a rope around her neck. We ripped our credentials out of the gunny sacking. Immediately he gave us an additional guide, a young *mozo* well-known to the sentries, to conduct us to the first Sandino *retén*.

And so, at the foot of the mountains on the Nicaraguan side, shortly before descending into the droning twilight of Limones, we were halted by two of the most poverty-stricken "bandits" I have ever seen. Captain Gilberto Herrero, the chief of the rich Limones sector, wore a shirt hanging from his back in tatters; his bare feet clung to stirrups made out of sticks tied by rawhides; his saddle-blankets were gunny sacking—but he had a gun and a full cartridge belt. Surely banditry should have brought him a better return here where the meadows are full of cattle and horses and the cribs are overflowing with corn, and coffee is piled high, ready for the shelling.

He had received his captainship for an attack single-handed on an American patrol of four marines. He had fallen on them with machetes, no gun, and cut them to pieces.

Herrero was bitterly suspicious of all Gringos—Americans. He eyed me with hostile misgiving. Sullenly he conducted us to sleeping quarters.

All the other people in the house where we were ordered to sleep, as well as the Sandinistas quartered there, were cordial, accepting my presence as a matter of course. The family in this house was risking all in the Sandino cause. Its members expected a marine incursion any moment.

"The 'pirates' may even come to-night," was the murmur. "They are circling Jalapa and they have just taken Jícaro." Both were a few leagues away.

Already most of the family's belongings had been sent up into a mountain hiding place. They expected to follow in a day or two with the rest of their things.

Herrero promised us an armed escort early the next morning before the aeroplanes would be abroad. A dozen men begged to be included in our escort, for all were eager to visit El Chipote, which loomed far across valleys and mountains, and from whose direction came occasional booming of cannon.

"El Chipote"—magical word. Its cloudy retreat, its crest, was the symbol of a people dreaming of freedom.

The house where we were quartered overlooked a beautiful valley opening down towards Ocotal and leading up toward Jícaro. Night fell. The valley was bathed in moonlight. Hill rose above hill, mountain on mountain to the far grim heights encircling El Chipote, the mysterious Sandino fortress. The soft air was redolent with the scent of *mesquite* and *manzanillo*.

Seated on the wide veranda I listened to stories of
American atrocities that made our own tales of German misdeeds seem tame—a reiterated lesson in the uni-
versality of war psychology; tales told in the low soft
Spanish of a patient people—a hum of voices melting
into southern, star-dappled night. . . .

A meal by carbide lights; bed on canvas cots covered
with clean lace-fringed sheets.

2

In this frontier area of Honduras and Nicaragua there
existed, at the time of the arrival of the Spaniards, two
Indian groups, the Taguzigalpas and the Tologalpas,
their domains divided by the Segovia or Coco River
which flows through territory over which Sandino had
been fighting the marines.

The Dominican friars early undertook the pacific
conquest of the Vera Paz zone in Guatemala with
marked success. Shortly after the colonial government
received an order from Philip III to undertake conquest of the territory covered by these two Nicaraguan
and Honduras tribes. The catechizing expedition, or-
ganized in the year 1610, was placed in charge of two
Franciscans, Vardelete and Monteagudo.

With an escort of twenty-five armed men under Captain Alonso Daza, a malicious but perspicacious fellow,
they advanced to the Honduras coast region, where the
missionaries at once began instruction and baptism, first
with the Lencas, then with the Taguacas of the Tolo-
galpa stock, founding a settlement.

At first the Tologalpas appeared very submissive. But one night, without warning, they fell upon the Spaniards and burned their houses. Daza, soldiers and priests fled, shirt-tails out, to Guatemala.

Two years passed. The Franciscans decided to make another attempt. The same Captain Daza went with them. They followed the same route and encountered the same Lencas and Taguacas. As on the first occasion the Indians showed themselves tame and submissive, as though they were incapable of breaking a dish. The Indians themselves invited the missionaries to advance and diffuse Christianity throughout the country-side, offering them friendship and coöperation.

Captain Daza made a reconnoitering expedition, leaving the friars near the coast. He encountered several tribes who showed hostility, but the Taguacas accompanying him assured him that this had no importance, so he continued to advance.

En route two Spaniards lost their way. They seized an Indian, ordering him to guide them. He proved fractious. They tied his hands, then nailed him to a tree, so that he died in terrible agony.

When Daza and his soldiers were well into the Segovia region, he sent an Indian commission to the priests, instructing them to follow his march and join him at a predetermined spot.

The priests immediately set out in canoes, and floated through a placid paradise. But, suddenly, at a turn in the river they heard an infernal cry. A cloud of Indians, painted all colors of the rainbow, wearing battle feathers and carrying enormous pikes, appeared on the banks. They shouted like demons. On a tall pike was the head of Daza and on smaller pikes were the heads of the rest of the soldiers. Their hands were nailed on boards.

The Franciscans offered no resistance. The end had come. With rosaries and crucifixes and eyes toward heaven, they prayed, waiting for death. They did not wait long.

1

EARLY IN THE MORNING, BE-
fore aeroplane time—for the
marines were accustomed to
drop bombs on any chance
travelers—I was conducted
from Limones to Los Encinos
by seven Sandino soldiers with red and black ribbons on
their hats.

Our trail passed between Jícaro and Jalapa, marines
in both directions, only a few leagues away. (All distances are reckoned in leagues—miles or kilometers in
this gigantic expanse of frontier region are quite too
small units.) All the way, there was talk of Sandino,
El Chipote, American attacks, Sandino victories, American atrocities against the civilian population. "Never
must the fight cease," was the common verdict. "They
may drive us into the highest mountains, the darkest
jungles, but never will we lie down before the invader."

We had just crossed an open ravine and dropped down
into a little *barranca* where three women with bundles
and an old man were preparing breakfast. They said
they had come in advance of a party going to Honduras.

Topping the *barranca* we came upon another group—
a poverty-stricken outfit with dirty bundles of soiled
clothing, primitive Indians. They were fleeing from the
war zone, declaring the marines were destroying everything.

At this moment, four men, mestizos in European

trousers, wearing shoes and Texas sombreros, armed with revolvers and cartridge belts, rode up. Siqueiros immediately questioned them in his inquisitorial way. They claimed to be miners from Murra, taking their wives to safety in Honduras. To Siqueiros' inquiries as to their sympathy for Sandino, they gave equivocal answers, probably not sure of our attitude.

"The sooner you join up with Sandino instead of running off to Honduras the better," declared Siqueiros sharply. "This is no time for Nicaraguans to run."

"As soon as we get our wives to safety we'll come back," they declared.

"Good. Your names?" demanded Siqueiros, pulling out a note book. He took down the name of the one who had been answering.

"Your permit to carry arms?" next demanded Siqueiros.

"What permit?" a bit resentfully.

"This is Sandino territory. No one goes armed here without his permission."

By this time I realized Siqueiros was starting trouble. We outnumbered the four men but Siqueiros had acted on his own initiative. We were scattered in such a way that the situation might prove difficult to handle. For my part, I was quite unarmed. My mule was about two yards in front of the group and I walked over and put myself on the far side of the animal, where I could observe everything.

"I have no permit," replied the heavy-set fellow.

Before the other could make a move, Siqueiros jerked the man's gun from the holster. "Sorry, you lose your gun." He twirled the gun about his fingers with a watchful eye on the other three.

I saw the next stranger brace his feet slightly apart, and move his hand, ready for a quick draw. Siqueiros undoubtedly noticed this also, but continued talking to the first man, upbraiding him further for running away.

"Very well," he said finally. "Here's your gun back," and he returned the weapon. "I'll write you a permit." On a slip of paper, Siqueiros wrote out a permit for the four men, filling in the names of each.

"Go," he said. "But remember your duty."

Thinking over the incident as we rode on, I concluded that Siqueiros had created a difficult situation in order to master it—for the sole purpose of impressing the Sandino escort with his courage and aggressiveness. Siqueiros' natural arrogance, his lust for leadership and preeminence, his overweening ego, had already made him assume command arbitrarily of the group, though theoretically he was merely being escorted.

He talked to the men about the necessity of keeping the present sector clear of marines in order to insure Sandino's communications with Honduras. To this end, he proposed to come back from Sandino's camp and organize a band of which he would be the leader. And he so imposed his personality that all agreed to follow him.

Further on we stopped at a friendly house, while we waited for an Indian runner to move on ahead to announce our coming to wayside houses and to the next Sandino *retén*. Things were in such a state that when people in Nuevo Segovia saw any one approaching, they either took to the hills or brought out their rifles and began shooting without warning. Our hosts thrust taffy candy made of sugar-cane syrup and small nuts into our hands and set out drinks. The Nicaraguans here, and it proved the same everywhere, are far more kindly and hospitable than the Hondureñans.

About an hour this side of Los Encinos two armed men slid down an embankment—Colonel Guadalupe Zelaya and an aide.

"You got off lucky," he announced. "I was just aiming at that gray coat [which I wore] when I happened to see a red and black ribbon."

"Didn't you get our message?" asked Herrero.

"Yes, but whoever saw any one but a Gringo wear a coat like that?"

"Quite right," replied Herrero, "Gringo he is."

The Colonel looked at me through slit eyes.

"It's all right," said Herrero. "He goes through."

2

Los Encinos was a picturesque *casería* (the marines later razed it to the ground), clambering up the two steep banks of a little stream. High mountains, covered by great forests of timber, rose close on every side. Here in Los Encinos, because of frequent aeroplane attacks and troop movement, all the women save a few octagenarians to do the cooking, had vanished. We dismounted before a long thatched house.

After I had stretched my legs a bit, Colonel Zelaya led me over to "the Englishman." Down the slope stood a log-hewn, well-roofed house within a solidly fenced clearing. And here lived a lone Englishman, with a big brood of beautiful-eyed girls, with a native wife. Here he sat on his gold mining claims, calmly smoking his pipe, an enormous Union Jack flying from the front yard, to warn the marines to be careful where they dropped their bombs. American troops had been there to try to browbeat him into leading them to El Chipote but he had refused; and while arguing with them, one of his girls had slipped off to bring the Sandinistas down upon them. Sandino troops now held the place. And though aeroplanes circled overhead, he sat under his Union Jack and smoked; and no one bothered him. The marines respected him as an Englishman. The Sandinistas admired his courage.

He was astounded at seeing me.

"Which cloud did you drop from! You've got your nerve. Any one of these fellows is likely to take a whang at an American."

He gave me my first decent meal since Tegucigalpa, and told me about marine movements.

"They came right before Chipote yesterday, in full force. A big drove of Sandino cattle couldn't get through. I doubt if Sandino will receive you. An American! Well, I'll be damned! What worries me is, any of these ignorant fellows is likely to pull a gun on you. They're simple-minded folk and irrational. I don't see how you got this far without trouble."

I told him Colonel Zelaya had had me keep in the middle of the group.

"There's a danger, certainly, of somebody sniping you. Zelaya's a good fellow. Keep close to him. If you've won his confidence you're in good hands. Take his advice, keep out of the lead, well in the center of the bunch."

He offered me his mule to go up to the next *retén*. I gave him my card.

Between puffs, he looked at it. "This I'll just keep as a little memento of the foolishness of mankind."

3

My new escort—most of the soldiers we had had turned back—was headed by Zelaya. He wore a gray shirt and a gray hat low over his black eyes. He was a coffee-grower, evidently a man of much influence in the community. Certainly he had personality—a crisp-tongued, straightforward man.

For long distances the horses' hoofs splashed silver as we ascended the beds of little streams in perpetual twilight cast by lofty trees, smothered with parasites, vines and gourds.

Finally we dropped down to a deserted farmhouse in a nook of meadow land, then through a gap.

"Now comes the dangerous part," declared Zelaya, as we swung around the nose of a cliff on a narrow trail, into the open. The late afternoon sun smote us full in the face. Blinking, we stared out across a vast ravine. Down, down it plunged, till the eye lost itself in a sea of jungle, then up, up, rising majestically. The trees on the far side, interspersed with jagged masses of rock and long scars of sliding gravel, were reduced to pigmy size. Up and up rose the opposite wall, lifting a mighty barrier against the crystal-clear gray-blue sky. Silence ruled the world. The afternoon was calm and peaceful, warm and drowsy. The cicadas shrilled and the dust rose about us from the hoofs of the animals.

"The dangerous part," repeated Zelaya, scanning the valley carefully, a bit apprehensively, with his sharp eyes. We all did the same. But not a movement. No air.

Not even the trembling of a leaf. We rode on along the brow of the cliff.

"Here," continued Zelaya, "we are in plain view. Anybody in the bush could pick us off." He smiled sternly.

But without mishap, after an hour of riding, we swung into a wooded valley. The sun was left behind. Twilight enveloped us. A damp air clung to us, laden with the moldy odor of leaves and rotting roots.

Gradually, though no word had been spoken, and no travelers had been met, I became subtly conscious that the military hold of Sandino on this region was already crumbling. As we advanced through the ravine, into the tangled mountains, a still, nameless terror overhung the world. The cannonading of the day before had ceased. The aeroplanes which had circled over these heights for months on end did not appear.

The world was hushed, gripped by unknown dangers. Menace grimaced from the crags. Terror leered from the matted tropical growths. Catastrophe twined around the trunks of the gigantic pines and *matapalos*.

Somewhere beyond were machine-guns and cannon and battle and limbs of dead men hanging from the trees, but all that came to us on this secret trail was an inexplicable silence—as though the whole countryside had died without even a final breath. No breeze—the air was deathly still.

The few houses we now passed on the upper stretches where several trails had joined the *camino real* were all deserted though animals stood in the corrals, and the cribs were full of corn—the banditry of Sandino, even at this early stage, showed restraint, though even bandits must eat.

·We went on. More deserted houses. Then dogs, dogs without masters, leapt past us in fright, whimpering. A little spaniel jumped into the brush, flattened its belly against the black earth and quivered pitifully. We began to meet refugees.

"The *Machos*—the Americans—have taken El Chipote," we were told—and all our plans fell into a jumble.

Where—now—was Sandino? Would his troops, just ahead in the town of Murra, be able to take us to him?

Other refugees. More details. Sandino had evacuated El Chipote without firing a shot. Avoiding a final fight, he had slipped out with all his supplies, dynamite, ammunition, guns, machine-guns intact, leaving the Americans a deserted mountain top guarded by dummy soldiers with sticks for guns. This then was the victory of the marines—the reward for months on end of skillful cautious approach—in proper observance of the latest Annapolis instructions. (The American press reported an extensive combat and many Sandinistas killed by aerial bombardment.)

4

Long after sundown we dropped into Murra, a mining town in the elbow of a cold dark stream, tight between cold gloomy mountain walls. Empty! Deserted! Not even a dog! The town was tomb-like, the doors swinging open in the wind. The ghostly place was gripped with nameless terror. The very mountains seemed empty, inexplicable. They seemed closing in on us, crushing us, growing darker and darker, more menacing.

Not a Sandino soldier anywhere. Not a soul to answer questions.

Where would we eat? Where would we sleep? Without a word, Zelaya—rifle slung across his back, jaw set—slouched low over his mule—rode on and on, grimly—for all we knew, right into a nest of machine-guns. Black mountain walls rose everywhere. The damp thickened. A mist closed in about us.

Rain again. Slowly at first, then quickening to a patter. Then torrents, great sluices of water from an unseen sky.

We climbed off our animals and floundered along a trail turned river, groping for foothold in muck, peering ahead for a path in murky black, pounding our animals on ahead—wearily—facing an unknown.

Hours passed. The rain poured. On and on. A weary plugging. Siqueiros and I had traveled all night and all day to reach Limones. We had traveled another fifteen hours to-day! And still we kept on, scrambling, slipping, falling in the mud and wet, drenched to the skin. The very fact of our endless on-going dulled our minds to further fear. Nothing mattered except the next step . . . the next step. . . .

A light!

We stumbled into a lone house on the mountainside.

Three male voices greeted us kindly. Welcome hands seized our blankets and bags, lifted off our saddles from our tired animals.

A mess of household belongings bulged from rawhide sacks ready for transportation on mule-back into the mountains. A sewing machine stood in solitary grandeur in the center of the empty littered room. A broken picture lay in one corner.

A makeshift supper was scraped together; steaming coffee, hot milk, beans and tortillas.

"The women," we were informed, "have already scurried off into the mountains. When a woman gets panicky you can't hold her. We light out to-morrow with the rest of what we can pack along. Soon, very soon, the cursed American *Machos* will be here and burn the house. They're burning all the houses."

"What's this place called?"

"San Pedro—ranch and mine."

"And where is Sandino?"

"God knows."

XXXVII THE THREAD BROKEN

1

THE ODYSSEY THAT BEGAN at the San Pedro ranch, after we lost track of the route which General Sandino had followed after his evacuation of El Chipote, led us ever deeper into the mountains in an ever-widening inland circle about the scene of action of the marines. On every hand loomed height after height, great crags and ridges, profound valleys and enormous precipices, all blanketed in the densest tropical vegetation, some days simmering under the hot, open tropical sky, at other times almost invisible in the whirl of tropical storms. Difficult mountains to cross, even if we had known the trail to take.

Immediately on our arrival in San Pedro that rainy night, sentries were set out. One of the three hosts, armed with flashlight and my oil-cloth cloak, made a two-hour trip through the rain, to where his father, Don Juan Colindres, was located in a secret nook with the women of his family.

Long after midnight Colindres appeared to talk with us. His uncle was a colonel with the Sandino forces, and in charge of a near-by *retén*. Colindres was not only an ardent Sandinista, he had direct connections with the forces. He read my documents, was duly impressed and promised to land us in Sandino's camp by two o'clock the following afternoon. "We will have to desert our

239

mounts and supplies and follow a short-cut trail," he decreed. "It's too dangerous to use horses."

We turned in on canvas cots, not even removing our soggy shoes.

Early in the morning, Don Juan, Siqueiros, myself and an Indian set out across the hills, past three well-timbered mine-shafts.

Colindres pointed out some curious holes. "The aeroplanes flew over here, and seeing this excavation, thought it an entrenchment, and bombarded it."

We topped a crest and descended into a huge ravine. On the other side, we spied several Indian *jacales*. We had hardly gone a few feet when a flash hit my eye—a quick flash gone in an instant, unrepeated. I jumped behind a tree, warning my companions. "Some one is down there in the valley with a gun."

We scanned the depths.

"I don't believe any one is there," finally declared Colindres. "Let's go on."

"There's at least one rifle down there," I insisted.

They laughed at me. "How do you know that flash was a rifle?"

Some instinct warned me. "Wait a few minutes longer," I urged. "Send the Indian ahead."

And so the three of us, Siqueiros, Colindres and myself sat down behind some thickets to chat. Said Colindres:

"Really, this climbing is a hard bet for a man of my years. I'm fifty-two but Beals here is so eager to get ahead—he puts patriotic Nicaraguans to shame."

"You don't look a day over forty-five," I exclaimed.

"Yes, I'm well preserved. I don't abuse my forces. Most men go to pieces over women, but I've always been moderate. I get along with five or six, but some men can't control their passions."

2

In half an hour our Indian showed up on the trail with two Sandino soldiers. They really had been about to take a shot at me when I jumped behind the tree.

Sandino, they told us, was now in El Remango, a lofty height back of El Chipote.

Don Juan whistled. "That ends our hopes for days."

Though we were close enough to both El Chipote and El Remango, the marines were now stationed between. To reach El Remango, without bumping into them, meant fully two days' marching by secret trails.

One of the soldiers offered to serve us as *chan*, or guide, as far as Zúngano, an intermediate *casería*. He shouldered my blanket and we set out.

On the other side of the valley we came to a cabin where two Indians were crushing juice out of sugar-cane by means of a primitive, handmade press with wooden rollers and an awkward, bent iron handle. Yellow jackets buzzed about everywhere.

We were offered some of the juice to drink—*caldo*, broth, it was called. We wanted food for the trip, for the Indians said everybody was fleeing; it might be hard to buy anything on ahead. They had nothing themselves but one of them set off for a house half a mile away in the forest to try for a chicken. I lay down on a bench made of rough branches and slept like a log.

Nearly an hour later the Indians returned empty-handed.

We set out over a scarcely visible trail, through mountain and jungle, into the wilderness. Here and there we left blazes on trees with our machetes, better to find the trail again should we have to beat a retreat.

The *jacales* we came upon were all deserted.

One hut was an exception. Here we were told that not a living soul remained in Zúngano; nor would we find a bite to eat. True, for from here on we were lucky to get a few tortillas; we were glad to toast green bananas or an occasional sweet potato. Now and then we sliced the outside of the "Suite" palm and ate the tender pith. Sometimes we got water from *bejucos de agua*. It came fizzing out of the cut stem like soda-water, fresh and cool. The few people we met were all loyal Sandinistas, fleeing ever deeper into the wilderness, to escape the hated marines. Their homes had been burnt, their crops destroyed. They were seeking safety, a new patch of ground to clear. But one and all, they vowed never to give up the struggle, and, if necessary, pass it on to their children. Here and there we came upon provisional lean-tos, still-warm camp-fires, heaps of fresh chicken feathers, left by the refugees.

In Little Mataguinea, a place I shall always remember because of the black, buzzard-like *macacalgas* screaming and circling about, we were told that marines had crossed our path just ahead in Zúngano. We could not possibly proceed.

But we also learned of a *retén* the other side of Zúngano, in charge of Colonel Colindres, uncle of our companion, and one of the most trusted Sandino officers.

We sent an Indian courier ahead with our letters, to be dispatched through Colindres to General Sandino.

Siqueiros suddenly became the doubting Thomas. He

talked seriously of turning back. But so long as there remained a glimmer of hope of reaching Sandino, I refused to listen. In fact the news of Colindres' *retén* quite reanimated me.

Our new stopping place was an open thatched hut, with wattle-woven walls on two sides, and a *tobanco* slung near the thatched roof. The other tenants were a dirty Indian couple, two squalling babies, and a bearded old man, sick with fever, his head bound up in a rag—all fleeing from the war zone.

They gave us food, toasted green bananas, a few beans, without salt—all they had.

That night we slept in the *tobanco*, on the hard swaying poles. Smoke half suffocated us. The thatch over our heads creaked with scorpions. But there was warmth and the mosquitoes, so ferocious down below, could not endure the smoke.

3

The next morning Colindres' reply arrived. Two soldiers and a *chan*, the last a bearded fellow, yellow with malaria, brought instructions to conduct us to the *retén*. We slung our blankets over our shoulders and set out.

One of the soldiers, Pedro Montoyo, viewed me with ugly hostility, mumbling something about "Yankees." He made me uneasy, so I took the trouble to explain my affair in detail. This somewhat appeased him, though from time to time he asked me sharp questions. He still revolved the whole mystery of my presence there in these mountains, behind the Sandino lines, over and over in his mind, with brooding Indian intensity.

"Most of those who have wanted to see the General," he said, "have wished to ask him to lay down his arms and let the marines stay in Nicaragua."

I assured him I had not come to offer Sandino advice of any sort, and added sharply that neither was it proper that one of Sandino's subordinates should concern himself regarding whom Sandino should or should not receive. Montoyo fell silent.

It so happened Montoyo was to remain by my side all the way to Sandino's camp. Before long he lost every trace of hostility. He became a staunch and unquestioning friend. He was ready to skirmish additional food supply for me—sugar-cane, oranges, fruit, roots, berries. From him I learned a great deal about the Commissariat of a Central American army. At times our forces looked like a walking sugar-cane field. Montoyo discovered my interest in the flora and told me the name of practically every plant which I examined, together with its medicinal uses—*zorrilla*, a root with a skunk-like smell, for headaches (better the headache, I decided); *coyol*, an insipid fruit; *golondrina*, for the eyes; *malva*, for the kidneys; cow's tongue, an urethral sedative; *dormilón*, the leaves of which closed tight with the slightest touch. With Montoyo's facts were mixed folk-lore and local superstitions. He told me of *cametillo*, an Atlantic coast plant: "If you give this plant to a person one day after it has been cut, he will die twenty-four hours later; if you give it to him a week after it has been cut, he will die a week later, and so on. The authorities shoot anybody with this plant in his possession"—(a rather strenuous pure food law and drugs law).

Before we parted, Montoyo came to wait on me hand

and foot. His last request was for my "likeness." "I want your picture to take with me into the battle of Jino-tega," he begged.

This, too, he must have felt was a real token of my esteem for him. For no Nicaraguan of humble origin cares to have his "likeness" in the hands of an unknown person. Terrible death-dealing magic can be worked with a "likeness."

XXXVIII   DEAD MEN'S CIGARETTES

1

THE FINAL APPROACH TO Colindres' camp was made at dusk, by hacking an entirely new path through the dense iron wall of the jungle across valley and ridge, a short distance from the American lines.

Wringing with sweat, we dropped into a clearing surrounded by jungle. A barracks harbored about thirty soldiers and a dozen camp Juanas, women who had tended to the cooking and washing in El Chipote. One of them, Teresa, a vivacious girl, with a little boy about five, addressed me boldly, "And you—you are an American!" I later learned she had been Sandino's mistress.

"How long since you have smoked?"

"Days on end."

"How does this strike you?" and she offered me two packs of Camels.

"How on earth—" I exclaimed.

"I took them off a dead marine," she replied nonchalantly.

A towel was bound about her head. She had been wounded in the forehead by shrapnel during a recent aeroplane bombardment. Lifting the make-shift bandage, she showed me an ugly star-shaped scar over her left eye, still red and raw.

Over the common camp skillet, steaming with

chicken and boiled potatoes in rich gravy, the two Colindres, Siqueiros and myself ate hungrily and discussed the problem of reaching Sandino.

"Your letters have gone forward," said Colonel Colindres. He was a young, round-faced officer who had served with Sandino longer than any one else; a member of a well-known Liberal family, claiming distant relationship with the president since elected in Honduras. He told me of the earlier stages of Sandino's career.

"I worked alongside Sandino in San Albino mines in Nuevo Segovia some years ago," he told me. "Even then Sandino had ideas about freeing the *patria* from foreign control, and I promised, if the hour came, to join him.

"We were with Vice-President Sacasa, when he established his government in Puerto Cabezas, I was with Sandino in his later battles throughout the Republic, in Yucapuca, in Trinidad; and when he took part in the attack on Chinandega. In spite of the American support of the Díaz faction, the Liberal arms were everywhere successful, because the country is overwhelmingly Liberal.

"One day, when we were still in the Puerto Cabezas, American battleships anchored, and three hundred marines landed without asking anybody's consent. The port, the seat of Sacasa's government, was declared a neutral zone. Everything was neutral zone where the Liberal forces were successful. Sacasa was ordered to deliver up his arms to the American forces—this, though Sacasa was the only legal president, for Díaz was put in by American coercion with a rump parliament, and not only a rump parliament, but a parliament containing many illegal members.

"When the marines appeared in Puerto Cabezas, Sandino was all for repelling them. Sacasa calmed him down. Thereupon Sandino, instead of delivering his arms, retired into the mosquito-infested marshes, where every drop of alkaline drinking water had to be secured by digging wells and straining out the mud. To him, here, the women of the town, even down to the prostitutes, smuggled out rifles. He secured some twenty-five Mosquito Indians to carry what he had salvaged down to Prinzalpoca through the most terrible marshes. From there he made his way up to Cabo de Gracias, and suffering untold hardships, with a small group, he ascended the Rio Coco into the mountains of Nueva Segovia.

"When the Stimson-Moncada agreement was made at Tititapa, Sandino disbanded his troops, but refused to deliver over his arms, which he oiled and buried in the forest. After thoroughly informing himself as to the terms of the agreement, he came to the conclusion that it represented not only a betrayal of the Liberal party, but of the Nicaraguan people; and he raised the banner of revolt in Nueva Segovia where he has remained nearly nine months. His experiences in Puerto Cabezas led him to fight for his country's sovereignty in the face of the world to make foreign intervention forever impossible."

2

Colindres was very skeptical about our catching up with Sandino. The marines were buzzing about everywhere. Many days, perhaps weeks, of travel might be ahead.

Again Siqueiros became pessimistic. Ever since the loss of Chipote, he had been down-hearted. He would remark that we were on a wild goose chase.

Now, "I'm for turning back. I'm not going a step further."

"I go on," was my reply. "So long as Sandino is alive I shall keep on his trail."

"But how will you get back alone?"

"As long as there is a chance, I keep on," I repeated.

"You don't realize the risk," said Siqueiros, nettled.

"I take it I am among friends. I throw myself absolutely on Colonel Colindres' protection."

"Well, I'm your friend also, but it's folly. How do we know whether Sandino got our papers?"

Hardly had he said this than an Indian courier arrived, panting. The reply was from General Sandino!

January 28, 1928.

Don Juan J. Colindres
ESTEEMED FRIEND:

I received your little note in which you advise me persons have arrived who wish to speak to me . . . have them proceed to the encampment of El Remango and from there the gentlemen mentioned will be conducted by Captain Pedro Altamirano who will take them to the place where I am to be found. Let their march be rapid in order that they may reach my camp soon. I greet you in company with your family.

Patria y Libertad
(*Signed*) A. C. SANDINO

P.S. Have them come before the battle of Jinotega which we intend to launch soon.

VALE

"Well, that puts a different face on the matter," admitted Siqueiros, "although—"

"I continue," I said.

"Then I stick too," Siqueiros decided, his arrogance and self-importance at once reviving.

That night, in a little cabin on the hill above the encampment, with my flashlight playing over the pages, Siqueiros read from his manuscript and the latest number of *Ariel*.

3

We broke camp early the following morning to make a forced march with the soldiers and the Juanas through risky country to El Remango. We circled the *retén* of El Retiro, where the marines were burning the houses. The smoke curled up over the side of the ridge.

On a densely wooded knob, quite by chance, we ran into General Echevarría, a Mexican. He had been a guerrilla fighter in Honduras for fifteen years; and was reckoned something of a poet. Originally he had brought twenty-five Honduras volunteers to Sandino's camp where he had subsequently served as official secretary.

He was a massive fellow, a red bandanna around his neck, a husky dagger stuck in the top of his right boot.

"Carleton Beals!" he exclaimed. "Why, I know all about you," and he gave me a typical Mexican *abrazo*. My stock went up with the soldiers.

Echevarría said he was taking a rest. "Chipote was all right; but I'm too heavy and too old to run up and down these mountains. The younger fellows will have to keep on. I'm here in a little cabin with my wife and dog. Later on, I'll rejoin Sandino. The marines are everywhere about, but I reckon they won't find me in this retreat. Why, I even couldn't find my wife for two days."

Siqueiros again broached the advisability of my turning back.

"I go on with you or without you," I replied doggedly, and from that moment sprang up an ill-feeling between us that was never entirely overcome. We dropped down into a valley, across a wide meadow, through a treacherous marsh, where one of the horses got mired in an *estero* and was extracted only after a half hour's cutting of branches. Then up mountain after mountain.

Finally, on a late but cold evening, under a brittle gray-green sky, we climbed a bald mountain knob swept by a remorseless wind from the great valleys beyond and below. Grinning rifles menaced us over log barricades tilting against the skyline. Red and black hat bands, bodies crouching low, waited.

This *retén*, one of the key outposts and almost inaccessible to attack, had been held since the beginning of hostilities. Its corrals were filled with animals—cows, pigs. There were a chicken coop and a number of outhouses clustering around the main barracks. Large fresh cowhides were pegged out on the side of the summit-slope to dry. Occasionally a pig broke loose and rooted at them. And here in El Remango, we found Captain Altamirano.

Captain Altamirano (later a colonel and later captured and executed) was a middle-aged soldier who had fought all over Nicaragua and Honduras. He was ponderous, slow and sure in thought, speech and act. He was dressed in white flannel trousers, a pink sash, and a lemon-colored shirt sans buttons, over which crisscrossed his cartridge belt. On one shoulder was slung a plaid cloth bag, and his face was covered with a week's growth óf beard. Here, too, was the column of thirty odd men which Sandino had disposed to accompany me to his encampment—wherever he might be found.

Captain Altamirano ordered our mules cared for, told the Juanas to serve us hot coffee, for we had arrived streaming with perspiration; but now in the face of the freezing wind, our clothes hung damp and stiff on our shivering bodies. The Captain personally arranged our bunks for the night, and shortly we were sitting down to hot food, a generous supper.

He, more than any of Sandino's followers, was branded as a ruthless, blood-thirsty bandit. No one was more kindly to us; no one struck me as being more honest.

XXXIX   SAN-DINO'S CAMP

1

THOUGH THE WIND HOWLED over El Remango, we spent the night convivially in the long barracks room. The soldiers were as free and easy as though the enemy were a thousand miles away instead of actually on the next ridge. The barracks room was made of driven poles and a high thatched roof. At one end stood the kitchen tables, heavy tree trunks split in half, or slabs of stone on wooden posts. By their side were the grinding *metates,* for making tortillas, the braziers and the adobe ovens, the fronts of them indented with features of human faces by some humorous artist. The barracks was lined with bunks, rawhide stretched over poles and the flaps pegged up against the walls as protection from the wind.

In a free wall space, the camp Juanas had set up a little shrine presided over by St. Anthony, decorated with colored tissue paper, before which burned a carbide lamp. From the smoky rafters dangled great loops of fresh and dried meat. Hung down, too, gourds with corn-cob plugs, terra-cotta jars, pieces of harness and home-made fiber ropes, long strips of rawhide. A baby squealed from a sisal hammock with multicolored tassels.

The soldiers, each with his rifle ready by his side, clustered in groups. Some were talking, telling stories—the attack on Ocotal, the surprise assault on the *Machos* in Las Cruces, the burning of the Hacienda El Hule and the violation of the women by the hated Gringos—and I, here in their midst, a *Macho*, a Yankee, a Gringo, yet treated with super-deference. Other soldiers, seated on sawed-off stumps, were reading by the light of the *ocote* torches—novels, the latest number of *Ariel*, stray newspapers. One fellow was making love to a Juana who wore a high red comb with sparkling glass diamonds. Another in white "pyjamas," grimy from use, roasted meat, using his ramrod as a spit. A guitarist thrummed a Sandino song, with simple Whitmanesque flavor and love of proper names, to the tune of the Mexican *La Casita*:

> *Yo soy de los defensores*
> *Que con sangre y no con flores*
> *Lucho por conquistar*
> *Mi segunda independencia*
> *Que traidores sin conciencia*
> *Han querido profanar.*
> *Es mi patria la sultana,*
> *Linda Centroamericana*
> *De los lagos y el pinar.*
> *No quiero ser esclavista*
> *Del nórdico expansionista*
> *Que nos viene á asesinar.*

Four verses of it.

To the sound of such music and words, we began to dance, and danced most of the night away—a crowded confusion of babble and smoke, song, smell, flame and color.

One of the Juanas, Blanca by name, found me a pillow, an extra blanket, and in the chill dawn reappeared with water in a *jícara,* for me to wash my face and hands. The reason for her sweet attentions became apparent. Captain Altamirano had ordered all the camp Juanas to remain behind; but little Blanca, who had thus served me, had a child of about three years, and was anxious to get down to some town. She had lost her man, and she hoped that I might intercede to let her accompany the escort as my companion. But the Captain was aware that the presence of women would delay our march and increase the risk, for we had to pass again close to localities occupied by the marines. Notwithstanding, General Siqueiros arrogantly insisted that a girl in whom he had become interested back in the *retén* of Colonel Colindres be allowed to proceed. Captain Altamirano, with a little show of bad grace, was obliged to accede. And indeed, Siqueiros, now that he saw the road open again to Sandino, lost all of his doubts, and suddenly conceived of himself as a full-fledged Sandino general. Instead of considering himself as having come on a mere mission, he now sailed ahead in his flowing raincoat and great peaked sombrero as the Generalissimo-in-chief of our little expedition, berating the soldiers and giving the Captain extended advice regarding discipline.

2

Sandino had taken most of the horses and mules with him, but Captain Altamirano managed to scare up three mounts, for Siqueiros, Colindres and myself. Mine was a big white horse with asthma, clumsier than a cow and completely indifferent to spur or quirt. The beast fell

twice on the steep muddy trail down from El Remango.
The second time I gave up the struggle and proceeded
on foot, over my ankles in mud.

Little by little, we worked our way down the precipitous mud-soaked trail to the lower valley. The cold of
the mountains was left behind. Making a great circle
to avoid Quilalí, where American marines were razing
the town, we toiled on over bare hills, with spiny cactus
and prickly acacias, here and there thorny bromelias,
and many *jícaras*, with hard unshelled fruit from which
carved drinking cups are made, a fruit the name of
which has passed into Italian—*chicchera*, tea-cups.

Following the sultry trail for sunbaked miles during
several days, then into thickening vegetation, finally
reaching the denser jungles of the river proper, we
stopped in the home of a woman several miles from the
river, whose son, a civilian, had been killed by an aeroplane bomb. "We made a very tiny coffin," she remarked
simply, without emotion, "because his legs had been
blown off."

When we asked for any attention, any milk, cheese—
for she had good cows—her invariable remark, uttered
with passion and flashing eyes, was, "For you, everything
I possess, everything!"

The following morning we ascended along the Rio
Coco, breakfasted in a river settlement, then, after
reconnoitering, for it was fully expected that the expedition might break lances with marines, we forded the
river directly into the *retén* of Colonel Guadalupe
Rivera, a grizzled soldier and well-to-do hacendado, who
had turned his place in Santa Cruz into a Sandino outpost. His wide, cool piazzas overlooked the river that
had witnessed so many operations of both marines and

Sandino troops. Here we stopped long enough to take a dip and scrub.

That scrub was a god-send, for I, as most of the soldiers, was suffering from *garrapatas,* a minute, brown tick, probably picked up from the brush where cows had passed. These *garrapatas* swarm on the tips of leaves and shoots, hind legs out, the claws on their feet ready to seize any passing animal. They bore into the skin and multiply incredibly, setting up an intolerable itching and making sleep well nigh impossible.

For days our customary greeting had been, "Did the *garrapatas* bother you much last night?"

My legs were a mass of tiny sores. Nevertheless I scrubbed myself ruthlessly with river sand, almost peeling off my skin. I washed and pounded my clothes. Since we had no time to let them dry, I wrung them out as well as possible and put them on again wet. But I scotched the *garrapatas*—they disappeared.

3

More jungles—humid, reeking. Great ceibas, caobas, pines, and guayacán trees, matted gourd vines, flouting leaves and flowers, purple and scarlet fungi, tangled *bejucos* with long nude arms, lichens and aerial plants, parasite feeding on parasite, down to the microscopic forms, the eternal hierarchy of the tropics, sadly repeated in the structure of human society. A soldier plucks $20 worth of purple orchids (N. Y. quotation) and sticks them in the red and black band of his sombrero. Troops of white-faced, screaming monkeys swing past, stopping now and then to grimace at us or throw

down a dead branch. Many tree mice scamper among
the limbs, and one carries a baby clinging to her teat
with its teeth. From the depths comes the roar of a lion
repeated at intervals, lugubrious, menacing. Huge macaws wing across the sky, crying hoarsely, flashing crim-
son. Now and then we hear the lovely whistle of the
"to-le-do." We ford and re-ford a north-flowing tribu-
tary. The soldiers, since leaving Rivera's *retén*, go better
provisioned—chunks of fresh meat, wrapped in banana
leaves, are slung on the muzzles of their guns.

The few people we met—for here, too, the population
in large part had fled their homes out of fear of the
marines—had not yet learned that Sandino had evacuated El Chipote.

We toiled along slots of muddy trails, the banks in
many places higher than our head, over a summit known
as Las Cruces into the gathering dark. Here Sandino
surprised quite a bunch of marines and slashed them to
pieces.

At one place a huge trunk has fallen across the trail.
Rivera, just ahead of me, dismounted. The pommel of
his high saddle just went under, grazing the trunk. I
risked slinging myself along the horse's side, only one leg
in the saddle. Rising up too soon, my back caught, rip-
ping the saddle off like a piece of paper. This saved my
life—though I barely dodged a frightened kick from
my horse.

The damage repaired, we dropped down near the
Jinotega Valley. Another night of driving rain, over a
road in which our horses rolled pitifully to their bellies
in mud. Colonel Colindres' girths broke and he took a
header into the slough. Siqueiros broke a stirrup and
struggled along on foot. We finally arrived at seven

o'clock to a supperless and freezing forced camp in a series of huts whose walls consisted of poles through which the wind howled dismally. For once Siqueiros did not read his manuscript, but instead dried his shoes over the fire. I slept on a chest with the rain driving into my face in fitful gusts.

The people here seemed hostile, especially an old man suffering with a toothache and wearing a dirty towel wrapped around his head and jaw. Siqueiros, to keep him from giving information, made him accompany us as a guide the next morning.

As the miles from his home increased, the old man's toothache became more unsupportable and his enthusiasm for Sandino more and more vociferously apparent. From time to time he begged to return to his home.

On toward Jinotega, where were stationed a hundred marines, we swung through a smiling open country of farms and meadows filled with cattle and wild horses. Our march took us within five miles of the plaza of Jinotega. Our little force advanced with an air of apprehension, scanning the sky for aeroplanes. The soldiers singled out the homes and farms of the *cachurecos* —Conservatives—and confiscated saddles and horses. Half the troop soon went mounted, some of them with rich-looking sheep-skin *pillones* on their saddles. Rivera and I rode on ahead alone. Rivera took off his red and black insignia and became an ordinary rancher riding down from the backwoods. He greeted numerous friends on the road. Several accompanied us and one tried to pump me as to the meaning of my presence.

"You are a journalist? Then probably you hope to see Sandino. There are rumors he is near by."

But I kept my own counsel. Finally we reached the

house of a cousin of Rivera, and he arranged for feeding the troops soon to appear.

The horses were tied up in an orchard, so as not to attract attention. After a few hours' rest, we hurried on, for the news of our presence in the vicinity had probably reached the marines in Jinotega.

4

Into the hills again, across upland meadows. After zigzagging over the noble crest of Yucapuca, we dropped down to a ranch house riddled with bullets. In this house, during earlier struggles, Sandino had maintained his headquarters for many weeks. The entire family, from grandfather to grandchild, a host of them, was enthusiastically pro-Sandino.

Learning that Sandino had arrived in San Rafael del Norte, we despatched an Indian courier post-haste.

At eight o'clock at night a courier from General Sandino, Colonel Santos J. Rivera, galloped into our camp with a message wrapped around the battery of his flashlight. Two hours would put us into San Rafael.

In a trice we had our horses saddled, and Colindres, Siqueiros, Rivera and I set out.

San Rafael del Norte is a small town of adobe walls and red tiles situated just over the Nueva Segovia line in the Department of Jinotega, on the high flank of the Yeli range. It lies in a narrow pass, through which flows a sparkling mountain stream. On the other side of the watershed, past the high crown of Yucapuca and a smiling populous valley lies Jinotega, capital of the Department. To the southwest the range stretches toward the Departments of Estelí and León; the whole region admirably suited for effective guerrilla warfare.

We swung round a bend. The red eye of a charcoal furnace glowed from the side of a mountain. Soon we were at the first sentry outpost.

"*Quién vive?*"

"*Viva Nicaragua!*"

"Give the countersign."

"Don't sell out the fatherland."

"Advance one by one to be recognized."

A youngish soldier in a dark green uniform and wearing smoked glasses took me in tow. "You are *el Americano?* A warm welcome, Sir."

Presently we were passing down the main street. Block after block the same peremptory challenge rang through the dark, and guns barred our passage until the final summons:

"Stick close to the wall; advance, one by one."

At the main sentry barracks, an entire company was lined up at attention. Their rifles snapped from ground to shoulder as we passed. After sundry haltings, we arrived to the sound of a night-splitting skirl of bugles. Sandino's troops were excellently disciplined. Later I mentioned this and the other evidence of good discipline to General Feland, in charge of marine operations:

"Probably some of those things were put on for my benefit."

"Not at all," was his reply. "Discipline is never put on at will for effect. It's hard enough pounding it into troops under the best of circumstances."

Colonel Estrada, of Sandino's general staff, informed

us that Sandino, because of a cold in his chest, would not see us till the following morning. We were escorted to the home of Colonel Rivera for the night.

In the bare parlor, with its portrait of Alfonso XIII, and members of the Colonel's family, with its phonograph and ring of home-made chairs, we were asked to sit down in the circle of Sandino's private staff and others of the command.

At my side was General Girón, a Guatemalan, former Commandant of Petén, a man with European training, later captured and executed by the marines. About fifty, he had a mobile face and lively gray eyes. Beside Siqueiros sat General Montoyo, from Honduras, a scarf wrapped tightly about his throat, for he was shaking with malaria.

After the customary formalities, we were taken off to dine. At Colonel Rivera's suggestion, we sent a note to Sandino, saying we were at his disposal and were well aware of military necessities; that if it were more convenient for him to receive us this same night, he should not imagine us too fatigued. Actually, I was weary from the two weeks' difficult forced travel in all sorts of inclement weather, at all hours of day and night, with improper food and no good places to sleep. However, the general sent back word again, begging to be excused on account of his illness and requested us to see him at —four A.M.!

On our return to the parlor, we were entertained by the camp guitarist, a member of Sandino's personal staff, who sang half a dozen patriotic camp songs, all of them directed against the "vile invader," "The cursed pirates":

Padre nuestro que estás en los cielos
¿Por qué no aniquiles el fuego del mal?

¿Por qué abandonas las rojas banderas?
¿Por qué á los pirates no puedes destruir?

Our Father who art in Heaven,
Why do you not annihilate the fire of evil?
Why do you abandon our banners?
Why can't you destroy the pirates?

About midnight, the officers withdrew, whereupon Colonel Rivera and his beautiful wife pulled out the family album, which we duly admired. Rivera had four children and the youngest, a little toddler just able to talk, he had taught to say, "Viva Sandino!"

Among the photographs was a series of the bombing of Chinandega by American pilots. Horrible scenes indeed! An entire street laid in ruins and sprinkled with mangled bodies; the tumbled walls of the hospital, broken bodies of patients flung about; a bank building and a smashed safe. Was it so long ago that we called the Germans Huns for destroying civilian populations without mercy?

Nearly two o'clock when we crawled into bed.

.

1

At a grim hour, the stri- dent *diana* of the bugler shrilled through the door and brought me out of bed fum- bling for matches and shoes. Two hours of rest. I was red- eyed and shaky. In less than half an hour General Sandino received me in his office in the rear of the main barracks. By the light of a lantern, we were served coffee and sweetbread by his wife, Blanca (at that time telegraph operator for the town), who spread out the cups on the red plaid cloth. As we talked the yellow tongue of the lantern flame grew feebler and finally faded into the light of common day.

Sandino was born on May 19, 1893, in Niquinohomo, a village of two thousand inhabitants in the Department of Masaya, three hours by train from Managua, the capital. His father, Gregorio Sandino, the owner of a coffee *finca,* is one of the leading men of the Depart- ment—a mild Liberal. General Sandino was educated in the village primary school and then sent to Granada to study in the Eastern Institute, after which he re- turned to the *finca* to help his father. He had a serious dispute with a prominent man of the locality and left for León, later for Honduras, where he worked in mines and for the banana companies in Ceiba. From there he drifted to Mexico, where he worked in Tampico for the Huasteca Oil Company.

In 1926, at the urgent pleading of his father, he returned to Niquinohomo. He brought back a number of books, among them various volumes on sociology and syndicalism—and strangely enough—a bulky Seventh Day Adventist tome, a fact confirmed by Sandino's mention to me, in a jocular vein, on several occasions, of this sect.

Sandino is short, probably not more than five feet. On the morning of our interview he was dressed in a new uniform of almost black khaki, and wore puttees, immaculately polished. A silk red and black handkerchief was knotted about his throat. His broad-brimmed Stetson, low over his forehead, was pinched into a shovel-like shape. Occasionally, as we conversed, he shoved his sombrero far back on his head and hitched his chair forward. The gesture revealed his straight black hair and full forehead. His face is straight-lined from temple to sharp-angled jawbone, which slants to an even firm jaw. His regular curved eyebrows are high above liquid black eyes without visible pupils, eyes of remarkable mobility and refraction to light—quick intense eyes. He is a man utterly without vices, with an unequivocal sense of justice, a keen eye for the welfare of the humblest soldier.

"Many battles have made our hearts hard, but our souls strong," is one of his pet sayings.

I am not sure of the first part of the epigram, for in every soldier and every officer to whom I talked, he had lighted fierce affection, blind loyalty; had instilled in every man his own burning hatred for the "invader."

"Death is but one little moment of discomfort; it is not to be taken too seriously," he repeated over and over again to his soldiers.

And another, "Death most quickly singles out him who is afraid of death."

A religious note in his thinking. Frequently he mentions God. "God is the ultimate arbiter of our battles." "If God wills it, we shall go on to victory." "God and our mountains fight for us."

His sayings, pithy and wise, run from tongue to tongue in his little army—ideas which are the wonder of simpler minds.

His most frequent gesture was the shaking of his forefinger, a full-armed motion behind it. Invariably he leaned forward as he spoke, and once or twice took to his feet, emphasizing a point with his whole body.

His utterance was remarkably fluid, precise, evenly modulated, his enunciation absolutely clear; his voice rarely changed pitch, even when he was visibly intent upon the subject matter. Not once during the four and a half hours during which we talked, almost continually without prompting from me, did he fumble for the form of expression or indicate any hesitancy regarding the themes he intended to discuss. His ideas are precisely, epigrammatically ordered. There was not a major problem in the whole Nicaraguan question that he dodged or that I even needed to raise. In military matters, however, he was quite too flamboyant and boastful, and exaggerated his successes.

"Where are all the aeroplanes I have heard so much about?" I asked.

He smiled. "At ten o'clock they will fly over San Rafael," he said. And at ten, as he had said, two bombing planes buzzed over the little town, circled lower and lower. Sandino's men were stationed in the door-

ways, rifles in hand. "Don't fire unless they bomb," were
his orders.

On the last approach, the planes roared over the very
roof tops, then were gone.

2

Among the Sandino troops I had noticed a rifle called
"Con-Con," which on examination proved to be a Russian model. How did Russian rifles get to Nicaragua?
Was Mr. Kellogg right when he accused Central America of Bolshevism?

These rifles have a curious history. When Miliukof's
revolution occurred in Russia, then Kerensky's coup,
the United States and allies still hoped to keep Russia
in the war; so a loan was made to Kerensky—to be spent
for war material in the United States. A large number
of Russian model rifles were turned out—but before
they could be turned over, Kerensky tumbled. The
October revolution occurred, the guns were on the War
Department's hands. Various attempts were made to
dump them.

A Costa Rican minister told me confidentially that
an American Cabinet secretary tried to turn a dirty
deal with these rifles. They would be sold at a song to
an intermediary, who would then sell them at an exces-
sive rate to Costa Rica. The Cabinet minister and our
secretary stood to split several million dollars, but the
Costa Rican indignantly refused the proposal.

The next opportunity to unload the Russian guns
occurred during the De La Huerta revolt in Mexico.
Our State Department sided with Obregón, and rushed

arms to him. Presto! The Russian rifles—some of which exploded in the hands of the users.

But some were good. And so Mexico, with proper irony, shipped them on to Nicaragua. Four boatloads were sent down to Sacasa, whom Mexico had recognized, and whom the United States was opposing—two boatloads by the Atlantic, two by the Pacific. One boat was called the *Con-Con*—hence the name of the rifles.

When Sandino, during the Liberal revolt, asked Sacasa for arms for Nuevo Segovia, and smuggled them out from Puerto Cabezas under the nose of American battleships, then trekked across the marshes, he received Con-Cons. The rest were bought back from Moncada at $10 a rifle in accordance with the Stimson agreement. What was then done with them, I don't know. But it seems very hard to get rid of these Russian model rifles! They keep coming back to us!—or their bullets do!

3

Stories of atrocities and violations of property naturally clustered around a figure officially declared an outlaw, just as many unjust stories have perched upon the marines. Certainly Nicaragua has a long heritage of cruelty not easily erased. Consider the following account by the old Spanish chronicler Oviedo:

In 1528, the treasurer, Alonzo de Perslta, and a man named Zurieta, and the brothers Ballas, left the City of León, each to visit the villages and Indians belonging to him. They never returned, having been destroyed by their own vassals. Hereupon Pedro Arias sent out soldiers to bring in some of the malefactors. They arrested

seventeen or eighteen caciques whom Pedro Arias caused
to be strangled by dogs. The execution took place in
the following manner, on Tuesday, the 16th of June
of the same year, in the public square of León: Each
cacique was armed with a stick, and told to defend himself against the dogs, and to kill them if he could. Five
or six young dogs were first set upon them, which their
masters wished to train, as they were yet without experience. They ran baying around the Indian, who
easily kept them off with his stick; but the moment he
thought himself conqueror, a couple of mastiffs, or well-
trained hounds, were sent against him, who threw him
in a moment. The other dogs then fell upon him, tearing out his entrails . . . In this manner the eighteen
were soon disposed of. They were from the valley of
Olocotón, and its vicinity. When the dogs were sated,
the dead bodies remained in the same place, it being
forbidden to carry them off, under penalty of being
served in like manner; otherwise the Indians would have
taken them away. They were left thus in order to
frighten the natives; but on the second day the stench
of the dead bodies became insupportable. And on the
fourth, it was so horrible that, being compelled to pass
there in going to the house of the governor, I begged
him to give permission to have them carried away;
which he did the more readily, since his house was
situated near the square.

Sandino at first religiously respected American lives
and property, but after four or five months declared
that since the marines showed no respect for patriotic
Nicaraguans, he would inflict reprisals at every opportunity. But that brutal acts emanated directly from
Sandino is not true. Numbers of people presumably
affected have rectified such charges in the press, declar-

ing Sandino has taken things merely out of actual necessity, sometimes paying for them with money, on other occasions leaving the customary revolutionary I O U's. The following letter from a wealthy Conservative coffee-grower is typical (*La Noticia*, February 12, 1928):

DIRECTOR OF *La Noticia*:

The information published in *La Noticia* of the 7th inst. is absolutely false, for not only have I not seen any of Sandino's people, but far less is it true that I have been held for ransom and a forced contribution of $2,000 exacted from me. I have precise information that in the places where he has passed, he has committed no acts of robbery and assassination such as your paper relates, but instead goes well-organized, in orderly manner, save for mules, which is the one thing he takes wherever he finds them.

(*Signed*) S. STADHAGEN

Sandino's first order on his arrival in San Rafael was that the first soldier touching anything not belonging to him would be shot. From my conversations with the shopkeepers of the town, Sandino's troops had been absolutely orderly and had paid for everything taken. Intoxicating liquors are not sold in any place controlled by the Sandino forces; the penalty for a man is shooting; for a woman, the burning of her house.

Sandino showed me the ledger of army expenditures. "Everything we take in and spend is faithfully recorded here."

While we were talking, Sandino suddenly noticed a dirty, ragged soldier near the door, who had been in the brush for a long time.

"Is that one of your men, Colonel?" he asked an aide abruptly.

"Yes."

Sandino pulled a five dollar bill from his pocket. "Go out and buy him a new shirt and trousers."

The Colonel hesitated. "The trouble is, there are five in this condition."

Sandino drew out ten dollars more.

"All I have at the moment. Tell the storekeepers we are poor and the money must go as far as possible. If it doesn't quite reach, tell him to send his bill for the balance to Mr. Coolidge."

1

SHORTLY BEFORE I WAS TO
leave Sandino's camp, Siqueiros came to me—agitated.

In his customary irritable
but decisive tone, he said, "I
must talk with you alone—
seriously."

I paced by his side to and
fro in Colonel Rivera's back garden. At first he did not
speak. Then suddenly, he stopped short and turned to
me impulsively. "Before we leave this camp," said
Siqueiros, "give me an *abrazo* for this is the last time you
will ever see me alive."

"What do you mean?"

Slowly, he said, "General Sandino is going to shoot
me." His quiet tone was unusual. He was tense, filled
with terror.

"Nonsense!" I exclaimed. "You have come with
proper credentials; he has treated you excellently. I
have been present every time Sandino has talked with
you. He's been courteous and thoughtful."

"You don't know our people."

How had Siqueiros come by this idea? I myself sensed
an uncanny power of domination in Sandino, something subtle, devious, not at all obvious. Certainly Sandino's domination over his men did not come through
his physical appearance; yet the lift of his finger was
law with men knowing only lawlessness. During our

interview, through some intricate Oriental mannerism (too recondite for me to comprehend), he had completely terrorized the arrogant General Siqueiros. Siqueiros' fear must have resulted from this same domination.

"Nonsense," I repeated, really believing he was in no danger. And I gave him the *abrazo* he wanted and half my money.

"Remember," he said solemnly.

"Nonsense," was my reply.

In July, six months later, Sandino ordered Siqueiros shot for treachery; documents were found on him arranging to betray Sandino to the marines.

2

My horse was saddled, my spurs strapped to my boots. Sandino's troops were mobilized, waiting only on my departure.

I rode to the barracks. Sandino stood grasping his red and black flag, a set look on his face. I dismounted, put out my hand. "General Sandino, you have received in your camp a man of the same race and country as those you are fighting. You have treated me with every consideration. I leave here most favorably impressed with the attention you have shown me. I am going, with your permission, from here to Managua, the capital of Nicaragua. My route I do not as yet know. As a newspaper man I reserve the privilege to interpret what I have heard and seen according to my own criterion. But in Managua I shall be asked many questions. In view of the fine treatment to me, I do not wish to injure you in a military sense in any way whatsoever. If there is anything of this nature—I should not write about or tell about, anything you feel would endanger you, rest assured it will not be told, not even hinted about."

Sandino's reply was: "You may go from here north, east, south or west. I shall give you as many men for an escort as you think necessary, or you may go entirely alone. You are absolutely free to tell to any one and every one anything and everything you have seen and heard without any restriction whatsoever. If you wish, ride straight to Jinotega, six leagues from here, and tell the first marine commandant you meet, everything you have seen and heard. In fact," he added with a little smile, "that would fit my plans admirably."

3

I swung out of San Rafael del Norte with Colonel Rivera at four in the afternoon. The sun was still hot. As we dropped lower and lower down the mountains into valleys ever widening, and the upland regions were definitely left behind, the country became dryer, but more cultivated, homes more frequent.

Rivera and I decided not to go to Jinotega. We would have arrived there after dark; and the marines had declared martial law with orders to fire on sight after ten o'clock. Instead we determined to drop over to the auto line at Metapa, or (as it is now called) Darío, for there was born Ruben Darío, the greatest Latin American poet.

We stopped to chat at various houses known to Rivera to be sympathetic to Sandino. We were in another world, for soon from here on, when Sandino's name was mentioned, it was with bated breath and a timorous glance around to guard against eavesdroppers. But with what enthusiasm we were received! Having just come from his camp—we were heroes.

Night fell warm and smooth—dreamlike as only tropic nights can be. To our nostrils came the fragrant scent of the flowers of the balloon-vine, draped from tree to tree. A great orange moon lifted over the rim of rolling hills. We rode through a wide valley, sometimes between open meadows or near the river between dense thickets, or along lanes of cactus requiring caution lest our clothes be torn to shreds.

No more peaceful scene could be imagined. Inconceivable that this country was being torn by war. Yet, a few hours' ride in any direction would have brought us to Sandino's outposts or to marine stations or upon the scene of possible combat.

In this valley Colonel Rivera had lived his boyhood; and under the influence of the great moon and the plated sky overhead and the silver miles stretching silent around us—save for the occasional howl of some lone dog—he told me of his youth, retouching sentimental chords.

Here in this valley in his youth Rivera fell in love, as perhaps a man falls in love only once in his lifetime; and he told me how, on warm nights like this, he had ridden for miles with a guitar under his arm to play at his love's doorstep. Of the junkets and excursions, the corn huskings and the house raisings. Then, after all, the girl had married some one else. Unable to endure the place any longer, he had gone away. Chance had taken him through this valley many times since; but never once had he seen her nor had he sought to see her. This, our present trip, was the first time in a year he had ridden this way; and the night had brought it all back to him, put a slight quiver in his voice, and an ache in my own breast, as his words flowed in and the silver trail unrolled before us like a magic carpet.

4

Towards nine o'clock, we came into a tiny settlement and whirled up to a wattle-woven house. A sorrowful uninterrupted monotone of voices. Rivera stood in his stirrups a moment, then turning to me, said in a low voice, "They are praying. Some one has died. Let us go; I had hoped to stop here."

For another hour we rode on. He was silent now. "From love to death, always but a step," was his remark.

Sitting upon the flat stones of another house by the roadside, we drank a warm brew of chocolate and ground corn. The simple folk with whom we talked here were all agog over Sandino. He had become ubiquitous. He had been seen here; he had been seen there. At night he had gone stalking along a ridge, god of the universe. Later I found the same mythology was believed everywhere I went in Nicaragua. At many a low doorstep I sat and talked over a *jícara* of chica corn beer, or a glass of yellowish palm wine; and there was no place Sandino had not been seen. He had fired the imagination of the humble people of Nicaragua. In every town Sandino had his Homer. He was of the constellation of Abd-el-Krim, Robin Hood, Villa, the untamed outlaws who knew only daring and great deeds, imbued ever with the tireless persistence to overcome insurmountable odds and confront successfully overwhelming power. His epos will grow—in Nicaragua, in Latin America, the wide world over. For heroes grow ever more heroic with time.

We rode on and on, forded a river several times and at last came to the house of a Liberal, Señor Vilches, a friend of Rivera's. Our horses were cared for. In the moonlight, we went down and bathed in the river, came back with our blood glowing. It was nearly midnight, but Vilches chatted endlessly. I could hardly keep my head up and my eyes open. For two weeks I had scarcely had any sleep, in some cases had ridden all night and all day. But at last, nearly two in the morning, we sat down to supper. My bed was stretched with canvas and over this was laid a sheet bordered by fully a foot of hand-embroidered lace. Almost a crime to spread my muddy poncho over it. Great stacks of corn, calabashes and chili were piled about the room, where even the chickens remained to roost. They rustled all night.

The following morning Vilches accompanied us as far as Trinidad, where he would branch off to an hacienda to get his wife. The news of Sandino in the vicinity led him to expect possible trouble—he preferred to have her by his side.

The morning grew hotter and hotter. While I was trying to fix my puttees, my horse took fright and gave me a bad fall on some rocks, an injury that gave me considerable pain for several years.

We expected to have to explain our presence to marines, but we swung through the high bluffs of Trinidad unaccosted. Avoiding the town, we separated from Vilches and went for a league beyond Trinidad to the little town of San Lorenzo, where Rivera had friends. On the way Rivera had shot an *iguana*, and our host, the principal store-keeper, had the tender meat cooked up for lunch, and I can well corroborate old Peter Martyr's eulogies:

These serpentes are lyke unto crocodiles, saving in bigness; they call them *guanas*. Unto that day none of owre men durste aduenture to taste of them, by reason of theyre horrible deformitie and lothsomnes. Yet the Adelentado being entysed by the pleasantness of the king's sister, Anacaona, determined to taste the serpentes. But when he felte the flesh thereof to be so delycate to his tongue, he fel to amayne without alfeare. The which thyng his companions perceiuing, were not behynde hym in greedyness; insomuch that they had now none other talke than of the sweetness of these serpentes, which they affirm to be of more pleasant taste than eyther our phesantes or partriches.

Afterwards we sat around the store talking about Sandino—though I had previously warned Rivera it would be much better for us to say we had come from Jinotega. But as any one who had seen Sandino wore a halo, Rivera could not keep his tongue from wagging.

A tall, frizzy-haired woman came in to make purchases. She listened to our talk, then said with a solemn shake of her head, "Ah, here one does not talk of Sandino, just the mention of his name is enough to get you in jail."

In San Lorenzo I had hoped to catch an auto down from Estelí, but as none came through, we decided to ride on to Sébaco, closer than Darío, and less dangerous for Rivera.

We saddled again and set off—a long, tiresome ride.

XLII   MARINE INTELLI-GENCE

1

I HOPED TO GET AN AUTO IMmediately on arriving in Sébaco. But dusk was already falling when we plodded down the dusty road between the homes into the lower part of the town. The only auto that came through was loaded to the gunwales.

We looked around for a place to stay. A young fellow accosted us, a local official, and demanded to see Rivera's permit to carry a gun. Rivera was a member of the Chamber of Deputies, hence could carry a gun; though being a Liberal he did not even dare to go to Managua to occupy his seat, despite the great protection to democracy given by the marines.

"Of course," said the youth arrogantly, "you are a Conservative?"

"Don't talk to me about politics," replied Rivera, "I am tending to my *rancho,* that's all. Where can we stay?"

"The only feasible place is the front *ramada* of Señor Hernández." He was another local official.

"I know him," whispered Rivera to me in sudden panic. "Years ago we had a bad quarrel. He is most bitter Conservative. We'll be sure to have trouble."

279

"I remain alone then—you'd better return this same night."

He was worried. "Are you sure you will be all right?"

"Perfectly," I reassured him, "merely a question of catching an auto—if not to-night, then to-morrow."

He took me over to the house, saluted his erstwhile enemy and hurriedly departed.

Señor Hernández told me he was glad to have me stay with him, but added, "I know that chap you were with. He's one of the worst Liberals about here. Where do you come from?" he demanded.

"From Jinotega," I lied.

"And where did you meet Colonel Rivera?"

"The marine Commandant in Jinotega recommended him to me as my guide."

"Oh, yes," said Hernández, satisfied; "of course for *such* things, men like that can be very useful."

While we were talking, the sheriff, who had demanded the gun permit from Rivera, dropped in with one of the local aldermen.

"Of course, you are a Conservative," they demanded, and in their tone was deathly rancor.

I assured them no intelligent man could be anything else. With that they insisted that I go over to the near-by store and have a drink with them. "The owner is a Liberal." The sheriff's tone implied that any one of that breed was worse than a rattlesnake. "But he's fairly decent and doesn't mix in politics."

The alderman declared I must remain over several days in Sébaco and see some of its historical landmarks; but I told him I had a Monday appointment with Chamorro, the political boss of the Conservative party, so that I would have to leave in the morning to get back in time. He was quite awed by my mention of the great Chamorro's name and agreed nothing should stand in the way of my fictitious appointment.

Every turn of phrase of these people made me realize how terribly bitter Nicaraguan politics had become, part of the aftermath of foreign control. On going out, no one paid for the drinks; the storeowner, being a Liberal, if he had objected, would have been run out of town.

2

When we had entered the store, a lean old muskrat of a man, about sixty, stood at the counter drinking potent sugar-cane *aguardiente* from a tall glass *with a straw*—a procedure which made me shudder. Shortly after, an old woman, stringy white hair hanging down over her walnut face, hobbled in with a knotted cane, angrily. Immediately she began railing and shaking her cane at the old man. For a second he stood petrified, then scuttled out with a little yelp.

"What's the trouble?" I demanded of my companions.

"He's the seventh son of the family," they responded, "and the bad egg. She's his mother; and every time he takes a drink she raises holy Ned. He has his accomplishments though. He can crack nuts with his toes."

"That's something worth seeing," I admitted. "Can't we get him back? I'll buy him another drink."

"Perhaps if his mother is invited too, she'll let him come," they suggested.

Presently they came shuffling back. I bought a quarter of a kilo of pecan nuts and scattered them about the floor. The old man kicked off his *guaraches,* and with a swooping motion of his foot and a prehensile clutch of his toes, he pounced on nut after nut and cracked each one instantly.

"He can also drive nails into the wall with his bare fist." The storekeeper pointed to the wall, covered with large nails. I bought some nails. The old man proceeded to drive in half a dozen, hammering them with his hard fist. His old mother stood by sipping her *aguardiente* through *her straw*, glowing with maternal pride at her aged son's accomplishments.

Supper of canned tuna and crackers from the store and hot chocolate prepared by Hernández' wife. My bed that night was a bench made of two narrow boards one higher than the other, making a very soft ridge where they joined.

My clothes were torn and mud-spattered, so early the following morning—Sunday—I went over to the store, bought a clean shirt and clean trousers—cheap workingmen's clothes, then proceeded to the river to take a swim. Suddenly I looked up to see a marine, rifle across his knees, watching me intently. I nodded to him, but he did not acknowledge my greeting, just sat there watching me with a suspicious expression as I dressed in my clean clothes.

He made no move to talk to me, so I went back to Hernández' house to wait for an auto. Hours passed but none came, only lumbering ox carts loaded with supplies creaked past, managed by drowsy marines.

Twice I sent one of Hernández' boys up to the high bluffs to the telegraph office to wire for an auto. Not even a reply! I walked up and down the dusty road. I watched Hernández, also a village barber, cut hair and shave. I followed a little procession carrying an image of Mary in pale blue silk through the village to collect money for Holy Week festivities. I watched an Indian girl, naked to the waist, spinning *pita* fiber on a hand-loom. Auto after auto passed by but all were full and did not even stop for my signal. I was willing to pay any price for transportation and was getting desperate.

Finally about noon I hailed a machine with a woman, four children and a *mozo* in addition to the chauffeur. At first they refused to take me. But the woman suddenly took pity on me, and told me I could have the front seat by the chauffeur. She, the *mozo* and all the children crowded into the back.

I then discovered why I had been unable to get an auto. News of Sandino's proximity to Jinotega had spread like wildfire. A combat was hourly expected. Everybody was rushing out of town. Every available auto had been commandeered. My new acquaintances asked me where I had come from.

"From a friend's hacienda near Trinidad."

"What news of Sandino there?"

"Everybody supposes him to be in Chipote."

"Impossible. He has been driven out of Chipote and is occupying San Rafael. They say he is within a few miles of Jinotega and is going to loot the city." The woman was nervous and distraught, half sick with worry. What would she have thought if I had told her I had just come from the camp of the terrible "bandit"?

The road in to Managua was chokingly dusty. The chauffeur complained bitterly. "The road is under repair by an American contractor. All he has done is to make it worse. It was well packed before. He's covered it with loose dirt. When the rainy season comes, not even an ox cart will be able to go through."

I could believe it. Already the marine trucks had cut his earth covering to pieces. Later in Managua, I was to meet the same contractor; solemnly he assured me that the roads to Managua and Estelí were in perfect shape to resist the rainy season. For his futile efforts, the Nicaraguan government was paying a pretty price.

3

In view of my disheveled appearance, I asked to be taken to a modest hotel. Even so, the hotel *mozo* was amused at my oilcloth *maleta*. Fortunately I had tossed away my broken straw hat just before entering the town.

The following morning I sallied forth to buy clothes. Ready made clothes simply cannot be bought in Managua, but I had the good fortune to find a fairly fitable palm beach suit that somebody had ordered and never called for. It would be about a week before I could get another made. I also bought a suit-case and putting in my belongings from the oilcloth *maleta*, I strolled up to the Hotel Lupone, the best hotel in Managua, hired a typewriter and set to work day and night on a series of articles.

I had been working several days when the hotel boy came up to my room. "Gentleman downstairs asks to come up to see you."

"His name?"

"He didn't give his name, he's a marine officer."

I cudgeled my brains—a marine officer?

"Shall I tell him to come up?" asked the boy.

"No, I'll come downstairs."

The boy led me to a burly fellow with a thick cow neck, fat wrinkles across the back.

He bellowed: "I am Lieutenant Larsen of the Intelligence Department."

I led him to a seat.

Again he bellowed. "How'd you get into Nicaragua?"

"None of your damn business." I stood up.

"Well," he added in a slightly less aggressive tone, "I just want to know, did you come by the east or the west coast?"

"None of your business," I repeated, about to go back to my room.

"Now look here—" he badgered.

It occurred to me to have some fun at the Lieutenant's expense. "It's none of your business, but as I have nothing to conceal—I came by the west coast."

"Then you came through Panama?"

"No, I came through Mexico, Guatemala, Salvador, and Honduras."

The Lieutenant glared at me accusingly. "Who do you know in Honduras?"

"I have many friends there."

"Well, who did you talk with?"

"If you really must know—" I drawled and gave him the name of old Doña Maria who had washed my clothes in the Hotel Roma.

He seemed relieved that I had not mentioned Froylán Turcios. "Through what port did you enter Nicaragua —Corinto?"

"No."

"Then you must have come through Tempisque"— (the port of entry on the Gulf of Fonseca).

"By the way," I interposed suavely, "what did you say your name was?"

"Larsen. So you came through Tempisque?" he persisted.

"Frankly, Lieutenant—er, by the way, what did you say your name was?"

"Larsen," he bellowed, visibly annoyed. "Did you or didn't you come through Tempisque?"

"Mr. Larsen, you know I don't speak Spanish very well, and all these names confuse me, they all sound so odd; but it sounded something like that."

The Lieutenant drew in an angry breath. "How does one get to the port of Tempisque?" he demanded.

"One takes a gasoline launch from Amapala and in about five hours one gets there."

"And so you came through Tempisque?"

"As I say, Lieutenant, the name of the place sounded something like that."

"Well, from Tempisque, where does one go?"

"I should judge, according to where one wants to go."

"I mean how does one get out of Tempisque?"

"Ordinarily, one takes horses to Chinandega."

"And so that's the way you came?"

"By the way, Mr.—, what did you say your name was?"

"Larsen," he bellowed, "*Lieutenant* Larsen."

"And whom did you say you represent?"

"Intelligence Department," he bellowed again. "Now did or didn't you come by way of Tempisque?"

"Lieutenant, don't you know that that's the business of the Nicaraguan Government to ascertain?"

His choler mounted, but he restrained himself.

"You are an American, ain't you? Well, I should think you'd wanna coöperate with us."

"As I told you, Lieutenant Larsen, I have nothing to conceal. The name of the place I entered sounded something like Tempisque, or Esquimula, or Canela, or something like that."

He switched the subject. "I just come to tell you—we know you intend to try to see Sandino and we can't give no guarantees."

"Don't you think you ought to wait till I ask?"

He snorted. "Well, *are* you going to try to see Sandino?"

"I did have the idea."

He bellowed again. "You'd better give it up. Better for you. It's dangerous. He hates Americans, he'd just kill you, that's all."

"That's my worry."

He ignored my comment. "Besides, we've got too much to do to look after Americans running around loose in the hills up there."

"As I say, Lieutenant, I did have the idea of going to see Sandino, but for the present I have abandoned it entirely."

The Lieutenant expanded with relief. He became more cordial. His insulting and aggressive tone changed. In a fatherly manner, he said, "You're darn wise not to go."

"Yes," I agreed, "all you say makes me believe that I had better abandon the project. It would be very difficult and dangerous. But don't you think that some one *ought* to go up and get his side of the story?"

The Lieutenant's tail-feathers stood up again. "Well, we can't give you no guarantees," he shouted.

."I must remind you again that I have not asked for any. Would you put any obstacles in my way?"

"I can't answer that question," he snorted angrily.

"But I've answered all of your questions," I replied mildly.

"Well, you'd have plenty of trouble getting through the American lines," he said in a tone of finality.

"I repeat, Lieutenant, er, what did you say your name was?"

He flew up to the rafters and squawked. "Larsen, L-A-R-S-E-N, Larsen," he repeated.

"All you say," I added, "makes me feel I have been wise in abandoning the idea of going to see Sandino at the present time. If in the future I change my mind, I shall let *you* know, Lieutenant Larsen."

He thumped his chest in surprise. "You will let *me* know?"

"With much pleasure. I have absolutely nothing to conceal."

He thought a moment. "Of course, you gotta passport?"

"Why don't you ask the Nicaraguan authorities?" I suggested. "An American citizen doesn't need a passport to enter Nicaragua. However, I don't mind telling you I have a passport in perfect order, visaed by the Nicaraguan consul in Salvador."

He stuck out his beefy hand. "Le' me see it."

"I'm very sorry, Mr. Larsen, but I intend to show it only to the proper authorities—namely, the proper Nicaraguan officials."

"Well, you got newspaper credentials, ain't you?" he demanded. "You can show me those, I guess."

"I have, but they are purely for professional pur-

288

poses, to show to anybody from whom I wish to secure information, or who is more informative than you have been. I am glad to show them, but *not to Lieutenant Larsen.*"

He became angry again. "You come right up with me to the American Legation," he ordered, "and present your passport and credentials."

"Lieutenant Larsen, I am very busy this morning. You have already taken up considerable of my time with no benefit to me and even less to yourself. I am unable to go with you to the Legation at the present moment."

"Well," he sputtered, "the Minister's free now. Why don't you come on up?"

"The Minister may be free, but *I* am not free."

"I'm telling you," he said menacingly, "you'll save yourself a whole lot of trouble, a hell of a lot of trouble. You'd better come up now and show your credentials. I'm giving you a straight tip." His tone was very threatening.

"I'm sorry, Lieutenant, I see no reason why an American citizen should not call upon his Minister—if he wants to. I see no reason why an American newspaper man should not call upon his Minister—if he believes he can secure authentic information. I intend to call upon Minister Eberhardt, but when *I* am ready and not before. I see no reason to pester him with useless questions before I am adequately informed regarding the situation here. Besides I am busy just now and I may be busy for some time to come."

"Well, if you won't come now," Larsen said, "will you go this afternoon?"

"Very unlikely. It might be this afternoon, or tomorrow, or—next week."

"If you went this afternoon, when could you go?"

"Certainly not before six or seven—and of course diplomats don't work at such hours."

"I'll be waiting here downstairs for you at six—*sharp*," said Larsen dictatorially, "and *the Minister will be ready to receive you.*"

"Lieutenant Larsen, don't waste your time. Managua is not a large place. I can easily find the Legation by myself. In short, I shall not go with you to the American Legation this afternoon, nor the day after to-morrow, nor the next week, in fact, never. Good-day, Sir."

"You'd better go up to-day, you'll save yourself a lot of trouble," he called after me threateningly.

XLIII UNDIPLO-
MATIC
LETTERS

1

Two days later, my work finished, I called at our Lega-tion. In spite of Larsen's threats nothing had hap-pened to me, nor did he re-turn.

Minister Eberhardt, tall, lean, genial, received me at once. I informed him I had come to Nicaragua to study the situation and write a series of articles.

With customary diplomatic reserve, he replied he would be glad to be of any possible service. "But I understand you are pretty much against our policy here."

"I have come with an open mind to be shown the true facts. And you are the first person in Managua upon whom I have called."

He was pleased at that and thawed out, repeating more positively he would be glad to be of any possible service.

"I hope to meet *all* the important people on the scene; I should like to meet President Díaz, Señor Chamorro, Moncada, etc."

"Quite possibly we can arrange the interviews."

"Thank you. I would prefer to get them myself. But I do want to meet *all* the important people on the scene." Abruptly I added, "Don't you think, Minister Eberhardt, that General Sandino is one of the important men on the scene?"

He was a bit taken aback. "Why . . . er . . . undoubtedly."

"He is the only one with whom I should like to have you arrange an interview."

He smiled patiently.

"Don't you believe somebody ought to go up and get his side of the story?" I persisted.

"I suppose so. But the marines have been trying to interview Sandino for almost a year. I imagine it would be a trifle *dangerous*."

"Would you put any obstacles in my way?"

Eberhardt tilted his head. "No, *we* would put no obstacles in your way. But I can't answer for the marines. Quite possibly they would not consider it convenient."

"Mr. Eberhardt, you are the first person on whom I have called in Managua, but you are not the first person I have called on in Nicaragua. I have already interviewed General Sandino."

"Impossible!—How did you do that?"

"Very simple. I hired a horse in Tegucigalpa, and rode overland for two weeks."

"And where did this interview take place?"

"In San Rafael del Norte, on February 2nd, five days ago."

Eberhardt began to realize I might really be telling the truth, fantastic though it sounded. "Wait a minute, until I call my assistant." He presented me to Dana Munro, the author of a sincere book on Central America; he still retained a studious air, but had now acquired the air of an apologist.

We chatted for a few moments. Eberhardt then called

in General McCoy (in charge of the elections). General McCoy called in his two chief assistants.

They fired questions at me—the details of my trip, Sandino, rural conditions.

"What does Sandino want?" demanded General McCoy. (Curious to be fighting a man for a year without even knowing his purpose.)

2

General McCoy is one of these iron-willed, super-logical, single-track types whose stern jaw carries not an ounce of compromise. After consultation with General Crowder, Kellogg, Hughes and others, he had formed an election program for Nicaragua. This program had become as holy as the Bible, not an "i" could be dotted, not a "t" be crossed; and General McCoy was now the Moses on the Sinai of Nicaragua with his decalogue on tablets of stone—an election law—"The McCoy Election Law" for the Nicaraguan people. This law, and its enforcement, he would pass and put into effect if all hell froze over. Nothing that he might discover on the Nicaraguan scene would cause him to alter by one iota the program he had mapped out.

Undoubtedly, without the unlimited backing of all the powers of the United States, General McCoy would have been an utter failure. With all the power of the United States behind him, he could have made the Nicaraguans build a ladder to Mars. General McCoy nevertheless prided himself on being a hard-headed realist. As a matter of fact, he had hit upon an ideal scheme for the salvation of Nicaragua—a utopian democratic perfection, which he was putting over with the faith of a Loyola and the same inquisitorial methods. A utopia about which he was utterly dogmatic—which he explained to me with fanatic zeal—as dogmatic, as undeviating as the most rabid Communist.

Ironically, there is a curious resemblance between the thought processes of the American Communist and the American Imperialist. Both move in a world of unreality. The Imperialist in Nicaragua, Haiti, or the Philippines can ignore local political realities because he has all power. The Communist ignores American political realities because he has no power. The Communist is fighting for a cause, the welfare of mankind. The Imperialist is also a crusader, fighting for the improvement of backward peoples. Both are dogmatic, earnest, sincere, sentimental. Both believe in the implantation of an ideal upon people by force. The apologists who drip greasy platitudes to oil the gun-carriages of our target-practice in Latin America are often hypocrites and bootlickers or plain racketeers; but our financial and political pro-consuls and our marine officers are fanatically sincere, imbued with a religious fervor of doing good. They are just as sincere as Mr. Thomas or Mr. Foster, and their convictions are just as unshakeable.

The credo of the Imperialist is simple; he believes that the United States represents the final word in human perfection; that all Americans are always honest, and that nearly all foreigners are devious and dishonest; that all Americans are brave and most foreigners cowards. He believes in good roads, sanitation, the strict enforcement of law, stability, work, machinery, efficiency, the punctilious payment of debts, and democracy. These things are written, never to be erased on the stone tablets handed down from the Sinai of his own American experience. They have, he feels, proven of worth in the United States, therefore, they must be equally advisable for all peoples. An extrovert, he does not analyze his own deeper motives nor does he see the contradiction between his faith in democracy and his fervent belief in his own race superiority. He never stops to try to reconcile his inner conviction that backward, dark peoples are incapable of progress, efficiency, honesty or democracy with his belief that the only possible way for a foreign people to be happy is to be standardized into the mold already created in the United States. Because of his faith in the value of lightness of skin, he hobnobs with the aristocratic Creoles who have exploited and betrayed their countries since the first days of independence. While devising and enforcing schemes for honest democratic elections, he is telling you that the only salvation for Mexico or Nicaragua is a good dictator. But he soon quarrels with the strong, wise and crooked men capable of becoming dictators (as did General McCoy with Emiliano Chamorro), because they cleverly block his own freedom of action, and turns to weaker sycophants like Adolfo Díaz, or Cuadro Pasos, or Moncada. The Imperialist at work abroad is muddle-headed but he is fantastically honest; the shining aura of the crusade always mantles all his acts.

This grows out of the situation in which the colonial administrator, the American business man, the marine officer and the financial expert finds himself. In case of intervention, as in Haiti or Nicaragua, political power is divorced from all organic connection with the politics, the government, and the culture against which it is exercised. Power, thus divorced, creates the possibility of irrational idealism and the implantation of alien systems of thought and action by force. So long as the force remains, they can be imposed; but those imposing them have no conception, because, among other things, they lack subtlety and imagination of the havoc this wreaks upon native ways of thought and character and habits. A native politician must play with and utilize the social forces and beliefs which exist in his country. The foreign ruler is freed from this necessity; and however well meaning his intention, the system of thought and life he imposes can never even be a good graft on the old stock; it is not even a good insecticide to kill old parasitisms; it is rather a new skin laid over old sores, while underneath, the corruption which otherwise might have been eliminated goes on eating more deeply into the tissues of the social life. This is why a bad native government is always, in the long run, probably better than the best foreign one.

Sometime after I left Nicaragua, the Nicaraguan parliament with a last despairing show of dignity refused to pass McCoy's law; and so President Díaz passed it by edict—cramming down legality by illegality and backed, of course, in the imposing of a pseudo-legality by illegal means by the marines, McCoy, and other representatives.

3

General McCoy was very much interested to know if a letter Admiral Sellers had dropped over the Sandino lines by aeroplane had arrived at its destination.

Without saying so, I had the original in my pocket.

Merely telling McCoy I had seen and read it, I gave him a brief resumé of the contents.

"The man is no fool!" exclaimed McCoy. "And has he replied to it?"

"He has." (I had his signed reply in my pocket.)

"Do you know whether it was sent?"

"General Sandino requested me to deliver the letter in person to Admiral Sellers, but I had to decline."

"Why?"

I smiled. "Probably you have heard of the famous Logan law passed about a century ago by the Congress of the United States? This law decrees that no unauthorized American citizen may conduct negotiations, carry messages, or give advice to any foreign government or to any foreigner with whom the American State Department has a controversy. It has many other blanket provisions which I do not recall, but that law made it impossible for me to bring a reply from Sandino to Admiral Sellers."

"But," protested McCoy, "we would never have used the law against *you*."

"Very kind, General McCoy, but I am not so sure that Admiral Sellers or Mr. Kellogg would be equally kind. Besides I do not care to violate the laws of my country."

"Quite admirable, quite admirable! But do you know the contents of his reply?"

"It is addressed to 'The American representative of Imperialism in Nicaragua,'" and I summarized his proposals and promises. "You know, General McCoy, as a newspaper man I have the right to gather any documentary evidence from any source in the world. I have an exact copy of Sandino's reply. If you want a copy of my copy you may have it, if you promise not to give it to the press. I will send it to you as soon as I return to my hotel."

He manifested his gratitude. He promptly cabled it to Washington; and President Coolidge announced pompously to the press: We now have Sandino's demands but do not find it opportune to make them public. McCoy also cabled to Sellers, then in Panama, and Sellers jumped on a battleship and hastened to Corinto.

4

I chatted with Eberhardt, the secretary, General McCoy and his aides for the better part of the morning. They would not have been so cordial had I been on my way to see Sandino instead of having already seen him. But scrambled eggs cannot be unscrambled.

They were all serious and honest gentlemen, "men of measured mirth"—conscientiously trying to carry out their assigned task.

All this builds up a corps of paid interventionists. However conscientious a man may be, if he is on the payroll of the Nicaraguan Government, the American Government and the New York bankers all at the same time, his financial advantages overreach those of the ordinary run of fellow human beings—the old story of the dead weight of bureaucracy.

Before leaving the Legation, I said to Eberhardt abruptly, "Who was that damn fool Lieutenant Larsen, who came down to my hotel two days ago and tried to browbeat me?"

"Oh!" protested Eberhardt. "We have nothing to do with him, nothing whatsoever. He is from the Intelligence Corps. Probably he has his duties to do. I know nothing whatever about him."

"I am glad to hear you have nothing to do with him, for if there are many more asses like him around, you certainly will mess things up around here."

"Well, we have nothing to do with him," repeated Eberhardt.

"Even if you have nothing to do with him, I consider it my obligation and my right to enter a formal protest here in the Legation and to you, our Minister, against such sort of treatment being accorded to an American citizen by an American official."

5

McCoy, Eberhardt, and other American officials assured me with ready nimbleness that we would hold a fair election and get out. We had descended upon Nicaragua with a swarm of armed marines, of American officials, of American experts, and colonial carpet-baggers, to impose American theories of government and democracy by force (a procedure contrary to these very theories). There were either some hare-brained utopians in the State Department or somebody was playing blindman's buff with the American public.

We are still in Nicaragua. We are likely to stay. We multiplied the machinery of American intervention; we multiplied lucrative jobs; and all this tends towards self-perpetuation. More and more machinery—customs collectors, High Commission, Claims Commission, Financial Experts, Election Overseers, Marine Officials, National Guard Officials—a corps of high paid representatives, and Nicaragua footing the bill. This very machinery, inevitably, in its desire for self-perpetuation, ever tends toward definite partisanship in local affairs. I found little enthusiasm in these men to better the economic condition of the mass of Nicaraguan people, to promote education—things that would ultimately provide a basis for orderly political succession. Instead —great avidity to get work on the claims from the last revolution—$16,000,000 had already been pegged up. If, according to past experiences, you are a New York banker, you can buy up claims at a fraction of their face value and have them recognized at face value plus interest; also if you are a Nicaraguan official in power your claims are largely recognized. But if you are a poor American or Nicaraguan, you may be informed: "New York now permits us to pay you ten percent upon the dollar."

General McCoy told me: "If the Government has to dig right in to pay these claims, this will teach the people how costly are revolutions." The people know that already. The real purpose is to keep heckling the Government financially, obliging it to place new loans at a ruinous rate to meet claims. Thus each government's strength is sapped so that revolutions cannot be dominated save by American marines. Sound reconstruction is made more difficult. A vicious circle.

Nicaragua at the time of my visit, after eighteen years of almost constant American meddling, much of which was attended by American financial, military and political control and by the employment of high-priced experts, was in a truly miserable condition. The argument for or against intervention cannot be based on its material benefits, actual or supposed, to a people;

yet it is significant that when I was there, its cities were dilapidated, its public buildings run down and dirty; that it had fewer miles of railway and roads than under Zelaya whom Knox, because of personal investments, overthrew in 1910; there are fewer schools. The north coast in Zelaya's time had over forty Government schools; to-day it hasn't half a dozen. The flourishing traffic of Zelaya's time up and down the great artery, the San Juan River and Lake Nicaragua, is to-day practically non-existent. I later made the trip at the risk of my life. The post-office service, and in fact nearly every public service, was a joke. Nicaragua, under our paternal tutelage for so many years, had become the most backward and miserable of all Central American Republics.

XLIV HOW THE NEWS IS MADE

1

I HAD RETURNED TO THE hotel and had sent McCoy a copy of Sandino's reply to Sellers when a knock sounded on my door. There stood Lieutenant Larsen. Very politely, he asked if he might talk with me. "I have a personal message from General Feland" (head of marine operations).

Obviously, he had tumbled to the fact that I had made a fool of him the other day. He came in as though walking on eggs. His courtesy could now be cut with a knife. "General McCoy phoned General Feland you had interviewed Sandino, and General Feland is very anxious to talk to you. He would greatly appreciate it if you would come up to see him. Of course, now understand, please, you are quite free not to come if you don't care to, but he would consider it a real favor if you drop in at your convenience. Remember, at your own convenience and at the hour most convenient to you; and if you don't want to you don't have to come at all."

"Have you had your lunch, Lieutenant Larsen? . . . Then I think we might go now and see the General. Perhaps you would be so kind as to accompany me."

"Well, yes, that would be fine."

"First, though, permit me to apologize for pulling the wool over your eyes the other day. I wished to tell my story to the Minister first."

He pounded his chest and boomed, "No, it is I who should apologize."

"To be perfectly frank with you, Lieutenant, I think you are right; I might also remark that I entered a formal protest at the Legation against your manner of browbeating me."—And I repeated the exact words I had used to the Minister.

"Furthermore, permit to give you some advice about running your job, so you won't be taken in so easily the next time. I take it that the function of the Intelligence Office is to gain information which will be of service to the marines and to the Government. Usually, one does not obtain information by browbeating people, unless the person is already behind bars. As I told you at the outset of our conversation, I had nothing to conceal, and if you had approached me like a gentleman, the chances are that I would have told you the whole story. You would have gone back to your office with the truth rather than a false account about which your superiors are probably now laughing. What is more, the marines in Nicaragua would have known the exact whereabouts of Sandino on the second of February—two days sooner than they know now."

(Up until the time that I arrived in Managua, the American authorities had not precise information as to Sandino's whereabouts since he had left Chipote. They knew the rebellious troops were in San Rafael del Norte but they had no assurance that Sandino was with them.)

"Probably," I continued to Larsen, "I am mistaken in thinking that the Intelligence Office has for its major function the securing of accurate information. Probably its function is to browbeat and threaten private citizens, but we have to admit that, in any case, the joke is. on you. After crossing five countries with the express object of interviewing Sandino, when the periodicals which I represented had announced the fact to the world, I discover you people did not know of my whereabouts or what I had been doing. That is an incredible commentary on the intelligence of the Intelligence Department."

I was not through with Mr. Larsen yet; and though he came to see me a number of times and was exceedingly polite and amiable, his thick bull-neck with its heavy wrinkles across the back annoyed me. I told the story liberally around Managua, till all Managua was laughing at him. Lieutenant Larsen suddenly found, so he told his superiors, that he could be much more useful nearer the front in Matagalpa.

2

The day I went to the Legation (since the game of Imperialism is a little more ruthless than even bridge parties), I decided to come boldly out in the open and lay all my cards on the table. For the same afternoon I cited the representatives of the local and foreign press and spilled just enough of the story to pique interest. It claimed the front page of the Nicaraguan newspapers for three days. This publicity at this moment was sufficient to prevent my being molested by either native or American authorities, as would have otherwise occurred.

At the time I arrived in Managua, a number of special correspondents had arrived on the scene. Prior to that, all the news had been sewed up in the customs office. Mr. Clifford D. Ham, American collector for fourteen years, represented the United Press and his assistant, Mr. Irving Lindbergh, the Associated Press. Customarily, these were the only two important newspaper men on the scene, thus insuring that only the strictest official versions would be sent out to the American public.

Mr. Ham, a typical pussyfooter, played me a trick. Before I knew he represented the United Press, he invited me to his office, *in his official capacity as customs collector*, and led me to tell much of my story which I otherwise would have reserved, and put it on the wire.

Fortunately, by the time I had arrived, the Sandino revolt had attracted various newspaper and movie men. There was, at the time, a standing offer of fifty thousand dollars to any one who would bring in five yards of film of Sandino's soldiers in action. The Associated Press now had, in addition to Lindbergh, an elderly individual whom the organization had definitely retired to Panama but who was now rushed up to Nicaragua, an honest though simple-minded gentleman, physically quite incapable of rustling around in the heat for the facts, so that most of his work was done by the other correspondents. Mr. Denny, of a New York daily, an unusually brilliant reporter, had been sent down to Bluefields on a battleship and then had been carried across to Managua in an army plane. He confided to me that in view of these and other courtesies he had dared not send out a single word which was not "official." Later he wrote a pseudo-liberal book *Dollars for Bullets* to exonerate our actions in Nicaragua. The Hearst people had sent down an executive, Mr. Williams, an official apologist, who went out of his way to twist every incident into a form which he thought would be highly agreeable to the American authorities on the scene—with an undue proportion of brains to maintain him in such a craven capacity. The *Chicago News* had sent down a slapstick youth who wrote only the gossip of the buddies, with definite orders to lay off all "political stuff."

Such was the source of all our information about Nicaragua.

3

General Feland, a powerful man with bushy eyebrows, took the cake for apathy. His drawling voice, his apparent lack of interest in everything, his completely bored air with his present job, the way he sat on the end of his spine in most unmilitary fashion—all betokened a supreme indifference to existence which placed him at once in quite a remote realm. I really wondered why he wanted to see me. To all my inquiries he droned: "You can get that information from Major Glass."

"And how will all this terminate?" I asked him.

"Oh, the bird will fall sometime," he drawled. "They all do sooner or later."

"If I remember, it was about seven years in the Philippines and seven years in Haiti, but now that we have more publicity on these things, I rather imagine you will get it in the neck if this lasts seven years in Nicaragua."

He grunted a languid unintelligible reply. "What do you think of Sandino?"

"He is not a bandit, call him a fool, a fanatic, an idealist, a patriot—according to your point of view; but certainly he is not a bandit."

Drawled the General: "Of course, in the army, we use the word 'bandit' in a technical sense, meaning the member of a band."

"Then Sousa is also a bandit?"

He did not deign to smile. I persisted. "In the publicity which you give out to the United States, of course, you explain to the dear public that you use the word 'bandit' in its technical sense; you have no ulterior motive in your reports?"

"Guess you've got us on the hip there," was his reply in the same indifferent tone.

He changed the subject. "There's only one thing I am interested in—how was that message of Admiral Sellers sent?"

I repeated what I had told General McCoy.

He smiled slightly. "I guess you are wise. There was another chap around here who had an idea to go up to see Sandino. We warned him to be careful about just such things."

"By the way," I asked, "can you give me details of the supply convoys Sandino has captured, or should I get that information from Major Glass?"

For the one and only time Feland threw off his apathy. He jerked upright. "That's a lie," he cried. "We haven't lost a single convoy, not one."

"How did Sandino get hold of American supplies, then—uniforms, guns, foodstuffs?"

"We lost no convoys," repeated Feland, and subsided to the end of his spine.

When I left, the General pulled himself painfully from his lounging position. "Come and see me again any time while you are here," he said with a show of cordiality, "and I will tell Major Glass to give you all the information that it is possible to give out."

I went out, convinced that the only reason Feland wished to see me was to try to pin the Logan act on me.

1

UNTHINKABLE TO LEAVE
Nicaragua without a look at
the route of the proposed
canal, which in great part
had served as an excuse
for our marine stupidities.

In Managua it was impossible to obtain definite information about traveling to the Atlantic coast—about
two hundred miles away as the crow flies, though earlier
in Nicaraguan history, the trans-continental route
across the country was one of the great traveled highways of the world. But now Nicaragua is virtually two
separate countries. All the political activities of the
country center on the Pacific coast. The entire region
from the lake across to the Atlantic is scarcely inhabited,
mountainous, swampy, full of impassable jungles. The
Atlantic is a distinct lumber and banana kingdom,
where as much English as Spanish is spoken. Easier to
go through Panama from Corinto to Bluefields than
straight across the country. No one could give me any
authentic information.

Nothing to do but set out . . . Sleepy Masaya on a
little lake—Nindiri. Beyond, the old volcano . . .
With wrinkled Juan, a Chorotegan Indian, up to the
red and yellow rock plateau on the edge of the wide
crater . . . site of ancient Indian sacrifices . . . circling long-tail *jijaves* . . . down through groves of

marañones, yellow-berry nanzis, nisperos, mameys.

Granada . . . A haphazard picturesque little place, faintly reminiscent of Italian towns. It was founded by Hernández de Córdoba in 1522; and Thomas Gage, the English monk who traveled through Nicaragua in 1665, calling the country "Mahomet's Paradise," tells us that the houses of Granada were fairer than those of León, the merchants were wealthy. They traded with Guatemala, Honduras, Salvador, Panama, Cartagena. The King's treasure often passed this way from Guatemala and Mexico to avoid Dutch and English buccaneers in the Gulf of Mexico. While Gage was there "in one day there entered six *requas* [three hundred mules each], from Salvador and Honduras alone, laden with indigo, cochineal and hides; and two days after, from Guatemala came in three more, one laden with silver, another with sugar and the other with indigo." In those days the city was one of the richest in the Americas, and on various occasions was attacked by French and English pirates.

Now it drowses in forgotten isolation. The old town was entirely burnt down by Walker and his filibusters in 1856, and was rebuilt in terraces, making abrupt breaks in the streets, so that modern traffic is very circumscribed. A stately municipal palace still dominates a tree-decked arcaded plaza, overlooked by the elaborate Conservative Club, where politicians sit all day long sipping cold drinks.

Granada has always been the Conservative center of Nicaragua; León, further north, the Liberal center. Granada is fanatically Catholic, feudal, made up of a wealthy merchant class. To the people of Granada, Protestant, Mason, Liberal, heretic, Jew, Bolshevik, are syn-

onymous words; periodically the front of the local
Protestant mission is bespattered with human excrement. León is Liberal, anti-clerical, middle-class; its
people are enlightened and aware of the modern world.
The feud between these two cities is centuries old; indeed is probably rooted in differences between the pre-
conquest Indian groups inhabiting the two regions. The
natives about León were quiet, settled, good-tempered,
cheerful, but ever-obliged to protect themselves from
the restless, treacherous, cruel inhabitants of the lake
region. An old Indian feud has been rechanneled into a
modern political feud.

2

One day at the Conservative Club next to my table was
seated a cold-cream-faced youth, wearing a spotless
Panama hat, immaculate pale blue silk shirt, lavender
tie, a blue serge coat and white flannels. From his pocket
cascaded a lilac silk handkerchief. He exuded perfume.
His black hair plastered down smooth and shiny—he
was too sweet for words.

Along the walk in front of the club piazza passed
a well-built girl with firm springy tread. She wore low
shoes. She looked strong. Her legs were sturdy. Her
physique, her bearing, her complexion, suggested she was
an American. The cold-creamed youth sipped through
his straw and eyed her languidly, then with growing interest.

Suddenly he galvanized into action, hurried down the
steps with his delicate cane and overtook the young lady

near the entrance to the adjacent hotel. In poor but intelligible English, he said:

"Mees, where I have the pleasure meeting you?"

She turned on him with wide blue eyes, looking him over scornfully from head to toe. She was half a head taller than he. "Beat it, bum!" she said in a clear, unmistakable Yankee tone that rang across the plaza.

He smiled wanly and said, "Mees, I am sure—"

She took one step forward. With a masculine jab from the shoulder, she cut him under the chin.

He fell flat in the thick dust which had accumulated during the long rainy season. A white cloud rose up from the place where he had disappeared. When he finally emerged, sputtering dust, his face was leprous, his white flannels ruined.

A titter rippled along the wide piazza of the club.

3

Every Tuesday morning the *Victoria,* a fifty-year-old ferry boat, left for San Carlos at the head of the San Juan River.

Tuesday morning, ready to embark, I discovered I had neglected to make necessary purchases—soap, quinine, and several other articles. Little time was left, so I gave a five-dollar bill to the hotel boy to buy what I needed, while I set out in one of the old-fashioned phaëtons, which rattled through the dusty streets, for the shore of the lake, where rows of palm trees stood stiff in the eternal breeze, fronds permanently bent landwards.

My baggage was duly carted down to the rickety

wharf. Time passed. The hotel boy did not show up. I
sent numerous urchins in search of him. "He made his
get-away," I thought to myself. "Five dollars was too
much for him."

But exactly two minutes before the boat was sched-
uled to pull out and the warning whistle was screech-
ing, he came tearing down the wharf, and pell-mell
through the crowd.

On the slip of paper I had given him, I had written
Palmolive soap, and though I had told him to get some
other kind if necessary, he had gone to every drug store
in Granada until he had found that particular brand.
Also, I had told him to get a small quantity of quinine;
but the tall package he brought me was big enough to
contain moth balls. He could not resist spending all of
the five dollars, so I had enough quinine for an army.

A twenty-four-hour trip across the lake, with stops
along the way. We threaded through a series of low
cone-islands, smiling and green, here and there a
thatched hut under tall palms, truly a fairyland picture.
To the right, its flank rising out of the lake, ridges running out from it like the legs of a lobster, towered
Momobacho, five thousand feet into the clear sky; and
far across to our left the riven hills and rough craters
of Chontales. We creaked past the larger islands—Zapatera, next Ometépec (two mountains). On the latter
are two swift rising volcanic cones, at the green base
of which could be espied occasional thatched Japanese-
like fishermen's huts; and here and there, where the lava
has weathered sufficiently, a stray corn patch.

On board was a marine sergeant to guard the mails.
He had done nothing else but ride this lake for six
months, and was sick of the job. Our passengers were a

motley assortment—Indian types, mestizos; negroes from the north coast, cattlemen, ranchers and voluptuous women of the tropics—dark eyes, sinuous bodies, clad in effective black or in light yellow or reds; and two American missionaries—one of whom lost his straw hat in the stiff breeze.

Much baggage was stacked on the hatchway—sacks, bundles, hand bags from brown pasteboard to alligator skin, woven *mecate* sacks, oranges, bird-cages. Birds and women kept up an incessant chattering in their shrill yet musical voices.

Later in the afternoon we arrived at San Jorge, the entry port for the town of Rivas. I had been seasick, but had soon gotten over it, and was now hungry. The boat had to remain here four hours unloading supplies and taking cargo, so I went ashore and ate a meal of rice and chicken on the beach under a thatched roof. An Indian woman cooked the food over a tin brazier in terra-cotta pots, and served pineapple juice in thick green native glasses.

Bathing suits had never been heard of in San Jorge and a big sign announced that men would bathe fifty yards to the right of the pier; women fifty yards to the left—anyone disobeying this would be turned over to the authorities.

The sun sank over the Rivas hills, touching the Orosi volcano far to the south with lavender. It was dark before our boat pulled out and slid into a strong off-shore cross current that churned us steadily. The moon came up over the islands. One of the passengers thrummed a guitar.

Few passengers were left. Among them was a large family of negroes of Syrian origin but long resident in

Bluefields. They spoke a queer sort of English, a queer sort of Spanish and a queer sort of French. With one of them, Tooker, a cordial young chap, employed by the radio corporation, I made friends; and he promptly took charge of me for the rest of the trip to Bluefields, tending to my meals and getting supplies. There were only two cabins on board, and one of these was occupied by the captain and the other by the marine officer, so we hired a cot from the steward and slept out on deck. Devilish cold, for the wind blew eternally.

Dawn found us at the other side of the lake, with Boqueta Island a golden glimmer in the early sun. We ran into the shadow of the hills to the little port of San Miguelito and lost the sun. The air was damp and cold. Here were large masses of pulpy floating plants on which egrets had alighted. A series of thatched roofs clambered from the sandy beach straight up the steep hill. The entire town was still in shadow, and the houses melted into the dense vegetation and gray mist on the hill crest. On this side of the lake everything was green and glistening.

About eleven we reached San Carlos with its ruined fort now draped with moss and maiden-hair ferns. San Carlos is set at the outlet of the San Juan River and the inlet of Rio Frio, haunt of the Guataro Indians. The day had become sizzling. The lake glistened, the vegetation gave back an intolerable sheen. The shore sands glowed and the houses glowed.

4

Transit down the river was made in a large scow pushed by a gasoline launch. Tooker transferred my baggage, then we reconnoitered the grass-grown town which ran uphill and tumbled downhill, dilapidated—a forgotten settlement, hodge-podge architecture, thatched roofs, tiles, rusted tins—a tangle of despair. Built by the English, the dwellings were of flimsy wood and adobe, many were rotting away. Scroll-work sagged, balconies hung broken. The population was just as hodge-podge —Melchora Indians, negroes, zambos, mestizos, a few whites—all in an equal state of patchwork, to judge by their multi-colored clothes.

After a meal of luscious *savalo* river fish, *tule* (a thickish gruel of parched corn, cacao and sugar), served in a carved gourd, and fried *plátanos,* no bread or tortillas, we bought supplies for the boat trip—canned goods, plenty of fruit, enormous watermelons, pineapples, oranges, bananas and limes and stowed them away in the cook's galley. Tooker also bought a few cakes of *chancaca,* or hard brown sugar.

Walking down the steep street in San Carlos, I was accosted by a heavy-set but simple individual: "Are you the man who went to Sandino's camp?"

"Yes."

"Were you accompanied by General Siqueiros?"

"And who are you, pray tell?"

"I am his brother." He looked around a bit apprehensively. "Is he going to join Sandino?" he inquired in a worried tone.

· "No," I replied, lying to relieve his preoccupation, "he just went with me as a guide."

The man's relief was manifest. "My brother is very impulsive. I was afraid he was going to be so foolish as to get mixed up in this trouble."

At the moment I thought of Siqueiros' last words to me, "Sandino is going to shoot me," and I have often wondered what his brother, the simple, unpretentious man who stopped me in the grass-grown cobbled street of San Carlos is thinking now. . . .

"Let us call on the Commandant," suggested Tooker.

"Why?"

"It is always customary in these parts."

"Is he a Conservative or a Liberal?"

"A Conservative."

"But I thought you were a Liberal?"

"Oh, yes, I call myself that, but on the Atlantic coast we are not really Liberals or Conservatives, we are *costeños*—we belong to the coast; which ever side wins in Managua, we are badly treated."

The Commandant, like all Central American commandants, was squat, fat, and very Indian. In his face lurked suspicion of everything and everybody. He had no use for Sandino, but was glad that he was stirring things up and making elections more difficult, because, as he put it, "Your marines are determined to elect Moncada, the cursed Liberal."

XLVI THE CANAL ROUTE

1

WE WERE SUPPOSED TO PULL out of sleepy San Carlos at one o'clock. But not until four did an Indian boy stand on the edge of the scow and blow a long shrill blast on a conch shell to announce our departure. The long *bongo*, or scow, had a small cook's galley; the rest of it was hollowed out for merchandise. About a third of it was roofed over to keep off the sun—the *chopa*. The wise travelers were those with hammocks to sling from side to side. The only accommodation for the passengers, as well as the chickens and one pig, was on top of the cargo —bales, smelly rawhides, a sewing machine, muddy banana suckers. I appropriated a bale and a box for my bed.

We shunted from the landing, past women washing bright clothes on the stones, and drifted on down. For the first twenty-five miles to the Toro rapids, the banks were fairly low; stretching acres of coarse *gamalote* grass, high cane, and palm trees; then we passed between the high impenetrable walls of the jungle, which line the river with scarcely a break until it flows into Greytown, walls which became higher and denser as we neared the sea.

On board was an American cattleman from up the San Carlos River on the Costa Rica side; also a German-American, one of those queer foreign types scattered around the San Juan River. Like others he had bought a cattle *hato* years ago when the canal was first started, and had vegetated there ever since, waiting hopefully for the day when it will finally be built and he will become rich. More than twenty years have passed, and people such as these are still waiting. They seize every stranger by the lapel and ask in a taut tone—"And the canal? When will they build the canal?"

Here and there a little inlet or a little knoll, surmounted by green farms, broke the monotony of the jungle. We stopped frequently to leave or collect mail, now and then to drop a passenger or take one aboard, or to handle freight. A lazy, slow going, with no effort on the part of the crew to hurry.

Long after dark, the launch shoved the scow and us under dense trees and disappeared up a side stream for more banana suckers. Not till an hour later did it come chugging back. It was late when we sighted the lights of El Castillo and drew up before the little landing. Rapids filled the night with their continuous roar. Boys seized our baggage, and we stumbled for about half a mile along a grassy lane and broken horse-car tracks to the house of a woman who put up travelers.

Most of the passengers remained to sleep on the scow. Four of us, however, were lodged in the large front *sala* of the whitewashed house fronting the river. The woman prepared hot chocolate for us—she had no coffee and no bread. Cots were set up for us, and the big hanging oil light was dimmed.

Not wishing to buy mosquito netting for what I imagined would be one night on the river, at the advice of a marine officer in Granada I had bought citronella to smear on my hands and face. But the buzzing mosquitoes sank their stingers into me all night long. I am now fully convinced that mosquitoes have a real fondness for citronella. The first thing I did in the morning was to take the bottle and hurl it into the river.

2

El Castillo lies at the foot of a hill somewhat resembling Chapultépec in Mexico. On its summit is a construction now called Castillo Viejo—Old Castle.

We sallied forth to reconnoiter. A damp, dripping morning—all mornings the year round are like this. As a result the town is eternally green and mossy, almost moldy. Grass and moss and fungus sprout from every roof and niche and cranny; the boards of the gray houses are soaked and rotted.

We clambered up from below "La Plataforma" where was located our lodging house along the abandoned track. A green lane twisted up toward the crest of the hill.

Just before reaching the castle, we came to two slabs of stone where had originally been buried Cannon and Grosse, the two American filibusters whom President Zelaya had shot in 1910 and whose death (though Zelaya was fully justified) gave Secretary Knox, who had business interests in Nicaragua, an excuse for supporting the revolution against him.

We struggled up the ascent beyond, steep and slippery and overgrown with shrubs and bushes. Around the brow of the hill ran a very wide and deep fosse with perpendicular masonry for its escarpments. We crossed this on a shaky plank which served as a causeway, and looked down from the high walls which dropped to the river, to the little settlement, to the great tropical trees. The far hum of the rapids floated up in the cool quiet morning. Below us were two tiers of chambers sunk in the solid rock. Here, too, tall trees lifted up their crowns as high as the level on which we stood. A slippery, dangerous, broken stairway led down into what had once been a powder magazine, and where garrisons had once been quartered. Another chamber had evidently served as a chapel for in it was a niche below which was a deep stone basin for holy water. The floors everywhere had been broken up, perhaps by seekers for treasure. On the western side of the construction where we had ascended to the main entrance, a glacis dropped down to the terrace, once the parade ground, the garden and the cemetery of the garrison To this day it serves as the cemetery of the town.

The Old Castle was built less than fifty years after the Conquest and was reconstructed in 1747 under royal orders by the Governor Intendant of Nicaragua and Costa Rica, for the defense of the river. Most advantageously situated. Boats coming up could be attacked at the very moment when they were obliged to struggle in the rapids below the town. An outlook sentinel box of stone dominates the northwestern bastion and in its narrow windows are still the grooves of the muskets of the sentinels.

In 1780, the English captured the fort by an expedition led by John Dolling, who hoped to gain possession of Lake Nicaragua and the cities of the Pacific and thus cut off communication between the Spanish colonies. The land forces were commanded by Colonel Polson, and they greatly outnumbered the Spanish garrison of two hundred and twenty-eight men officered by Juan de Ayssa. Nevertheless, the English were obliged to besiege the castle for many weeks. The garrison finally capitulated and in "consideration of the gallant defense of the fort," Ayssa was permitted to march out with muskets and side arms, torches lighted, colors flying, drums beating. They were promised vessels and provisions to convey them to any port of Spain or America agreed upon.

Of this English expedition up the San Juan ten ultimately survived; and in January, 1781, the English abandoned the castle and withdrew to Jamaica.

Perhaps worthy of a separate paragraph is the fact that near here, Nelson lost his eye.

3

Our landlady had told us that we could take a bath in the morning in the bathhouse. Before each of the houses along the river on high stilts stood a combination toilet and bathhouse composed of two rooms. After taking one look at it, and observing that the water for the bath was drawn from the river, I decided to go without a bath, hot though it had now become at eight in the morning. Drinking water, to my dismay, was also drawn from the river.

We had to lay around El Castillo until three o'clock that afternoon. The tug was obliged to return up the river to get another scow loaded with banana suckers. It did not return until afternoon. Time is no object in these parts. But presently we were quivering and darting through the foaming rapids, fascinatingly white in contrast to the dark walls of vegetation on either side. The unfortunate sequel of the delay was, we did not reach the most beautiful part of the river, the San Carlos junction, until after nightfall. Here the river widens out and is broken by small islands. Yet even at night the myriad expanse of channels, the towering jungle, the shimmering moonlight, the velvet emptiness of lost inlets—made the spot incredibly beautiful.

We kept on in the night, with occasional stops before dim houses on the bluffs—barking of dogs, swinging of lanterns, sound of voices.

I had spread my blankets on the roof of the launch, the only level place I could discover. Its chief disadvantage was that the whistle of the launch was beside my ear and that driving rain soon drove me to the floor of the launch, my head now near the motor.

We laid up at the Sarapique junction about midnight. Though there had been trillions of mosquitoes at Castillo, here not a single insect bothered us. At this season, this is the only place on the entire river not infested with mosquitoes, hence is usually chosen as the over-night stopping place.

When I woke up, I discovered I had been sleeping with my shoulder and head in a pool of engine oil. The upper third of my blanket was soaked and dripping with black oil; my clothes were smeared.

Next day the vegetation was truly stupendous; at some points it reaches fully 150 feet in height, two solid walls of high trees and matted vines. Here and there were the white trunks of ceropias, great-leaved Heliconiae, slender palms striving to reach above the thick growth, but doomed to everlasting twilight. Great alligators sunning themselves on the low mud bank, with mouths wide open and running with saliva, now and then slipped off into the water with a heavy splash, sometimes with a bull-like bellow; here and there, floating motionless in the river, they looked exactly like logs. Pink herons stood near the shore; macaws screamed and squawked among the trees.

1

AT THE WHARF IN GREY-
town I was greeted by an
elderly American, Mr. Bland.
His tanned face beamed from
under a broad straw hat.

"You are Mistah Beals," he
announced. "My niggah boy"—and he indicated a little
stooped negro with kinky white locks—"will take you'
baggage ovah to the hotel. Ah heah you intention gawin'
Costa Rica. The quickest and best way is ovahland, suh.
Now while my boy takes you' baggage to the hotel, suppose we go ovah yondah and have a few drinks?" On the
way, he expounded the many advantages of the proposed
route.

Mr. Bland's ready information about myself and my
plans amazed me. There is no telegraph or radio office
in Greytown. Here I had been traveling for days through
the wilderness of Nicaragua to arrive at Greytown and
have Mr. Bland call me by my name and inform me
about my own plans.

"Tell me," I demanded, "how you know so much
about me."

"Well," he drawled in the quaint darky English of
the port, "they's not so many fo'nahs comin' down the
rivah now; and Ah read in the papah you was prospectin'
to go ovah the route of the canal befoh you left Nicaragua. And so Ah just spiced two and two togethah, suh,
and figu'd out you'd be a young fellow nobody seen

around these heah pa'ts befoh; and like as not any one
comin' into Greytown would most likely be set on goin'
to Costa Rica."

Mr. Bland was another stranded specimen long settled
in Greytown, waiting for the canal. With every other
breath he repeated, "Are they goin' to build the canal,
suh? When do you think they'll begin? It's mighty high
time, suh, we folk was makin' a rise."

In contrast to these hopes of prosperity, the old English settlement was more run-down at the heel than
even San Carlos, though in 1868, that remarkable and
little known genius, Thomas Belt, had called it "one
of the neatest tropical towns I have visited." Every one
of the wooden houses was rotting, warped out of all
proportion, the gingerbread work broken and fallen,
upstairs piazzas sagging dangerously. Half the houses
were abandoned, their windows broken, the roofs fallen
in, here and there were heaps of charred ruins. In one
pile of black beams I saw a big safe. These houses, I
was told, had been burned down to get the insurance.
Many had once been covered with galvanized tin; but
these roofs were rapidly disappearing, carried off to the
more prosperous community of Bluefields. The unpro-
tected walls were tottering. Not a house, save the customs office in charge of a courteous, alert negro, had
a fresh coat of paint. The streets, once paved with cobblestones, were cushions of green grass; and the jungle,
which circles the town, seemed to be pushing in, preparing to strangle it. But the walls were covered with
festoons of pink *vegésina* creepers; every branch was
draped with moss, aerial plants, ferns, orchids. Great
arms hung on forks of branches, letting long cords
dangle to the ground; and the lianas looped from tree

to tree like a gigantic tangle of yarn. These and the mass of palms, bread-fruit, nancito (native olive), orange, mango and guayava trees made of the place a bower of beauty despite its ruinous state.

The region is alive with birds, canaries, parrots in large screaming flocks; velvet black toucans, splashed with fiery red; and the olive-green mot-mots, moving their long queer tails from side to side.

Mr. Bland, as we walked to the hotel, continued to impress upon me the advantages of taking the overland route to Costa Rica. The same negro "boy," the little old man of the shrill voice, who had taken my baggage to the hotel, would serve as my guide for ten dollars.

Our two-story hotel proved one of the better preserved buildings, and an elderly, delightful and hospitable negress, Susan, kept it spick and span.

2

In the hotel I met Stacomb and a German rancher named Wolff—from up the river.

Stacomb, an employee, so he said, of the United Fruit Company, was a breezy fellow, half under the weather from alcoholic *copitas;* obviously, a daredevil adventurer, a handsome reckless type, hail-fellow-well-met!

He had already made up his mind to go overland to Costa Rica—he and the German. The German was also a "canal-hopper," an old-time resident. They invited me to join them on their trip. But Stacomb's invitation, for some undefinable reason, aroused distrust in me.

He invited me out to drink. Realizing this was an all-day all-night avocation with him, I avoided the fiery white *agua* and kept to beer. I suspected Stacomb was trying his best to make me drink to excess.

"What made you take the trip down the San Juan?" he inquired.

"To see the canal route and as much of Nicaragua as possible."

My answer did not satisfy him. Apparently my presence in Greytown worried him exceedingly. He doubted both that I had been to see Sandino and that I was a newspaper man. I could not for the moment fathom his purpose or why he should thus doubt me. I myself questioned his being an employee of the United Fruit Company; I believed him rather to be a mere adventurer. The German, Wolff, was also an odd number. Why were they so anxious to have me accompany them? Stacomb's motive could not be robbery, for he seemed to have plenty of money, indeed he flashed a roll of greenbacks as big as my fist, and seemed, though insistent on ferreting into my personal affairs, to be most anxious to get on the good side of me. And he was a most likeable daredevil.

Finding he could get no further information out of me through drinking, he next offered to provide me with ladies in any quantity I should desire. Quality was not mentioned.

At the hotel and during lunch, Stacomb and Wolff talked in German. I pretended not to speak the language, hoping if anything out of the way was designed against me, I might get a hint of it. But their conversation was innocent enough.

If Stacomb had been a Nicaraguan his motive might have been to get hold of the information which I had gathered and to steal the articles which I had written, or prevent them being sent out; something I still thought

might be attempted before I left the country—and one
of the reasons I was considering crossing overland into
Costa Rica instead of going up to Bluefields. But this
could scarcely be Stacomb's motive. I decided to put
all my cards on the table.

I took him up to my room and showed him the photographs which I had taken on my trip to Sandino, showed
him the articles which I had written and pointed to all
the documents in my suitcase and told him that he was
quite at liberty to look them over. "No, no," he exclaimed shamefacedly, waving everything aside.

"Now, what's your game?" I demanded bluntly.

He laughed heartily. "The joke's on me all right. I
thought your newspaper gag was a bluff, that you were
really an employee of the Cuyamel Fruit Company and
that you had been spying on us in the bush."

He went on to explain that there was open war between the United Fruit Company and the Cuyamel,
that the United Fruit was attempting to open up new
banana railway lines on the Costa Rica side in the direction of San Carlos, clear to Lake Nicaragua, and that
the Cuyamel had managed to block their attempts to
get a concession and was bothering them in every way
possible. Said Stacomb, "I hoped to get you drunk and
get some information out of you, or to give you a good
time to-night for the same purpose, and then if you
wouldn't come across and lay your cards on the table,
when we went overland to Costa Rica I was going to
see to it that our *mozo* went by a different route, whereupon I would have lost you [which might have meant
death] and gone on to San José with your baggage. Now
that we really know each other, we can have a good
time and a good trip."

XLVIII   LADIES FOR STRAN-GERS

1

Stacomb was not the only one in Greytown who desired to provide me with pleasure. I waş greatly behind in my work, so that night I sat down in the restaurant of the hotel to do typing. Susan had given me directions how to put out the center lamp and close up the place when I went to bed. Because of the terrific heat I was working with the door open. Difficult to decide which was worse, the heat with the door closed, or the mosquitoes which swarmed around me and stung mercilessly through the back of my shirt as I typed. Yet even with the door open, the heat bellied in from the jungles and with it, a clogging stench of tar and rotten fruit and the queer odor of nigger-town.

While I was thus typing, a little wretch of a fellow, the secretary of the local commandant, came in. This little spider talked to me in a sly, unctuous way. I was beginning to think everybody acted suspiciously in Greytown, including Bland, who had greeted me by name. The little secretary hemmed and hawed around, trying to insinuate something, I could not quite make out what. Finally, quite exasperated, I turned on him. "What the hell do you want anyway?"

He stroked my arm. "No, no," he said. "It's only this. As an official of the community I feel that it is my duty to see that all the guests of the town leave Grey-town with proper impression of its hospitality."

"Well?" I countered.

"For that reason I suggest that we have a few bottles of beer and we will play the phonograph and have a good time."

"I happen to be busy."

"Then I'll come a little later on. Shall I tell them to send over the beer?"

"I'll see when you come back," I replied, and went on with my work.

He was gone about ten minutes, then appeared on the scene with a pretty little Indian girl to whom he introduced me. Ignoring my interest in my work, he set the phonograph going raucously, then said to me brazenly, "This music will not disturb your work, will it?"

After a few pieces, he added, "Why don't you dance with my friend?"

The little girl had been looking at me quite reproachfully for my indifference, and so I pushed back my work and danced with her.

The music had attracted quite a crowd of bystanders at the open door.

After several dances, the secretary sidled over to me and with a wink said, "How about the beer? Shall I go over and get it?"

It was stifling. A bottle of beer was tempting.

"All right," I said. "How much do you need?"

"Well, it is so much a bottle," he answered, naming a price double what I had paid earlier in the day. In a whisper in my ear he added: "You must treat her nice."

The girl, at the sight of money, immediately cried,

"Andrés, I'll go for the beer." But the secretary fairly snatched the bill from my hand. She tried to wrench it away from him by pure force. A wrestling match ensued to see which should go. Both showed a ferocious and disgusting sort of greed.

Most annoying was the crowd of bystanders at the door. Playing a dangerous game in Nicaragua, I wished to avoid any possible tangles with the authorities. I was, perhaps, over-suspicious of everybody.

The secretary now dragged the girl over to the corner of the room and told her something which mollified her. Then he came back to me. "You had better get more beer than we planned," he said. "I'm going to ask her sister over."

After all, he was secretary to the Commandant and knowing these countries I realized he might make trouble for me. I gave him the money. The girl flew at him again and tried to snatch it away from him. He finally shook her off and went away alone. I sat there talking with her. She had grown very sullen.

A fellow from among the crowd at the door—a young chap, cap drawn over his eyes—I could not quite make out whether he was a Nicaraguan or a foreigner—came over and in a very important tone requested to speak to me.

"A very serious matter indeed," he declared. There was a twist to his words as though he wished to warn me of impending trouble.

All these events seemed quite unusual. The greedy attitude of the Commandant's secretary made me think that avarice had been his only motive in the whole matter, plus a quaint desire to please me. Or might there be something else?

It was unbearably hot, difficult to think straight. The room seemed uncannily bright with the big oil lamp, around which tropical insects were fluttering and falling. Outside was the mysterious pulse of the moist tropics.

I knew those jungles. Around Greytown they are dense and swampy. I had drifted around them in a *pit-pan*, which Tooker had called "a bread-trough; not a canoe," a sort of dug-out in which natives had brought fruit to the first sail vessels of the Spanish conquerors, centuries ago.

In those jungles there were no clearings, no comfortable roads, only dank solitudes, home of the tapir, the wild boar, the monkey and the panther. There wing wild macaws and screaming birds from cotton-wood ceiba to palm and iron-wood; huge emerald serpents coil over the limbs of huge *matapalos;* and from it came the rank odor of rotting vegetation, of precious gum, and powerfully scented flowers. Queer poisonous emanations, deathly vegetations, carnivorous plants, mortiferous insects—always an overhanging menace of malaria, yellow-fever, and queer diseases uncharted by science.

Earlier in the day I had seen how the jungle had wrapped its arms around the machinery and dredges left behind from the initial attempt to build a canal forty years before.

This fellow with his whispering voice suddenly seemed to me the messenger of the jungle, a ghost of its multiple diseases.

He drew me to one side. He had been drinking. Instead of telling me outright what he wanted, he, too, began with a long wheedling prelude as to how I was an estimable person with generous instincts and few such persons came to those parts. I burst out, "What do you want, anyway?"

He was taken aback and stuttered his request: "Why don't you let me in on this party?" he demanded. "You can tell the girl to get some one else and we can all have a good time."

I laughed. His request was so simple—after my odd imaginings. But I was also out of sorts.

"And who are you?" I demanded sharply.

"Oh, I've been hanging around this town for a while," was his vague reply.

Something in his shifty manner angered me. "There isn't going to be any party. And I'll have to ask you to leave this room for I'm going to close up."

"No party!" he exclaimed dazedly.

"No," I snapped.

I closed the doors in his face and those of the rest of the bystanders. Some trick of nerves, always occurring in these hot climates, now made me furious at everything and everybody. I was still boiling at the petty larceny tactics of the secretary. I thought of the struggle with the girl over the money. Shoddy. My anger mounted. I turned to the girl. "Kindly go out and see what has happened to the beer."

"How will we get in then? Shall I knock?"

"You can knock if you wish," I said. "But I doubt if any one will answer because I'm going upstairs to bed." . . .

Stacomb was certainly not wasting his time. Through the flimsy partition which separated his room from mine I heard the pop of champagne corks. I crawled under my mosquito netting and tossed about, oppressed by the heat and uneasy thoughts.

2

Stacomb was full of practical jokes. Bland liked his fiery *agua* and the four of us, Stacomb, the German, Bland and myself had gathered in the corner grocery store. Stacomb turned the subject of conversation to revolutions, how easy it was to start revolution in Nicaragua, and suggested that we might all try our hand. Bland caught the cue and in a humorous vein carried on the idea. And so we began making plans for staging a revolution then and there in Greytown. Bland, in a loud voice, told us the important part he would play in the undertaking, and that he should be put in charge of the city hall. His glass of *agua* in hand, he dissertated volubly.

Suddenly, a bare-foot policeman in blue dungarees and carrying a home-hewn stick tapped Bland on the arm, saying quietly, "The Commandant orders you to come over to his office."

Bland turned pale. With shaking hand, he sat his glass of *agua* down untasted. With a despairing glance at us, mutely, he let the bare-foot policeman lead him off. We trailed behind him over to the office of the Commandant.

Sotto voce Stacomb told me he had cooked up a little joke. The Commandant was in on the farce.

As we stepped into the office, the secretary of the night before glared at me balefully; but quickly averting his glance, he jumped up unctuously and pumped my hand. He was sorry he had come back so late with the beer. Why had I gone to bed? All in a low voice, so that the Commandant could not hear.

The Commandant turned upon old man Bland sharply. "You have been brought here for uttering seditious remarks and attempting to foment a revolution. What have you to say?"

Bland stuttered. "Your Honor, I assure you . . ."

The Commandant cut him short, called his secretary. "Kindly take down this testimony. Gentlemen, I should like your testimony regarding the remarks of Mr. Bland. Is it true that he said so and so?"

Very seriously Stacomb repeated the remarks Bland had made. The secretary copied them down. The Commandant next turned to me and asked me if I swore to the same statement. Then Wolff.

"Your testimony will be taken later," he told Bland. Turning to the policeman, he said, "Take Señor Bland off to jail pending further investigations."

"Your Honor," protested Bland frantically. But the policeman propelled him firmly through the door.

Laughing heartily, the Commandant produced a bottle and poured out drinks for us.

"You know, Bland is a good old codger, harms nobody. But every once in a while I have to scare him into sobriety, or the poor fellow would drink himself into the grave."

Calling another policeman, he wrote an order for Bland's release, stamped it and sent it over to the jail. Bland could not have remained in the place more than five minutes. He reappeared on the scene thoroughly frightened.

"Your Honor," he began. "This is all a mistake."

The Commandant turned on him severely. "I realize that you had been drinking and probably were not aware of the seditious character of your remarks. I am taking into consideration that you have been a worthy and law-abiding citizen of this community. It was probably a moment of indiscretion on your part. On the insistence of these gentlemen I have decided to free you, but kindly understand that you are under constant surveillance and that you are to comport yourself properly in the future, or the law will take its course. Now, if I catch you taking another drink, I'll run you in. If solemnly you promise not to touch anything, I'll let you out on good behavior."

Bland raised his tremulous hand. "Not a drop, Your Honor."

"That's all, you may go."

Bland crumpled his hat, looked around at all of us helplessly and went out.

With this final gesture Stacomb and Wolff departed from Greytown through the jungles to Costa Rica and San José. I had decided to take a boat to Bluefields.

"I'll be in San José before you," called Stacomb, waving good-by.

That evening Bland came over to the hotel to talk with me.

"Well," I remarked. "You were lucky to get off so easily."

He resumed an air of bravado. "They couldn't do anything to me. I'm an American."

Maybe he's right!

XLIX BLUE-FIELDS

1

DAY AFTER DAY, TRANSIT OF the dangerous San Juan bar was postponed. No boat would venture across until conditions were entirely propitious. The traditional entrance to Greytown was by the southern branch of the delta known as the Colorado River; but this bar was now even more dangerous. The last vessel to cross it had swamped with thirty passengers, all of whom were devoured by sharks which abound near the surf. The local Chinese tie a long rope to a tree on shore, then wade into the surf and with great dexterity harpoon the sharks as they swim up.

Even on the bar we were choosing, many lives had been lost, and I had been warned against crossing it by President Díaz himself. Finally word came to be ready at six the following morning.

We stepped from Susan's hotel in a misty rain—"the pride o' the mo'nin', suh"—and accompanied the old negress' ample ground-swishing skirts and apple-green teamster's umbrella to the little wharf. The crew of our little blue boat was not even awake. We piled our luggage on a hatchway, our future bed; and waited, shivering under a canvas. The day brightened. But departure was indefinitely postponed; there were still some banana suckers to be loaded, so we went back to Susan's for coffee.

About noon three vessels zigzagged out through the bayous along a channel barely visible through the thick growth of aquatic plants which covered the sluggish lagoons several feet thick. Presently we were in the open, running toward the bar. The vessel in front of us was already tossing like a peanut shell; but before we could observe how it maneuvered the crossing, our own boat was lurching. We had to cling tight. A number of the passengers, including a man scaling from smallpox, were already disgustingly seasick. Suddenly our boat literally stood on end, jerked, eased down, stood on end again. The prow hit the bar with a mighty crack; the whole boat shuddered and creaked; a huge wave swept upon us in a great green wall; we keeled half over. Then, like a horse leaping obstacles, the boat seemed to back off and shoot forward with dizzy speed. We heaved up and down, huge swell after swell. But we were safely across, and staring, with considerable relief, at the smoother waters, where dozens of sharks were slicing about, and not far off a turtle, fully six feet across, swimming like a floating island.

Rough going. We ran into Monkey Point cove to avoid a storm, lay up all night, and finally hove to in Bluefields lagoon late the following morning.

Another grass-grown town of wooden houses, sheet-iron roofs and board walks. A winding muddy street curved up from the launch landing, past the extensive buildings of the Moravian mission to the main stores, the radio station and the Tropical Club.

The port was under a temporary reign of terror. The marine captain, provisionally in command, had a brutal record in Haiti and was perpetuating it here. Any citizen who fell into his hands was beaten into jelly. A

Chinaman, whom he had arrested, was beaten up with gun-butts and poked with bayonets as soon as he arrived inside the barracks fence. Screaming, he made for the low picket fence which opened on the main business street, was shot down, and a bayonet run through his belly. He had been arrested for a minor offense. Though the captain had a wife in Bluefields, he lived across the river quite openly with one of the lowest prostitutes in town; and the resident Americans had not only black-balled him for membership in the Tropical Club, but had ordered him off the premises. Nevertheless, he brazenly made himself at home in the place. He had run one American correspondent out of town and had beaten up another badly.

On departing for Limón in a little cocoanut steamer, our baggage was inspected by marines who could speak no word of Spanish. One called to the other, "If you run across a good kodak, Jim, you know I want one." And I gathered from their joking, they had recently confiscated a portable phonograph.

The marine leaned over my suit-case. I reached down and put my kodak on top of it. "Suppose you take this one," I suggested.

He looked up, grinning. "You're one of these fresh guys, aren't you?"

Next to me was a young newly married Nicaraguan couple going to visit relatives in Costa Rica. They had a black case full of stereopticon slides, pictures of the family and scenes of Nicaragua, which they were taking with them as a present.

"Ho, Jim," shouted the marine, "I've hit it." He paid no attention to the rest of their belongings, made a sign to them to shut up their baggage.

339

In Spanish, the Nicaraguan asked the marine why he was keeping the case.

"Aw, shut your trap," blustered the marine. His crony, Jim, came over to look at the prize.

I stepped over to the couple, almost in tears, to translate. To the marine I said, "These people want to know if they can lock up the case also."

"What 'n hell are you butting in for?" demanded the marine. "This ain't none of your damn business."

"I'm making it my business. Why are you taking that case?"

"Regulations."

"Regulations, my eye. Let's see your regulations. Go call the officer in charge."

Meanwhile Jim had opened the case. "Say, Tom, this ain't no kodak, just some fool slides. You don't want this."

"Call the officer in charge," I repeated.

The marine turned to me. "I thought it was a kodak. We have orders to confiscate all kodaks." He gave the case back.

"If that is the regulation, then I demand that you confiscate my kodak," I told the marine.

"If you know what's good for you, you'll go on board and shut up."

I was half inclined to look up the officer in charge, but the time of sailing was short; and I doubted if I would get any satisfaction anyhow. Probably if I insisted they would be only too glad to hold me for a witness.

2

We rolled down to Limón, our gunwales awash with every wave. The boat was weighted down to the level of the sea by 10,000 cocoanuts, bound for Panama, then the United States, to make gas-mask charcoal. Even the bunks were full of cocoanuts. I sat on cocoanuts, ate cocoanuts, slept on cocoanuts, dreamed cocoanuts . . .

The train inland from gray-walled, rain-soaked Limón wound through jungles, banana plantations, clap-board negro settlements wallowing in mud, to the plateau and San José, the neat little capital of a country that boasts more school teachers than soldiers.

Here I received mail. A letter from Venditti of Hotel Roma in Tegucigalpa explained lengthily that the day after my departure two policemen had come to the hotel to look for me, then an officer, finally the chief of police himself. Venditti, not knowing my plans, had assumed I had committed some misdemeanor, but hastened to assure me he was my loyal friend. Probably through Minister Summerlin, the Honduras authorities had learned that I was en route to Sandino's camp, and were intent upon stopping me.

Immediately I sent a long radio collect to the chief of police (11 cents a word), stating I had heard he had been to my hotel looking for me, that if there was any reason why I should present myself in his office, I would, however inconvenient, pass through Honduras on my way back to the United States; please wire me accordingly. He paid for the cable but did not reply. Whereupon I sent him a second message telling him I was em-

barking on the Pan American steamer, *Corinto*, to go to
San José, Guatemala, that when the boat stopped at
Amapala, I would go ashore to give him ample oppor-
tunity to arrest me.

In Puntarenas, the little Pacific port of Costa Rica,
while seated in the charming hotel dining room, set on
stilts over the harbor waters, the hotel proprietor came
to me, asking whether he could speak to me privately.

He led me into his office. "First of all, I want to tell
you how proud I am to meet you; second, to warn you,
two secret service men are following you."

"That wouldn't surprise me. Who are they?"

"Do you remember a fat man sitting two tables down
from you?"

I laughed. "He certainly looked the part."

"Well, one is an agent of President Adolfo Díaz of
Nicaragua; the other is an agent of Mr. Davis, your
Minister in Costa Rica."

"Thank you very much for the warning; but what
should I do about it? Is it not quite possible that Mr.
Davis' man is here, not to spy on me, but for some
routine matter in connection with the arrival of the
steamer?"

"I know what I'm talking about," repeated the proprietor. "And, also, I want to warn you, don't go ashore
in Corinto, Nicaragua; you'll get into trouble."

"Thank you again for the warning, but I have a legal
right to go ashore in Corinto, and if I feel in the humor,
I shall certainly exercise it. Any trouble that might be
made for me would prove a decided boomerang for the
authors."

"Of course that's up to you. But remember, I warned
you. There are more ways than one of making you trou-

ble. Merely an ordinary dog-fight just before the boat leaves, and you are detained as a witness . . . I am certain you are going to have difficulties somewhere along the line, and I am pretty sure an attempt will be made to make you miss your boat in Corinto."

By now I was not particularly *persona grata* in any of the little countries along the route. I had a score to settle with Honduras; the Minister of Salvador in Costa Rica, incensed at an interiew I had given to the press in San José regarding the treatment I had received on embarking in La Unión, answered in an open letter that when I had passed through, Salvador was under martial law; that foreigners had been implicated in recent disturbances, so the government had been obliged to take precautions with regard to all suspicious characters; but now that martial law had been lifted, I or any one else could travel through without the slightest molestation. No mention of the stolen money.

I replied tersely, thanking the Minister for his information that I could now travel in such safety through Salvador but that hereafter I would reserve my visits for more civilized countries like Costa Rica.

As per schedule, I went ashore in Amapala, sending word up to the military Commandant (enclosing copies of my telegrams to the chief of police) that he would find me eating in such and such a restaurant. I did not have the pleasure of meeting the Commandant and re-embarked unmolested on the *Corinto*.

3

Three days later we reached Corinto, Nicaragua. Though I did not put too much stock in the hotel keeper's remarks, a warning is a warning, and so I had taken pains to cultivate the acquaintance of two fellow passengers: the executive of a tire company and a cigarette salesman. I was determined to go ashore in Corinto, but by keeping in their company, would at least have witnesses. I induced them to go with me to the telegraph and post offices, and to walk with me as far as the pier on my return.

I had already ascertained that the port was in charge of a National Guard corps under the command of Colonel Bleasdale. I had heard about Bleasdale over in Bluefields—from one of his buddies; he was reputed to be the bravest man in the entire marine corps; he literally ate cold steel and fire, and enjoyed it. Now, when I got back on board boat, the steward told me: "Colonel Bleasdale was on board to ask whether you were among the passengers."

Shortly after, when I was leaning over the rail, the steward came up to me to point out a lean officer on the wharf, directing the handling of some supplies: "That's Colonel Bleasdale."

I immediately walked down the gangplank and strolled over beside him, striking up a casual conversation. How long had he been in Nicaragua? . . . Did he like it? . . . Our conversation branched out. Soon he became aware I was not a casual tourist, but well acquainted with Nicaraguan affairs. Presently, I went a step further, and said, "That action in C——, when you walked up to a machine-gun, pistol in hand, and drove out the Sandinistas . . ."

He turned on me. "Who the devil are you anyway?"

"Here's my card, Colonel Bleasdale, good-day." And I walked back on board.

From the deck, I saw he was still looking at the card.

The following morning, Bleasdale and his aide came on board to look for me; he would like to talk to me about Sandino. I was playing chess with the ship's doctor, and told him I would be glad to do so as soon as I finished the game.

He perched on the arm of a near-by chair. But as the game dragged on, he became restless. "I'm rather busy. Why don't you come to the barracks for supper. We eat at six; the boat doesn't leave until ten. You will have plenty of time to make it."

A warning is a warning. Was this a ruse to make me miss the boat? Or was his invitation in good faith?

"I'm sorry," I replied. "But I have invited friends to eat with me on board. Why don't you and your aide join us? It will be a pleasant change from barrack fare."

I imagined I saw a little frown of annoyance, but he said quickly, "I'll be glad to come."

After lunch, during the hot siesta time when the coast was clear, I dashed down to the hotel at the foot of the pier, where my two friends were stopping.

"You have to come on board and have dinner with me to-night," I announced.

The tire man groaned. "We're sick of that fare. Come and eat with us in the hotel."

I explained that Colonel Bleasdale was coming aboard

and that he might have some interesting tales to tell, so they accepted the invitation.

"This is a nasty job we have here," said Bleasdale that night. "We're going to get it in the neck from the American public whether we succeed or fail." And he went into a long argument to justify marine intervention. He dilated upon the trials and tribulations of the Nicaraguans. "We are only trying to help them out," was his clinching argument.

"It seems to me the only ones you are helping out are a bunch of lickspittle politicians," was my retort.

But that night at ten, when the *Corinto* swung out of the harbor past an American battleship, it carried its full list of passengers.

L GUATEMALA HO!

1

MY REAL SURPRISE CAME IN San José, Guatemala. I had planned to cross from there to Suchiate, Mexico. But when I went down to the purser's office to present my passport to the military port Commandant to get my landing card, that fat, black official handed it over his shoulder at me. "This isn't worth anything."

Up until that time, I had imagined that Mr. Kellogg's signature would take me anywhere in the world. "The reason?" I inquired.

"It's not worth anything," repeated his fat nibs in an insulting tone.

"It bears the Guatemala visa; it is entirely in order. I demand to know the reason why I am not permitted to land."

"You can't land," repeated the Commandant, annoyed.

Over his shoulder, I read a telegram signed by President Chacón, denying me the right to set foot in Guatemala.

"Thank you for your courtesy," I said sarcastically, and went upstairs. The situation was unpleasant, because the *Corinto* was making an extra run to load coffee. Instead of proceeding to San Francisco and touching at Mexico, as was customary, it went only to the next port—Champerico—then returned to New York

347

via Panama. It had taken us ten days to get from Puntarenas to San José; I saw myself marooned on board for
at least a month longer.

Where had this thrust come from? I doubted that the
Guatemalan authorities would take such a step without
being instructed to do so by the American authorities.
On the other hand, I doubted if our Minister Geissler,
despite his having been incensed over a previous article
of mine, would dare to make such a move. I determined,
in any case, to make a real fight to get off the boat.

Through the purser I sent a message to the American
Consul on shore, who in turn remitted it to Geissler.
Then from the ship's radio office, I began sending messages: one to Geissler, giving the numbers of my passport, visa and vaccination certificate. I also radioed an
account of the affair to the three leading dailies of
Guatemala City, all of which were then running articles
of mine; and similar messages to the leading dailies of
all Central America, well knowing the petty jealousy
between these countries would cause them to severely
censor the act of the Guatemalan government. To President Chacón I merely sent copies of my newspaper messages, "out of courtesy to the government he represented."

Geissler immediately wired back he was going to the
Foreign Office to try to get permission for me to land.
The Guatemalan authorities held up his wire twenty-
four hours. Learning of this, Geissler sent his subsequent
messages via the railway company's private wire. I was
soon in receipt of his message that he had secured permission for me to get off the boat in Champerico.

Our boat lay in San José three days. As the harbor
is too shallow for large-draft vessels to come up to the

wharf, all merchandise is sent ashore in lighters. Too heavy a sea was running to allow the lighters to come alongside.

Hence another telegram from Geissler informing me that on finding out the boat was still in San José, he had returned to the Foreign Office and had secured permission for me to land at once. Geissler showed himself most energetic and most thoughtful throughout the whole affair.

More for the amusement of the thing than anything else, I sent the fat Commandant a letter, advising him that I would hold him and his government responsible in court of law for my loss of passage money, loss of time, inconvenience to my personal affairs, and for the injuries to the good name of myself and the papers I represented, then ended by thanking him for his great courtesy when he had looked at my passport. Now, when the captain advised me I was free to land, despite this and Geissler's telegram, I decided to be a bit cantankerous myself, and sent back word I would not leave the boat until either the Commandant came aboard or he sent a written message I was quite free to go ashore.

The message was soon forthcoming. I was rowed to the wharf through a dangerous sea of high breakers. After being nearly capsized by a huge launch, I was strapped in a chair and swung up by derrick to the wharf.

2

I have already described the ridiculous formalities to enter Guatemala; before going to a hotel, I had to go to the Commandant to get my passport stamped and signed.

He looked at it, handed it back with a grunt.

"Please stamp it," I said, returning it to him.

"It's all right as it is," he said surlily.

I had noticed on his desk another telegram, also signed by Chacón, instructing the Commandant to let me land and allowing me forty-eight hours in which to cross the country; so I was pretty well able to say anything I pleased. In any case, I would insist that my passport be properly stamped.

"I've already told you it's all right," he repeated.

"Unfortunately, I happen to know the Guatemalan regulations," I replied. "To show legal entry I must have your seal and signature. What are you trying to put over on me? Are you looking for a pretext to get me into trouble further on? I do not intend to leave this office until you have complied with your duty."

At that he sat down and stamped it.

"Thank you again for your great courtesy," I said drily.

He looked at me balefully from under his puffy lids. "I received your letter," he snapped. "It didn't frighten me at all."

"My dear sir, it was not meant to frighten you; it was merely a formality."

"What is more," he went on, "I was not obliged to give you any explanation why you couldn't land. I am a soldier. I merely obey superior orders. I don't have to give any explanation to anybody."

"Ah!" I exclaimed. "Superior military orders. Then Guatemala is a military dictatorship."

"Not at all," he retorted. "It's a civilian government . . ."

"Democratically elected," I finished for him. "And if that is the case, why are travelers received by military men obeying military orders? If Guatemala truly has a civilian government, why are not civilians put in charge of immigration offices, men who have the training and intelligence to treat travelers decently and courteously. Why—"

He flew into a towering rage; his fat belly fairly quivered beneath his frowsy uniform. "You'll take the first train out of here in the morning," he shouted.

San José is the world's jumping-off place; a more miserable cess-pool was never made by God or man. "Señor Commandant," I replied, "have no fears. Do you think I want to stay any longer in this dirty little hole than I have to? I would be overjoyed to leave here this very moment."

After putting my bags in the hotel, I called upon our Consul to thank him for his efforts in my behalf.

"Where is your luggage?" he asked. . . . "You can't stay at the hotel; bring it right up here."

"But I am quite comfortable—"

"I don't want to insist, but I think it absolutely necessary that you sleep at the consulate to-night. You will save yourself a lot of trouble."

Later I learned the people of the town were planning to stage a pro-Sandino demonstration. The Consul probably not only wished to checkmate this, but was quite right in fearing this might have served as a pretext for my arrest.

In any case, the Consul's home was far more pleasant than the stuffy little hotel where I would have tossed, annoyed by mosquitoes and the terrible stench of hot oil, mire and garbage. We sat comfortably over our high-balls on the wide screened-in second-floor veranda over-looking the ocean, savoring the fresh clean breeze from the Pacific. . . .

Within two days, the dawn of Suchiate "received the visit of the Sun"; and within a week, Mexico City had "sunk into the light of her royal lover," and in that place, I drove "the last spike" in my Odyssey.

INDEX

INDEX

Abd-el-Krim, 276
Acatenango, place, 62
Administración de Rentas, 74
Aguirre, Juan, 55
Agurcia, Colonel Pable, 126
Alcohol, 171, 270
Alhambra, *café*, 81
Altamirano, Captain Pedro, 249, 251 f., 255
Alvarado, Pedro de, 50 f., 52, 140, 169, 173. *See conquistadores*
Amapala, 108, 116, 189, 286, 342, 343
Amatique Gulf, 142
American, battleships, 268
  imperialist, 294 f., 297
  intervention, 299, 300, 346
  legation, 75, 289
  loans, 191
  press, 236. *See* newspapers
Americans, general, 140, 310
  business men, 121 f., 133 f., 283, 324 f., 326-329, 333, 334, 336, 339
  captains, 109 ff.
  consul, 351 f.
  missionaries, 44
Amezquita, Bartolomé, 35
Amolongo, place, 60
Amoya, place, 71
Anathema, the, 98
Andalucians, 87. *See* national types
Antigua, place, 49, 52, 53, 55, 56, 176
Aparicio, 127 f.
Argüello, Marcelino, 115
Arias, Pedro, 268 f.
Ariel, 190, 191, 193, 250, 254. *See* newspapers
Arteaga, Bernardino de, 51 f.
Atrocities, 224, 226, 229, 254, 263, 268, 339
Association of Nicaragua Independence, 183
Associated Press, 305. *See* newspapers
Aztec, 87. *See* Indians
Ayssa, Juan de, 321

Aycinena, Marquis, 71, 72
Ayutla, place, 25

Bahona Paz, 122, 132. *See* Honduras
Baldwin Locomotive Works, 106
Ballas, Brothers, 268
Bandits, 84, 235, 306
Banana, general, 37, 68, 78, 88, 134, 135, 175, 265
  rule, 117, 120 f., 145, 176
  labor, 121, 139
  ports, 140, 141, 192
  cars, 149, 150
  fields, 151, 341
  railroads, 153, 328
  country, 171, 308
  suckers, 317, 318, 321, 337
Bankers, 76, 295, 298, 300
Baron Banana, 143 f., 145 ff., 151, 154, 172, 175
Barrios, 30
Barrios, Gerardo, 97
Bathing, 26, 321
Beer. *See* drinks
Belize, place, 139
Belitz, place, 175
Belt, Thomas, 325
Beluchistan, place, 163
Benavente, Luís, 73
Berrospe, Gabriel Sánchez de, 35, 167
Birds, 83, 116, 117, 131, 151, 152, 242, 258, 314, 323, 326, 332
Bland, Mr., 324 f., 326, 329, 334 ff.
Blanca, 255
Bleasdale, Colonel, 344 ff.
Bluefields, place, 305, 308, 314, 325, 328, 338, 339, 344
Bolshevik, 117
Bonillas, President, 121, 189, 193. *See* Honduras
Boqueta Island, 314
Borrachita, 18
Breves, 56, 57
British Honduras, 139
Bugles, 11, 261, 264. *See* musical instruments

INDEX

Cabañas, Trinidad, 97, 125 f.
Cabo de Gracias, place, 248
Cabrera, 30, 34, 76
Cachureco, 202, 259. *See* conservatives
Cacique, 63, 64, 65, 165, 269
Calles, Plutarco Elías, 156
Calonitos, mountain, 73
Campeche, place, 151
Canaanites, 157
"Canal-hoper," 318, 325, 326
Cannon, 319
Canela, place, 287
Capo de Oro, place, 141
Cárdenas, Francisco, 136, 139 f.
Carías, 121, 122, 123, 132
Caribbean gales, 139
Carmona, Señor, 206
Carrera, 30, 31, 33, 125 f. *See* Honduras
Carson, Mr. and Mrs., 106, 117 f.
Cartagena, place, 309
Caruana, 40-43
Catholic strike, 69. *See* church
Castaño, Quirio, 158 f.
Castellanos, Victoriano, 128
Castillo, Viejo, 319, 320
Castro, Señor Francisco, 81 f.
Casual workers, 38. *See* labor
Cedros, place, 193
Ceiba, place, 120, 264
Celestuia, 68
Central America, general, 25, 105, 111,
    112, 117, 118, 135, 137, 292
    U. S. in, 122 f., 179
    union of, 125, 170, 175
    population of, 139
    conquest of, 173
Central American, customs, 77, 105,
    188
    Confederation of Labor, 82
    commandants, 316
    press, 348
Central Americans, 117. *See* national
    types
Cepile, hill, 122
Cerna, President, 72. *See* Guatemala
Cerro Quemado, mountain, 169
Chacón, President, 40, 347, 348, 350.
    See Guatemala
Chamorro, Emiliano, 123, 194, 280,
    281. *See* Nicaragua, 291, 295
Champerico, place, 347, 348
Chapéton, Colonel, 127

Charros, 14. *See* dress
Chapultépec, place, 319
Chiapanecas, 165, 166
Chiapas, 17. *See* Indians
Chiapas, province, 14, 16, 30, 151,
    155, 157, 159
Chiba, 87. *See* Indians
Chicago, 10
Chicago News, 306. *See* newspapers
Chichén Itzá, place, 151, 152, 167
"Child of the Sun," 50
Chicle, 171, 175
Chimaltenango, 36
Chimandega, place, 247, 286
Chinantla Indians, 51 f. *See* Indians
Chinese, 22, 146, 337, 339
Chiquimula, province, 126, 158, 161
Chocolate, 155. *See* drinks
Choutales, mountain, 312
Choroteganos. *See* Toltec
Chowder, General, 293
Christ of Esquipulas, 159 ff., 162
Christmas, Lee, 134 f.
Church, the, 40, 42, 69, 105, 226
Churches, 47, 53, 73, 162
Citlaltepetl (*See* Mt. Orizaba and
    Quetzalcoatl), 11
Class distinctions, *haciendados,* 14
    ladinos, 29, 59, 175, 176
    mestizos, 14, 29, 90, 230, 313, 314
    general, 102
Climate, Mexico, 12, 17, 18, 20, 22
    Guatemala, 38, 77, 83, 118, 133,
        135, 137, 139, 153, 171
    Salvador, 178
    Honduras, 196, 202, 221, 314
    Nicaragua, 319, 329
Coatépec, 106
Cocoanut, 34, 44, 88. *See* drink
Cocullos, 131
Coffee. *See* food
    in Guatemala, 37, 38, 171
    ranches, 37, 131
    planters, 87
    rule, 107, 171, 176
Colindres, Colonel, 242, 243, 246 ff.,
    249, 256, 259, 260
Colindres, Don Juan, 239 ff.
Colindres, President, 121, 247. *See*
    Honduras
Colombia, 112
Colon, 139
Colorado River, 337

Comayagua, place, 119, 124, 126, 129, 130, 159
Comitán, 165
Commandant of Greytown, 334 ff.
Commandant's secretary, 330-333, 334
Commissions, 299
Concessions, coffee, 38, 77
    banana, 120, 150
    Honduras, 191
Conchagua, island, 114, 116, 130
Conchagüita, island, 116
"Con-Con," 267, 268
Conquistador, 50, 51, 87, 140, 166, 332
Conservative party, in Guatemala, 31, 33
    in Honduras, 121, 125
    in Nicaragua, 277 f., 309
Conservatives, in Guatemala, 31, 33
    in Honduras, 121, 125, 202
    in Nicaragua, 209, 247, 259, 270, 279, 316
Coolidge, President, 271, 298
Copán, ruins, 151, 157
Córdoba, place, 9, 10, 12
Córdoba, Hernández, 309
Córdoba, Matias de, 177
Corinto, place, 285, 298, 308, 342, 343, 344
Corinto, S.S., 342, 343, 346, 347
Corpus Christi Day, 48
Cortez, 50
Coseguïna, island, 111 f.
Costa Rica, general, 317, 324, 325, 328, 339
    population, 87
    government, 88, 111, 177
    order in, 88
    banana rule in, 117
    road to, 326
    U. S. and, 267
    history of, 320
Costenos, 316
Council of the Indies, 57, 163, 168
Coyote, 10
Cravioto, Ambassador, 69
Creoles, 87, 295. See national types
Creole tradition, 87
Cruz Brothers, 31 f. See revolution
Cruz, Field Marshal, 72
Cuba, 56, 158, 184
Cuidad Real, place, 155
Cumatz, 59. See disease

Customs. See taxation
    Guatemala, 21, 28
    Salvador, 85, 103, 183
    Honduras, 120
    Nicaragua, 186 ff., 299, 325
Cuyamel Fruit Company, 120, 135, 328

Danlí, place, 202, 206, 211, 219
Darío, place, 274, 278
Darío, Ruben, 274
Davis, U. S. Minister, 342
Daza, Captain Alonso, 226 ff.
Dennis, Laurence, 123
Denny, Mr., 305
Diario del Salvador, 179. See newspapers
Díaz, President Adolfo, 184, 247, 291, 295. See Nicaragua, 296, 337, 342
Díaz, Bernal, 53
Díaz epoch, 37. See peon
Dictamen, the, 9 f. See newspapers
Dictators, in Guatemala, 30, 31, 33, 34, 72, 76, 81
    in Honduras, 111, 121
    in Salvador, 183
    Nicaragua, 295
Dictatorships, in Guatemala, 31, 35, 81, 350
    in Salvador, 87, 105
    in Honduras, 121
    general theory of, 140
    banana, 145
Die Woche, 88. See newspapers
Dipilto Range, the, 222
Diseases, in general, 140, 174, 202, 332
    malaria, 14, 36, 38, 170 f., 185, 243, 262, 332
    cumatz, 59
    plague, 115
    yellow fever, 118, 332
    eye, 124
    scrofula, 124
    syphilis, 171
    small-pox, 338
Divorce, 46
Doctor Méndez, 66
"Dollars for Bullets," 305
Dolling, John, 320
Dominicans, 164, 226
Doña Isabella, 139, 142
Doña Maria, 286, 326
Don José, 202 f.
Don Martín, 62, 64

Don 'Simón, 195, 197, 198, 200, 202, 204 ff.
Don Vicente, 63
Dress, 10, 11, 14, 16, 49
Quiché, 49 f., 172
soldiers, 105
Drink. See food
tequila, 17
tepacho, 18
beer, 24, 27, 44, 94
cocoanut milk, 44, 88
chocolate, 155, 276, 318
Drunkenness, 104
Dutch buccaneers, 309

Earthquake, 115
Eastern Institute, 264
Eberhardt, U. S. Minister, 289, 291 f., 298 f., 302
Echevarria, General, 250
El Baruche, hill, 122
El Castillo, place, 318, 319, 321
El Chipote, mountain, 181, 192, 222, 225. See Sandino, 229, 258, 283, 302
Marines at, 233, 236, 248, 250
Juanas at, 246
Election overseers, 299
El Fiscal, place, 34
El Hule hacienda, 224, 254
El Imparcial, 70. See newspapers
El Modelo, house, 93
El Remango, place, 241, 249, 250, 251, 253, 256. See Sandino
El Retiro, place, 250
El Tigre, island, 115, 116
Enaguas, 16. See dress
England, 126
English, the, 315, 320 f., 325
English, language, 308, 314
"Englishman, the," 233
English pirates, 116, 309
Escobar, José Bernado, 31 ff. See Guatemala
Escuapa, place, 221, 222
Escuela de Cristo, 71
Escuintla, place, 36, 44, 47
"Especiales." See taxation, 120
Espirito Santo Mountain, 143
Esquimula, place, 287
Esquipulas, place, 158 f., 161
Estelí, place, 261, 278, 284
Estrada, Colonel, 262

Eucharistic Congress, 43
Eye infections, 124. See diseases

Feland, General, 261, 302, 306 f.
Ferns, 325. See flowers
Ferrera, Colonel Francisco, 111. See Honduras
Ferrera, General Gregorio, 123
Feudalism, 38
"Fig of Adam," 144
Figueroa, Pedro Pardo de, 160 f.
Fincas, 38, 52, 88, 173, 206, 264
Financial experts, 299
Florencia, Francisco de, 55
Flores, Vice-President, 170
Flowers. See trees, moss, ferns
general, 10, 16, 44, 54, 88, 118, 256, 325
orchids, 11, 257, 325
of the jungle, 131, 257, 332
medicinal, 244
vines, 275, 325
Food. See drink
meals, 13, 197, 199, 238, 282, 313, 315
tacos, 16
mole, 17, 18
tortillas, 16, 197, 206, 222, 238, 242, 253
mangos, 44, 54, 88
fruit, 37, 44, 94, 106, 173, 242, 315
meat, 16, 106, 202, 206, 254, 277 f.
fish, 17, 130, 155, 276, 318
cheese, 16, 130, 206
general, 83, 94, 173, 202, 242, 277, 315
Food
milk, 9
eggs, 10, 16
chicken, 16
tortillas, 16
meat, 16
cheese, 16, 130
chili, 16
mole (turkey), 17
fish, 17, 130
coffee, 22
peas, 94
mangos, 44
cocoanut, 44
drink
tequila, 17
tepacho (pineapple), 18
beer, 24, 27, 44, 94

Forced labor, 38, 39
Foreign experts, 103
Foster, Mr., 294
Four-leaf clover, 172, 175, 176
France, 40, 86
Franciscans, 162, 226 ff.
Fray Diego de Landa, 55
Fray Gómez Fernández de Cordoba, 158
Free plebescite, 122
French, language, 314
French pirates, 309

Gage, Thomas, 53, 309
Gallegos, 87. See conquistadores
Gallegos, Rafael, 111. See Costa Rica
Galvez, President, 73, 111. See Guatemala
García, Juan, 159 f.
Garoba, island, 116
Garrapatas, 257
Gas-mask charcoal, 341
Geissler, Arthur, 69, 75 ff., 81, 348
Genoese, 57
German-American, 317 f.
German Electric Company, 169
German, language, 327
Germans, 14, 38, 88, 89, 172
Girón, General, 262
Glass, Major, 306, 307
Gogol's Russia, 37
Gold, 21
Gomez, 80 f.
Gonzales, Gil, 140
Gourd, 88. See musical instruments
Government. See dictatorships
  Guatemala, 28, 31, 87
  Salvador, 97, 105, 172, 175, 177, 183
  Honduras, 87, 119, 121, 125, 128, 189, 192, 247
  Costa Rica, 88, 111, 177
Goyena, Rafael García, 70, 176
Granada, place, 264, 309
Greytown, 317, 324, 325, 327, 329, 330, 332, 334, 337
Gringos, 207, 225, 232, 254
Grosse, 319
Guajiniquil trees, 37. See trees
Guanas. See food, 278
Guarumo trees, 116. See trees
Guardiola, General Santos, 126 ff.
Guataros, 314. See Indians

Guatemala, topography, 23, 29, 30, 44, 171
  and Mexico, 23, 26, 29, 30, 178
  red-tape, 28, 349 f.
  political history, 31, 32, 33, 35, 126, 132, 164 f., 171, 175, 177
  presidents, 40, 72, 73, 111
  marriage laws, 45
  handicrafts, 48, 170
  dictators of, 31, 34, 35, 72, 76, 81, 350 f.
  bishops of, 56
  racial divisions, 56, 77, 170 f.
  the inquisition in, 59
  army, 75, 176
  finances, 76
  labor laws, 76, 79
  government, 28, 31, 87, 145, 175
  economic divisions, 171, 175
  Quiché civilization, 172-179
  Spanish in, 226
  general, 157, 158, 163, 165, 166, 167, 169, 193, 285, 309
Guatemala City, settled, 52
  churches, 73
  water supply, 47
  dailies, 348
  general, 27, 48, 68, 72, 82, 126, 164, 175 f.
"Guatemala," by Guillermo Rodríguez, 38
Guatemalan consul, 135 f., 139
Gulf of Fonesca, 108, 111, 118, 122, 190, 285
Gulf of Mexico, 309
Gutiérrez, President Rafael López, 121. See Honduras
Guzmán, Fuentes, 53, 176
Guzmán government, 101
Guzmán, Joaquín Eufrasio, 97

Haiti, 294, 295, 306, 338
Handicrafts, textiles, 49
  carving, 54, 207
  Salvador, 86
  Quiché, 170, 173
  Guatemala, 173
Haciendados, 14. See class distinctions
Ham, Clifford D., 304 f.
Hearst newspapers, 305. See newspapers
Hercules, 157
Hernández, Colonel, 69, 79, 80
Hernández, Emilio, 193

INDEX

Hernández, Señor, 279, 282
Herrero, Captain Gilberto, 224, 225, 232
Honduras', political history, 87, 119, 121 f., 125, 126, 128, 189, 192, 247
  races in, 87
  capitol, 108
  population, 117, 119
  banana rule in, 117, 120
  revenues, 120
  topography, 130, 137, 309
  and United States, 122, 179, 190, 191, 192
  and Sandino, 191
  Spanish conquest of, 226
  women of, 209
  and Beals, 343
  general, 71, 121, 134, 151, 157, 178, 179, 229, 250, 251, 285, 341
Honduras etiquette, 203
Honduras mines, 36
Hondureñans, 117, 120, 232. See national types
Honduras Sierras, the, 116
Hotels, in Guatemala, 24, 47, 143, 145, 148
  in Honduras, 121, 136, 189, 193, 341
  in Salvador, 89, 94, 106, 178
  in Nicaragua, 284
Huasteca Oil Company, 264
Huelmetenango, place, 167
Huëhuëchos, dance, 174
Huehuetlán, place, 157
Huerta, de la, revolt, 69, 267. See revolutions
Huete, 121
Hughes, Charles E., 293
Huipiles, 16. See dress
Hunahpuh, volcano, 44

Ignacio, 204
Indian, forced-labor, 38 f.
  allies, 164
  runners, 41 f., 190, 231, 242
  refugees, 229, 243
  feud, 310
  types, 9, 313, 316, 330 f.
  general, 11, 23, 132, 152, 243
Indianism, 176
Indian. See national types
  in Guatemala, 41

Indian (Cont.)
  Quichés, 29, 49, 76, 77, 78, 83, 87, 169, 172-175, 198
  Micos, 51
  Chinautlans, 51
  Pipiles, 87
  Mayas, 87, 166
  Toltec, 87
  Chibas, 87
  in Honduras, 117, 119, 133, 198
  Olanchanos, 127
  Central American, 140
  Banana, 146, 147, 151
  Lacandónes, 163
  Puchutlas, 163
  Tlaxcaltecans, 173
  Mexican, 174
  Taguzigalpas, 226
  Tologalpas, 226
  Lencas, 226 f.
  Taguacas, 226 f.
  Mosquitos, 248
  Chorotegans, 308
  Guataros, 314
Indian Spanish, 90
Inglasera, island, 116
International Railway, 106
Inter-Oceanic Railway, 34
Inquisition, the, 59
Isidro, 211 f.
Isla de los Pájaros, 116
Italy, 86
Izamal, 56

Jacaleapa, place, 196, 206
Jaime, 65 f.
Jalapa, place, 72, 181, 225, 229
Jamaica, 112, 121, 147, 311
Japanese, 14, 147
Java, 163
Jefe Politicos, 38 f., 65, 176
Jews, 29 f.
Jícaro, place, 225, 229, 237
Jilotepeque, valley, 50
Jim, 148 ff.
Jiménez, 167
Jinotega, place, 259, 260, 261, 274, 277, 279
  Battle of, 245, 249
  Valley of, 258
Joyaбaj, place, 173
Juan, 308
Juanas, 246, 250, 252, 253, 254 f.

INDEX

Juarros, Domingo, 176
Jutiapa, place, 37
Junta de Notables, 172

Kaiser, Koffee, 172, 175
Kellogg, Secretary of State, 267, 293, 297, 347
Kerensky, 267
King Canec, 168
King of Spain, 71, 164, 169
Knox, U. S. Secretary, 301, 319

La Casita, song, 254
Labor. See wages
    peon, 37, 38
    forced, 38 f.
    casual, 38
    banana, 121
    government supplied, 39
Labor laws, 76, 79
Labor union, 80
Labor unrest, 117
Lacandón expedition, 165, 167
Lacandónes, 163-168. See Indians
La Chabela, house, 92
Ladinos, 29, 59, 175, 176. See class distinctions
"La Esperanza," 136, 142, 145
Lagoon of the Idols, 151 f.
Lajos, 121
Lake Amatitlán, 44
Lake Itzá, 167
Lake Nicaragua, 117, 301, 320, 327
Lake of Petén, 163, 165
Landivar, Rafael, 53, 177
"Lands of doom," 140, 142
La Noticia, 270. See newspapers
La Parroquia, place, 33
"La Plataforma," 319
Larsen, Lieutenant, 285-290, 298, 302 ff.
Las Almeas, island, 116
Las Cruces, mountain, 254, 258
Latin American, 23, 25, 46, 76, 276. See Central America
Latin frontiers, 23
Las Casas, Bartolomé de, 53
La Unión, place, 96, 106, 108, 113, 114, 118, 179, 185, 343
La Viuda, 23
Leal, Barrios, 35, 167
Lencas, 226 f. See Indians

León, place, 112, 264, 268, 269, 309
    Department of, 261
    Liberal center, 310
Liberalism, 33, 72, 125, 309
Liberals, Guatemala, 31, 32, 170
    Costa Rica, 88
    Honduras, 121, 125, 128
    Nicaragua, 206, 209, 247, 269, 277, 279, 280, 316
Limón, place, 339, 341
Limones, place, 224, 229
Lindbergh, Charles, 183
Lindbergh, Irving, 305
Little Mataguinea, place, 242
Little theater movement, 69
Livingston, place, 176
Logan law, 297, 307
Lola, 90-96
Los Altos, mountain, 173, 177
Los Amates, place, 150
Los Encinos, place, 229, 232
Lost Soul, 109 f.
Loyola, 294
Lumber, 308
Lundo y Goicoechea, Antonio, 176
Lusitanians, 57

Madriz, Francisco Gomez de la, 35. See visitadors
Magarita, 184-186, 189
Mahomet's Paradise, 309
Malaria, 14, 36, 38, 170 f., 185, 243, 262, 332. See diseases
Malespín, Francisco, 97 ff., 101
Managua, place, 264, 273, 279, 283, 284, 290, 291, 302, 303, 305, 307, 316
Mangos. See food
Manuel Aladaña, 170
Mariano, 216, 220
Marimbas, 18, 48, 154, 173. See musical instruments
Marine captain, the, 339
Marine, tactics, 250, 256, 274
    outpost, 275
    officers, 295, 299, 302, 314, 338, 344
    guard, 312
Marines, general, 117, 122, 201, 225, 229, 232, 233, 238, 242, 248, 256, 260
    in Nicaragua, 183, 191, 247, 279, 282, 294, 296, 299, 300, 312, 316

Marines *(Cont.)*
  and Sandino, 178, 190, 207, 222,
    244, 254, 258, 269, 292, 303
  in Chipote, 236, 241
  and Secret Service, 303
  and Nicaragua Canal, 308
  in Bluefields, 338 ff.
Markets, 48, 49, 53 f., 86
Marriage, 45, 109
Marroquín, Francisco, 53, 56, 176
Martín, President, 111. *See* Salvador
Martínez, Juan Antonio, 31. *See* Guatemala
Martínez, Rafael Arévalo, 170 f., 173
Martyr, Peter, 278
Masaya, place, 264, 308
Masons, 189, 190
Mayan Society, The, 163
Mayapan, ruins, 151
Maya-Quiché, ruins, 151
Mayas, 87, 166. *See* Indians
McCoy, General, 293 f., 296 f., 298, 299, 300, 302, 307
McCoy Election Law, 293 f., 295, 296
Mena revolt, 192. *See* revolutions
Méndez, General, 129
Mestizos, 14, 29, 90, 199, 230, 313, 314. *See* class distinctions
Mérida, place, 167
Metapa, place, 274
Mexico, and Guatemala, 23, 26, 29, 30, 76, 178, 347
  army officers, 105
  Díaz epoch, 37
  church in, 40, 159
  government, 43, 50, 117
  and United States, 122, 191, 295
  and Sandino, 264
  and de la Huerta, 267
  Indians in, 174
  border of, 176
  general, 21, 49, 309
Mexico City, 9, 15, 52, 178, 352
Mexican characteristics, 174
  train, 17
  food, 13
  influence, 76, 117, 118
Mexican constitution of 1917, 80
"Mexicanos," suburb, 91
Miangüera, island, 116
Mico, place, 50
Mico Indians, 51 f. *See* Indians
Micos, Augustus, 59

Miliukof's revolution, 267. *See* revolution
Militarism, 105
"Milwaukee, The," 122, 123
Minatitlán oil fields, 14
Minister of Salvador, 343
Miracles, 56, 160, 161
Missionaries, 45, 313, 338
Mitla, ruins, 152
Mitlán, place, 157
Mole, 18. *See* food
Momobacho, mountain, 312
Moncada, José María, 123, 268, 291, 295, 316
Monkey Point cove, 338
Monteagudo, 226
Montejo, 124
Montes, Francisco, 128
Montoyo, General, 262
Montoyo, Pedro, 243 ff.
Morales, Cristobal, 158
Morales, Franklin S., 121, 122
Moravian mission, 338
Morazán, President-general, 111
Morséli, place, 200, 202, 204
Moses of Nicaragua, 293
Mosquitoes, 20, 133, 318, 322, 329, 352
Mosquitos, 248. *See* Indians
Mosquito Coast, 126
Moss, 319, 325. *See* flowers
Montagua, river, 50, 153
Mountain of the Star, 11
Mount Orizaba, 11
Muluá, place, 40, 41, 169
Munro, Dana, 292, 298
Murciélago Theater, 69
Murra, place, 236
Musical instruments, bugles, 11, 145, 261, 264
  marinbas, 18, 146, 154, 173
  gourds, 88
  piano, 13
  drums, 145
  guitars, 254, 262, 317

Nahuala Santa Catarina, place, 172
Nahualin, 62-69
Nat Chan, 158
National Guard, 299, 344
National types. *See* Indians and negroes
  of mixed blood, 15, 140, 199
  Vera Cruzano, 17

National types (*Cont.*)
Creoles, 87, 295
Gallegos, 87
Andalucians, 87
in Salvador, 106
Hondureñans, 117, 119, 232
Japanese, 147
Chinese, 146
Nicarguans, 231
Spanish, 117, 119
Negro blood, 106
Negro custom officials, 325
Negroes, Honduras, 117, 119, 133
Jamaica, 121, 139
British Honduras, 139
banana, 146
Nicaragua, 313, 315
of Syrian origin, 313
Nelson, 321
News, 304 ff.
Newspapers, Central American, 9 f.,
52, 70, 179, 190, 270, 348
Die Woche, 88
censorship of, 183, 304 f.
American, 236, 306
A. P., 305
U. P., 305
Hearst, 305
New York, 347
Nicaragua, disorder in, 87, 123, 172,
192, 300
government, 97, 184, 249, 281, 301
looted, 117
and United States, 123, 268, 286,
288, 293 f., 295, 296, 299 ff., 306,
319, 344, 346
and Sandino, 178, 181, 266, 268, 276
population, 231, 240, 327, 301
Spanish conquest of, 326
education, 300
commerce, 301, 309
press, 306
political divisions, 308
topography, 324
general, 111, 157, 183, 222, 224,
244 f., 251, 268, 305, 309, 320,
327, 329
Nicaragua Autonomist Association, 178
Nicaragua canal, 308, 318, 324, 325,
327. *See* canal-hoper
Nicaraguan utopia, 294
Nicaragua Railway Line, 108
Nindiri, place, 308

Nirvana, 152
Niquinohomo, place, 264, 265
Niquiranos. *See* Toltec
Nuestra, Señora de Izamal, 56
Nuevo Segovia, place, 181, 231, 247,
248, 260, 268
Nufio, General José Dolores, 126
Núñez, Dr. José, 111, 112
Nut-cracker, the, 281 f.

Obregón, Alvaro, 12, 156, 267
Ollas, 11. *See* dress
Ococingo, place, 167
Ocotal, place, 207, 225, 254
October revolution, 267
Olanchano. *See* Indians, 127
Olocotón, valley, 269
Ometépec, island, 117, 312
Ordóñez hacienda, 211
Orellana, President, 30, 40, 69 f., 75,
76, 77, 81, 144. *See* Guatemala
Oviedo, 268

Paid interventionists, 298
Palencia, place, 73
Palenke, place, 157
Palenque, ruins, 151
Palín, 44, 173
Palmolive soap, 312
Paludismol, 14
Pan-American Railway, 16, 28. *See*
railroads
Panajachel, place, 36
Panama, 298, 305, 309, 341, 348
Paredes, Mariano, 32, 125. *See* Guatemala
Pasos Cuadro, 295
Patulul, place, 36
Patzún, place, 36
Pecacho, hill, 118, 119, 122
Peon, 37, 38, 45, 175. *See* labor
Perry, Juan, 115
Perslta, Alonzo de, 268
Perspire, place, 118
Petén, Province, conquest of, 163-168
general, 171, 175, 176, 262
Petroleum, 77, 163
Philip II, 56
Philip III, 226
Philippines, 294, 306
Pierson, Mr., 106, 107
Pinüela, island, 116
Pipiles, 87. *See* Indians

Pirigayo, island, 116
Pius V, 57
Plague, 115 f. See diseases
Police, 104
Polson, Colonel, 320
Prinzalpoca, place, 248
Protestant mission, 310
Pyramid of Cholula, 157
Puchutla, place, 165
Puchutlas, 163-168. See Indians
Puebla, place, 156
Puerto Barrios, 40, 135, 136, 148, 150, 154
  banana port, 143, 144, 145 f.
Puerto Cabezas, 247, 248, 268
Puerto Cortés, place, 117, 120, 134, 135, 136
Puntarenas, place, 342, 348
Punterillos, place, 131

"Queen's Own," 9
Queen Victoria, 126
Querétaro Constitution, 80
Quetzal, the, 25, 152, 169, 173
Quetzalcoatl, 11
Quetzal Falls, 62
Quetzaltenango, 40, 41, 169 f., 172, 175
Quezada, Rodriguez de, 164
Quiché Indians. See Indians
  general, 29, 77, 78, 87, 169, 198
  dress, 49 f., 178
  civilization, 172-175
  speech, 170, 174
Quiché Sierras, 169
Quilali, place, 256
Quinónez, Pedro Ramírez de, 164
Quintanilla, Luís, 69
Quiriguá, place, 150, 152, 154, 155

Railroads, 16, 28, 41, 77, 120, 130, 153
Rebozos, 10, 49. See dress
Renwick, W. W., 183
Retlahulen, province, 172
Revolution, in Mexico, 10, 12, 69, 269
  in Guatemala, 31, 72, 76
  in Salvador, 111
  in Honduras, 121
  in Nicaragua, 192, 300, 305, 334
  Miliukof's, 267
  October, 267
Rio Coco, 248, 256
Rio Frio, 314

Rivas, place, 313
Rivas, General, 180-182, 184-187, 189, 190
Rivera, Colonel Guadalupe, 256 f., 258, 259, 260
Rivera, Colonel Santos, 260, 262, 263, 272, 274, 275 f., 277, 278, 279
Robin Hood, 276
Rodo, 190
Rodriguitos, place, 33
Rodríguez, Guillermo, 38
Romero, M., 116
Romero, Vicente, 115
Rosario mine, the, 196, 198
Rubber, 175
Russian rifles, 267 f.

Small-pox, 338. See diseases
Sabana, Grande, place, 118
Sacatepéquez, province, 59, 61
Sacasa, Vice-President, 247, 268
St. Anthony, 253
Sailors' patois, 138
Salvador, and Guatemala, 86
  and the church, 86
  population, 87
  government, 87, 97, 101, 105, 111, 183
  Army, 87, 105
  loans, 103
  revolution, 111
  and United States, 179, 183
  and Beals, 343
  general. 58, 83, 109, 126, 128, 154, 159, 178, 193, 197, 285, 309
Salvador Cathedral, 99
Salvador city, 100, 103, 105, 167
San Albino mines, 247
San Borja, university, 52
San Carlos, place, 311, 314, 315, 316, 317, 322, 325, 327
San Cristobal, place, 173
Sandinistas, 200, 222, 225, 233, 236, 239, 242, 259, 275, 276, 345
Sandino, Blanca, 264
Sandino, General Augusto Cesar, and Honduras, 211
  and U. S. Marines, 207, 231, 236, 248, 58, 287 f., 307, 345
  mistress, 246
  wife, 264
  life, 247 f., 264 f.
  character, 265 f., 270 f., 272 f.

INDEX

Sandino, General Augusto Cesar (*Cont.*)
  interview with, 265-271, 273 f., 302
  myth about, 276, 278, 283
  and Admiral Sellers, 296 ff.
  and U. S. Intelligence Office, 304
  estimate of, 306
  general, 178, 233, 236, 238, 241,
    242, 246, 250, 255, 256, 267, 277,
    292, 305, 327
  and prohibition, 270
  and atrocities, 268, 269 f.
Sandino, Georgio, 264
Sandino songs, 254, 255 f.
Sandino's representatives, 179, 192
  camps, 182, 193, 195, 225, 239, 250,
    260, 275, 315, 341
  soldiers, 241, 253, 265
  underground, 210
  officers, 224 f., 239, 242, 249, 255,
    256, 261, 262
  victories, 229
  territory, 222, 230, 235, 243
  bandits, 235, 252, 306
  policy towards U. S., 269
San Felipe, castle of, 71
San Francisco, 347
San Gerónimo Junction, 16, 35
Sanitation, 103
San Jacinto, mountain, 196, 198
San Jorge, place, 313
San José, Costa Rica, 177, 341, 336,
  343
San José, Guatemala, 176, 342, 347,
  348, 351
San José press, 343. *See* newspapers
San Juan River, 301, 311, 314, 318,
  321, 327, 337
San Juancito, place, 200
San Lorenzo, place, 108, 118, 189,
  277, 278
San Miguel, place, 101
San Miguelito, place, 314
San Migüel Usupantán, place, 173
San Miguel, volcano, 111
San Pascual Bailón, 60 f.
San Pedro, Honduras, 133, 136
San Pedro, ranch, 238 f.
San Pedro Sacatepequez, place, 62,
  173
San Rafael de Norte, place, 260, 266,
  270, 274, 283, 292, 303
San Rosario, place, 133, 134
Santa Ana, 58

Santa Carmen Parroquia, place, 48
Santa Cruz, place, 257
Santa María, volcano, 38
Santa María, mountain, 169, 172
Santana, place, 85, 88
Santa Rosa, place, 18
Santa Tomás, university, 52
San Tomás Chicastenango, place, 172,
  173
Santiago, 62-67
Sarapique junction, 322
Schwartz banking interests, 76
Sculpture, Virgin of the Coro, 55
  Nuestra Señora de Izamal, 56
Scrofula, 124. *See* diseases
Sébaco, place, 278, 279, 280
Sellers, Admiral, 296, 297, 298, 302,
  307
Segovia River, 226. *See* Rio Coco
Seventh Day Adventist, 265
Sharks, 337
Sirena, island, 116
Sierras, 116
Sitio del Ninol, 88
Siqueiros, General Santos, life, 192
  Beal's guide, 193-199 f., 202-204,
    206-218, 221 f., 230, 237, 240
  timidity, 242, 246, 248 ff., 251
  traitor, 272 f., 315 f.
  general, 255, 256, 259, 260
Soil, 38, 114, 116
Sonora, place, 156
Solares, General Antonio, 72 ff., 74
Soldiers, in Salvador, 105
  in Guatemala, 75, 176
  with Sandino, 241, 253
Sousa, 307
Spaniards, 19, 133, 140, 163-168,
  226
Spanish blood, 117, 119. *See* national
  types
Spanish colonies, 320
Spanish language, 16, 23, 45, 54, 86,
  90, 170, 207, 226, 308, 314, 339
Spanish instructors, 87
Squier, E. G., 130
Stacomb, 326-329, 333, 334 ff.
Standard Fruit Co., 120, 137
State Department, 75, 76, 122, 267,
  297, 299
Stimson-Moncada agreement, 248, 268
Suchiate, place, 19, 347, 352
Suchiate River, 20

INDEX

Summerlin, Arthur, 123, 183, 188, 190, 341
Susan, 326, 329, 337
Syphilis, 171. *See* diseases

Tabasco, place, 157, 163
Tacos, 16. *See* food
Taguacas, 226 f. *See* Indians
Taguzigalpas, 226. *See* Indians
Tamalería Nocturna, 86
Tampico, place, 264
Tapachula, place, 19
Tata Tonino, 72
Taxation. *See* customs
    method of, 53
    Nicaragua, 108
Tegucigalpa, place, 108, 118, 119, 121, 122, 123, 127, 178, 179, 182, 183, 188, 189, 192, 196, 233, 292
Tehuana women, 16, 17. *See* Indians
Tehuantepec, Isthmus of, 12, 16
Tejada, Lico, 32
Tela, place, 120, 192
Teupacentl, place, 208
Tempisque, place, 190, 285, 286, 287
Teotihuacán, place, 152
Tepacho, 18. *See* drink
Tepoctum, river, 158, 159
Tequila, 17. *See* drink
Teresa, 246
Textiles, 49. *See* handicrafts
Thomas, Mr., 294
Tierra Blanca junction, 12, 13
Tititapa, place, 248
Tlaxcaltecans, 173. *See* Indians
Toguacas, 226 f. *See* Indians
Toledo, place, 141
Tologalpas, 226, 227. *See* Indians
Toltecs, 87. *See* Indians
Tonatiuth, 50
Toolser, 314, 315, 316, 332
Topiltépec, place, 165
Toro rapids, 317
Torres, Eugenia, 191
Torres, General, 224
Tortillas. *See* food
Tosta, General Vicente, 122, 123, 132, 191, 193
Totonicapán, place, 173
Tranceschs, Miguel, 176
Trees, sapotes, 11
    cottonwood, 23
    bamboo, 131

Trees (*Cont.*)
    mangrove, 117
    jungle, 12, 30, 131, 234, 320, 322
    pines, 130, 235, 257
    ceibas, 146, 157, 332
    hardwood, 151, 171
    palm, 154, 311, 312, 317, 322, 326, 332
    caobas, 257
    guayacáns, 257
    palos de sope, 257
    ironwood, 332
    ceropia, 322
    heliconiae, 322
    orange, 326
    nancito, 326
    guayava, 326
Trinidad, place, 247, 277, 283
Tropical Club, 338, 339
Tropical Radio Corporation, 120
Trujillo, place, 120
Turcios, Froylán, 179, 180, 183, 187, 188, 189-193, 196, 211, 213, 285
Tzakaliá, place, 170

Ubeda, Beatriz Plácida, 71
United Fruit Company and the papal delegate, 40 f., 117
    in Honduras, 120, 121
    in Guatemala, 143
    Organization, 144, 148, 153
    in Nicaragua, 326, 327
    and the Cuyamel, 328
United Press, 305. *See* newspapers
United States, and bananas, 144
    and cocoanuts, 341
    as Caliban, 190
    and Russia, 267
    in Central America, 176, 183, 190, 191, 222, 341
    general, 117, 122, 295, 298
U. S. Intelligence Department, 285, 299, 302
U. S. policy in Honduras, 122, 179
    in Nicaragua, 123, 177, 222, 247, 268, 293, 299
    in Salvador, 179
    in Mexico, 267
Ursua y Arismendi, Martín de, 167 f.
Utatlán, place, 157
Uxmal, ruins, 151

Vardelete, 226

Vásquez, Francisco, 176
Vendetti, 189, 193 f., 341
Vera Cruz, place, 9, 14, 112
Vera Cruzanos, 17. *See* national types
Vera Paz, place, 163, 166, 167, 226
Victoria, the, 311
Vilches, Señor, 277
Villa, 276
Villalpando, Bernardo de, 56 ff.
Virgin of Lourdes, 159
Virgin of the Coro, 55
Visitadors, Sánchez de Berrospe, 35
   Gómez de la Madriz, 35. *See* Guate-
   mala
Viteri, Bishop, 97 ff.
Volcán de la Unión, 111
Volcanic eruption, 112 ff.
Votán, 172
Votán, Balum, 155 ff.
Votanites, 157

Wages, peon, 37
   forced-labor, 39
   teamster, 79
   Mozo, 80
   street-car conductor, 80
   farmer, 80
   machinist, 110
   banana, 121
Waldorf salad, 147
Walker, 126, 309
War Department (U. S.), 267
Washington, 298
Washington treaties, 75, 123
Wells, Sumner, 122
Wild animals, 13, 258, 323, 332, 337 f.,
   338

Williams, Mr., 305
Wolff, 326 f., 334 ff.
Women, 10 f., 313
Wood carving, 54. *See* handicrafts
Workmen's association, 79
Workers' homes, 79

Xahob Tun, dance, 174
Xibalbay, place, 157, 158
Ximenes, Francisco, 176

Yellow fever, 118, 332. *See* diseases
Yánez, Enrique, 210-214, 216
"Yankees," 243, 254
Yeli, mountain, 260
"Yellow-pig-tail," 107
Yojoa, lake, 130
Yucapuca, place, 247
Yucapuca, mountains, 260, 261
Yucatán, 55, 151, 157, 163, 166,
   167

Zacapa, place, 158
Zacate, 49. *See* handicrafts
Zacatillo, island, 116
Zacatlán, place, 157
Zambos, 315. *See* national types
Zamora, Dr. José Jesús, 178-180, 182-
   184
Zapatera, island, 312
Zapiain, Pedro, 176
Zapotec, 16
Zelaya, Colonel Guadalupe, 232 f.,
   234, 237, 300
Zihüapate, 173
Zúngano, place, 241, 242
Zurieta, 268